Praise for the *Thru Hiker's Guide to America*

"A guide to some tempting trails, Schlimmer knows what he's talking about—The Lighten Up! section is worth its weight and then some. Read it. Believe it. Achieve it."

—Andrea Lankford
Appalachian Trail thru-hiker,
retired National Park Service ranger,
author of Biking the Arizona Trail

"Just glancing through the table of contents stirs the imagination and fires the wanderlust within. Every distance hiker will find this unique book to be an informative and useful tool for trip planning.

—Chuck Wilson
Eastern Continental Trail thru-hiker,
Florida Trail Association
long-distance hiker coordinator

"The *Thru Hiker's Guide to America* is more than a guidebook. . . . It's a book of dreams for everyone who has ever hungered for more after a two-, five-, or even seven-day backpacking trip."

—Dr. Larry Soroka
Adirondack Experience program
director at Plattsburgh State University

"I'm impressed with the scope of the project Schlimmer tackled. He gives very practical straightforward information to the reader in a format that is entertaining and easily understood. I also like the tone set in the *Thru Hiker's Guide to America* in terms of wilderness ethics, and adventuring in wilderness on its own terms."

—Mark Simon
Wilderness Education program director
at Potsdam State University

thru hiker's guide to america

25 incredible trails you can hike in one to eight weeks

e. schlimmer

Ragged Mountain Press / McGraw-Hill

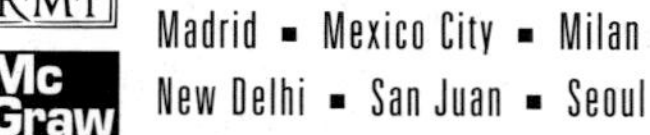

Camden, Maine ▪ New York ▪ Chicago
San Francisco ▪ Lisbon ▪ London
Madrid ▪ Mexico City ▪ Milan
New Delhi ▪ San Juan ▪ Seoul
Singapore ▪ Sydney ▪ Toronto

The McGraw·Hill Companies

1 2 3 4 5 6 7 8 9 10 DOC DOC 0 9 8 7 6 5

Library of Congress Cataloging-in-Publication Data
Schlimmer, E. (Erik)
Thru hiker's guide to America : 25 incredible trails you can hike in one to eight weeks / E. Schlimmer.
p. cm.
Includes bibliographical references and index.
ISBN 0-07-143364-3
1. Hiking—United States—Guidebooks. 2. Trails—United States—Guidebooks. 3. United States—Guidebooks. I. Title: Thru hiker's guide to America. II. Title.
GV199.4.S35 2005
796.51'0973—dc22
2004028075

Questions regarding the content of this book should be addressed to
Ragged Mountain Press
P.O. Box 220
Camden, ME 04843
www.raggedmountainpress.com

Questions regarding the ordering of this book should be addressed to
The McGraw-Hill Companies
Customer Service Department
P.O. Box 547
Blacklick, OH 43004
Retail customers: 1-800-262-4729
Bookstores: 1-800-722-4726

Page ii photo by Tim Barnett/Getty Images.
Maps by Jason Smith.

For all the underdogs.

JASON SMITH

contents

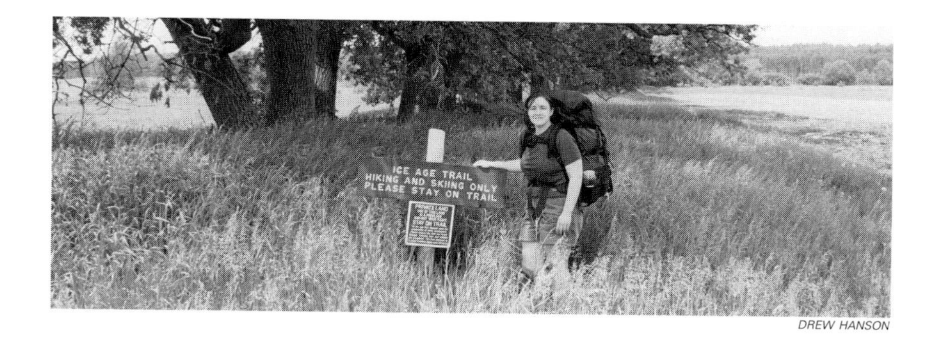

DREW HANSON

trail listing by distance

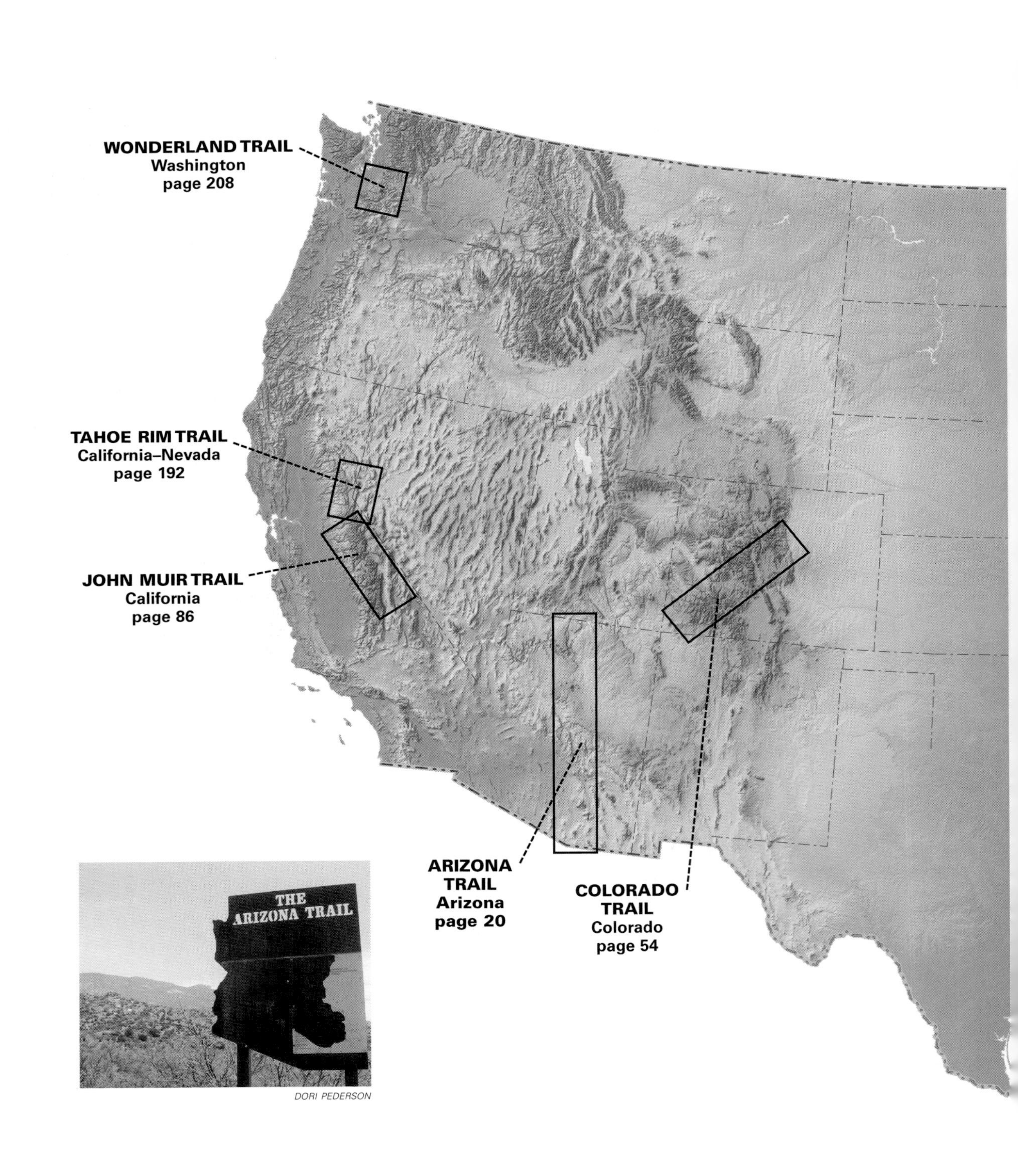

DORI PEDERSON

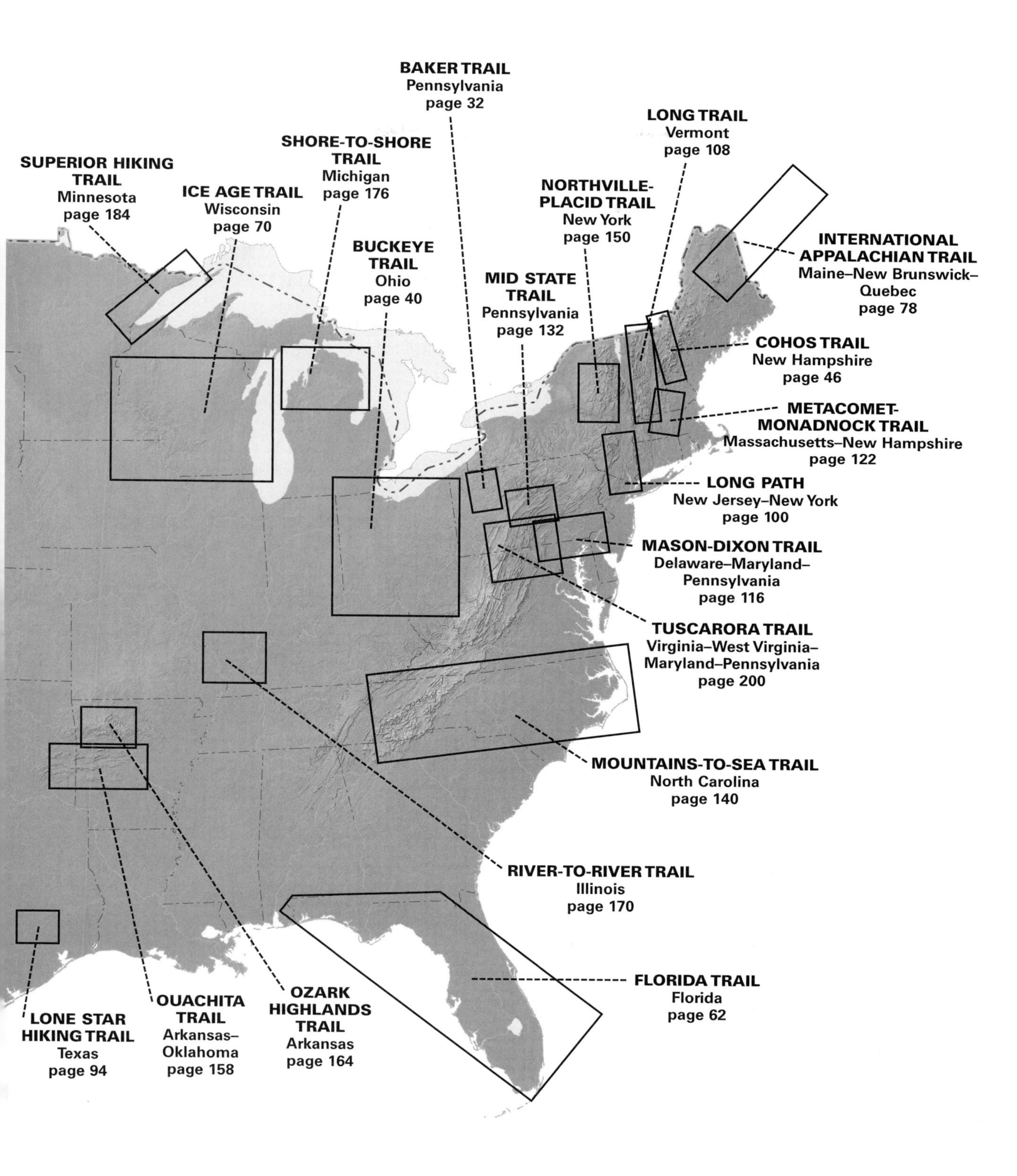

BAKER TRAIL
Pennsylvania
page 32
LONG TRAIL
Vermont
page 108
SHORE-TO-SHORE
TRAIL
Michigan
page 176
SUPERIOR HIKING
TRAIL
Minnesota
page 184
ICE AGE TRAIL
Wisconsin
page 70
NORTHVILLE-
PLACID TRAIL
New York
page 150
INTERNATIONAL
APPALACHIAN TRAIL
Maine–New Brunswick–
Quebec
page 78
BUCKEYE
TRAIL
Ohio
page 40
MID STATE
TRAIL
Pennsylvania
page 132
COHOS TRAIL
New Hampshire
page 46
METACOMET-
MONADNOCK TRAIL
Massachusetts–New Hampshire
page 122
LONG PATH
New Jersey–New York
page 100
MASON-DIXON TRAIL
Delaware–Maryland–
Pennsylvania
page 116
TUSCARORA TRAIL
Virginia–West Virginia–
Maryland–Pennsylvania
page 200
MOUNTAINS-TO-SEA TRAIL
North Carolina
page 140
RIVER-TO-RIVER TRAIL
Illinois
page 170
FLORIDA TRAIL
Florida
page 62
LONE STAR
HIKING TRAIL
Texas
page 94
OUACHITA
TRAIL
Arkansas–
Oklahoma
page 158
OZARK
HIGHLANDS
TRAIL
Arkansas
page 164

acknowledgments

Christy Blanchard gave me the idea to write this book, so without her suggestion this guide would not exist. The following members of the long-distance hiking community, in both professional and recreational capacities, gave me valuable feedback, photos, "In Their Own Words" write-ups, and sage advice: Jan Hancock and Andrea Lankford (Arizona Trail); Gary Dill, Herb Hulls, and James Sprague, (Buckeye Trail); Jim Ritchie (Baker Trail); Kim Robert Nilsen (Cohos Trail); Chuck Wilson (Colorado Trail and Florida Trail); Brigit Brown, Drew Hanson, and Tim Malzhan (Ice Age Trail); Dick Anderson and Will Richard (International Appalachian Trail); Karen Connelly and Ryman McLane (John Muir Trail); National Forests and Grasslands in Texas, Gay Ippolito, and Paul Morgan (Lone Star Hiking Trail); Ed Walsh (Long Path); Green Mountain Club, Ed Rolfe, and Jeff McCanna (Long Trail); Jim Hooper (Mason-Dixon Trail); Chris Ryan (Metacomet-Monadnock Trail); Tom Thwaites (Mid State Trail); Jeff Brewer (Mountains-to-Sea Trail); Rich Vertigan (Northville-Placid Trail); Tim Ernst (Ouachita Trail and Ozark Highlands Trail); John O'Dell (River-to-River Trail); Al and Katie Fritzler (Shore-to-Shore Trail); Gayle

JEFFERY CASE

JIM RITCHIE

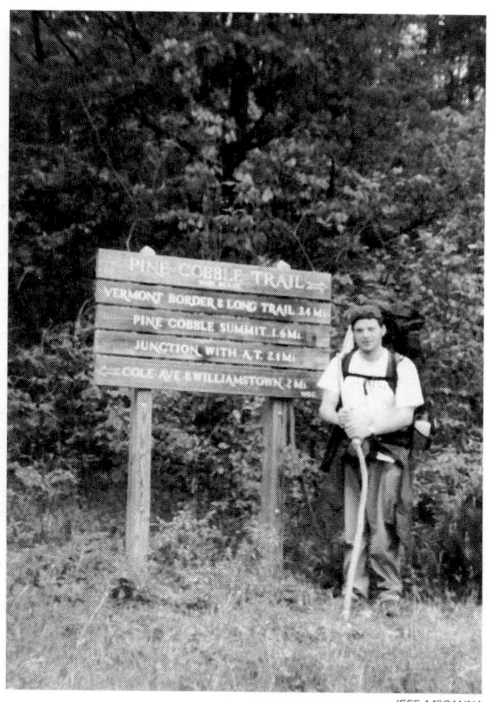

JEFF McCANNA

Coyer (Superior Hiking Trail); Steve Andersen and Tim Hauserman (Tahoe Rim Trail); Don Desrosiers (Tuscarora Trail); M. Shawn Lutgen (Wonderland Trail). The Lord gave me legs, eyes, fingers, and feet, plus all my other parts so I could hike, reflect, and write about the wonderful world He created. Christy, Mother and Bill, Nick and Tammy, Queeny, Sean and Buddy, and my grandparents let me sleep on their couches while I worked on this book, which was greatly appreciated, especially during those cold North Country winters. Many individuals and various institutions let me use their computers for research and writing. My grandparents were incredibly supportive as usual, which was nice when I had only forty dollars in my bank account and decided to go bushwhacking instead of going to work. Trail officialdom and friends gave helpful writing style suggestions. Pickle, Redbone, and all the other paratroopers out there drank all the beer I would have drunk if I had not decided to write instead. The crew at the Wooden Ski and Wheel in Plattsburgh, New York, gave me a setting like a home away from home. Kelly O'Connor and Dr. Kathleen Camelo, both of the State University of New York at Plattsburgh, helped me through some gravely difficult times, and I can never thank them enough for their care. I'm sure their empathy and talents are appreciated by many besides me. Many people kept asking how the book was coming along and offered their assistance and encouragement, which helped motivate me to keep hiking, researching, and writing. So I say to everyone above and to all my comrades elsewhere: thank you!

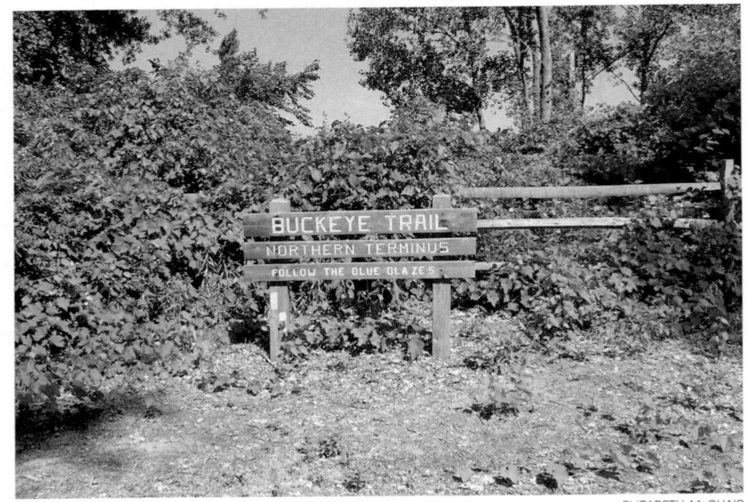

ELIZABETH McQUAID

introduction

I neared the southern terminus of the 1,300-mile Florida National Scenic Trail, deep within the Everglades, in April 2002. Fifty-five days prior I had started walking from the trail's northern terminus, on the far end of the Panhandle near Pensacola, a stone's throw from Alabama. A dear friend flew all the way from upstate New York to finish the last eight miles of the trail with me, an act that was greatly appreciated to say the least. The day after the ceremonious completion of my longest hike to date, my friend suggested I write a book about my experiences on this trail. But I didn't want to write a book about myself or just about this trail. "Yeah, I did this and that on the Florida Trail, and I hope you don't think I'm conceited, but I did this, too. Oh, and I hope you care." Instead, I decided to write about trails themselves; I would share what I had gleaned from the Florida Trail and so many other trails during my years of hiking and mountaineering throughout the United States.

I came up with seven major trail requirements as criteria for inclusion:

1. The trail needed to be at least a hundred miles long. (The only exception to this rule was the 95-mile Wonderland Trail, but there are exceptions to most rules I make.)

2. I didn't want to include really long trails, so I decided to set the upper limit at 1,300 miles.

3. I chose trails that showed their own personality and related to specific entities, such as communities, rivers, mountains, lakes, and even political borders, among other features.

4. I wanted to discuss different kinds of trails all over North America, from flat to mountainous, tough to easy, wilderness to multiple-use.

5. Paths that a lot of people had not heard of were certainly worthy of mention, but more famous trails could not go unrepresented either. No matter how famous or little known a trail was before I found it, it had a fair chance of being picked.

6. A trail could be included only if it had a feeling of wildness. Generally, the trail needed to stray from massive development for

extended distances, because the guide would be written primarily for hikers.

7. If a trail was not currently routed end to end on the ground, on a map, or in a guidebook, it was not described. An exception was if someone had thru-hiked the trail already, the trail could be selected despite the lack of accurate guidebooks and maps. (Such was the case with the Arizona Trail and the Shore-to-Shore Trail.)

Then came the research. I increased my breadth of long-distance hiking by traveling and walking sections of the trails I would later write about. I dedicated more than two years to thru-hiking and section-hiking trails I had not set foot on before. For the trails I did not entirely cover end to end on my own, I spent upward of ten hours a day surfing the Internet, reading guidebooks, reviewing magazine and newspaper articles, and examining trail maps until I couldn't see straight. I also went through all my old hiking journals, photos, and on-the-trail e-mails to refresh my memory of trails I had already hiked. Then I talked with U.S. Forest Service employees, trail club presidents and members, writers, photographers, volunteers, and experienced long-distance hikers so I could pass on their trail knowledge to you.

Based on my trail criteria, the long-distance giants—the Appalachian Trail, the Continental Divide Trail, and the Pacific Crest Trail—didn't qualify. Only 10 to 15 percent of those who start a thru-hike of the Appalachian Trail complete their goal. In today's technology- and drudgery-based society, many goals in life are difficult to achieve or simply unrewarding if they are actually met. Why should we make long-distance hiking as unrewarding as the "real world"? Self-fulfillment and rewards are more obtainable on a shorter path than they are on an overly long trail. The goals in this book are reasonable and within reach of many hikers.

The result of my research is twenty-five separate trails in twenty-six states and two Canadian provinces. The shortest trail is the Wonderland Trail, at 95 miles; the longest ones are the Florida Trail and the Buckeye Trail, each covering about 1,300 miles. The average trail length is a hair over 400 miles. Additional long-distance trails are listed under "Other Long-Distance Adventures." Just because each of these trails did not get its own chapter doesn't mean it's not worth hiking. Choosing which trail to hike simply depends on what kind of adventure you're looking for, and where.

The *Thru Hiker's Guide to America* is written for college students who have Spring Break coming up and want to do something other than irreparable harm to their liver and brain cells. It's written for the recent Appalachian Trail thru-hiker who wants to take a trip of more reasonable length, perhaps closer to home. And it's designed for the husband-and-wife team who have a month of vacation time saved up and would rather not go to the Caribbean or the Yucatan Peninsula like all the other tourists. Instead, they want adventure! They want to go to places like Mayhem Swamp, Rough Butt Bald, Devil's Gulch, Poverty Mountain, Greasy Creek, the Armageddon Trail, and Alligator Alley.

LIGHTEN UP!

I care about you. I want you to have more fun on your next hiking trip than on your last one. To do so, I'm going to let you in on something.

You carry too much stuff. It's time to cut down.

With fewer things and lighter gear, you'll hike farther yet feel better at the end of the day. To make my point clear, let me tell you two stories about two very different hikers.

THE FORD F-350

In August 2004, I was day-hiking the beautiful flanks of Saddleback Mountain, a 4,000-foot peak on a section of the Appalachian Trail in western Maine. It was an ungodly hot day by Maine standards, and after four miles I had already taken off my shirt, rolled up my pants, crafted a homemade sweatband, and finished the two quarts of water I had set out with.

In the midst of an evergreen and paper birch forest, I approached a lean-to. Lying in and around the shelter were the usual accoutrements of lean-to life: a shovel, discarded paperbacks, a register book, a length of cord, and a book of matches. Muddy boots and brightly colored gear were strewn about the shelter floor. I could smell ramen noodles, dirty socks, and stale wood smoke.

As I drew nearer, a deep-throated "woof" issued from a gray, long-haired dog. I thought it was odd for a dog to be left unattended, but then, from behind a fire ring, stirred a wiry, thoroughly bearded young man. Sporting a threadbare thermal top, muddied shorts, and a well-worn pair of black sandals, he could only have been an Appalachian Trail thru-hiker, headed north toward Mount Katahdin. I expected this resident of the trail to rise and greet me, or at least give me a cheery, rhetorical "How's it goin'?" but all I heard from him was, "Hey, man . . . awwww." With an expression of pain creasing his upper cheeks, he remained prone next to the fire ring. I asked if he was okay. As he attempted to rise, he assured me he was "gonna make it." My years in the woods, either as a backcountry ranger or a trail crew leader, caused me to immediately start "assessing the patient." So, I asked him what happened.

He grimaced and spoke. "I was hitching into Rangeley when this big-ass, four-wheel-drive, white Ford F-350 pickup pulled over to give me a ride. I didn't take time to put down the tailgate; I just heaved my pack over it into the bed. Since then, my back has been totally messed up. Man, I'm hurtin'."

Listening, I began taking a secret inventory of the thru-hiker's belongings—the colorful gear strewn about the lean-to. It was a lightweight backpacker's nightmare.

His kitchen consisted of a blackened white-gas stove with its 22-ounce red metal fuel bottle, pump assembly, and silver windscreen. Nearby there were a few pots for cooking (each with a lid), a few stuff sacks, pot grips, a scrubby, an insulated mug, and some metal spoons. A torn Ziplock bag held more books than I bought in college. Subjects varied from edible plants to geology; there were also

Appalachian Trail guides, and maps for sections of trail we were nowhere near. A pile of clothes exceeded the size of a county fair's prize-winning watermelon. In this mountain of fabric I spotted a heavy-duty waterproof/breathable jacket, rain pants, shorts, socks, thermal tops and bottoms, and multiple pieces of clothing that shared duplicate purposes. I also saw a hefty pair of leather stompers futilely airing out in the humid, stagnant August air.

On a clothesline hung a two-person, four-season orange tent that looked as though it was designed to survive a year pitched on the side of Mount Everest. Next to the tent hung a mummy-style dark green sleeping bag as thick as a mattress you might find in a penthouse suite at the Ritz. I figured that this sleeping bag was rated for 20° F. No wonder it was hanging up and not being used; the air temperature was 80°. Below the clothesline lay our immobilized thru-hiker on two sleeping pads—one a self-inflating air mattress, the other a durable closed-cell foam pad. Finally, hanging on a wooden peg was a gargantuan, overly built, internal-frame pack made by a well-known Montana-based outdoor company. The thru-hiker had almost the same build I did, and still I surmised that he and I could easily have used this 5,500-cubic-inch pack as a hasty shelter if we needed to. Empty, the thing resembled more of a collapsed yurt than a backpack.

I totaled the weight of this poor boy's load and estimated that even Hercules would have thrown out his back had he tried to hoist it over the tailgate of a truck. After walking 2,000 miles and climbing nearly half a million vertical feet through thirteen individual states, this long-distance hiker may have ruined his chance for a successful end-to-end trip.

After filling my water bottles at the nearby spring and giving him a peppermint Altoid as a get-well-soon gift, I left him with a few stretching recommendations and wishes of good luck.

THE ENLIGHTENING

By contrast, I offer Seymour, a long-distance hiker friend who thru-hiked the 135-mile Northville-Placid Trail in 1995 with a pack that weighed about as much as a Navy destroyer's anchor. It was his first long-distance trail hike, and he brought about as much gear in his 5,500-cubic-inch internal-frame pack as our disabled Appalachian Trail thru-hiker had hoisted into the F-350. Part of Seymour's packing list even included a twenty-six-ounce jar of spaghetti sauce, full-size window thermometer, 20° sleeping bag, a self-inflating air mattress fit for a king, and a Rambo knife. By the end of his Northville-Placid Trail trip, he had averaged only fourteen miles a day though he hiked as hard as he could. By the end of the expedition, Seymour was simply exhausted and needed a day or two to recover from his blisters, sore shoulders, bruised hip bones, and tired legs.

But Seymour was soon back on the long-distance hiking scene, covering Vermont's 270-mile Long Trail. This time he brought much less gear. He refused to bring all the gear that his local outdoor gear store's customer service representatives told him he "needed," and he even ditched the Rambo knife and braved the wilds with

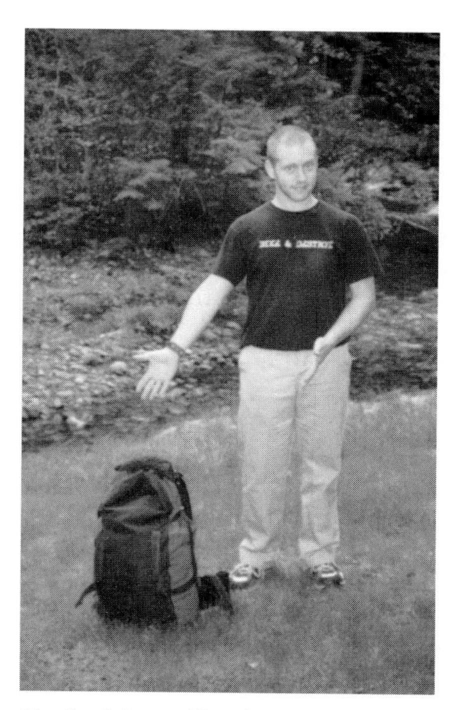

The "enlightened" author with his twelve-pound pack. (PETE PRICE)

only his two fists. He wore a pack that was only 3,700 cubic inches in size. On this thru-hike he averaged seventeen miles a day and didn't feel exhausted every evening. He sometimes even went for a short stroll after dinner. Even so, by the time Seymour reached Canada, the northern terminus of the Long Trail, he felt pretty beat. His pack was still too heavy. It was at this point that his *enlightenment* began.

In 2002, Seymour, who obviously had become attached to long-distance hiking, upped the ante and hiked the 1,300-mile Florida Trail end to end. He might have even established a new fastest traverse time of the Florida Trail by averaging twenty-two miles a day. His speedy traverse was mostly due to the fact that he brought even less gear than he did on the Long Trail. When he took his first step from the northern terminus of the Florida Trail, his pack was the size of a day pack: less than 3,000 cubic inches. He reported feeling "fresh as a daisy" at the end of most days of hiking, and had spring in his step even at the end of some twenty-six-mile days.

When some people told Seymour that the only reason he could hike twenty-two miles a day was because the Florida Trail was flat, he proved his critics wrong by thru-hiking the very mountainous and muddy 160-mile Cohos Trail in 2003, establishing a new fastest traverse time and averaging twenty-one miles a day. He then blazed the 120-mile Metacomet-Monadnock Trail in 2004, again averaging twenty-two miles a day even though he had to climb more than 23,000 vertical feet end to end. On these hikes Seymour was not racing. (He hates competition in the woods.) He just kept a slow, steady pace, which enabled him to take fewer rests and average more than two miles per hour. He used fewer calories per mile carrying a lightweight pack than on the Northville-Placid Trail while carrying a heavy pack, so he had energy left over at the end of the day. He could use it that evening on his after-dinner stroll or save it for the next day of backpacking.

Seymour says he owes his high daily mileage to "thorough planning, good health, the right attitude, and a lightweight pack." He can now hike any distance from early spring to late fall with a complete pack weight of approximately twelve pounds. (Pack weight is the weight of the pack with everything in it except food and water.) Our injured Appalachian Trail thru-hiker wore a pack that weighed six pounds when it was completely empty.

These two hikers—the injured Appalachian Trail thru-hiker and my buddy Seymour—demonstrate two completely different takes on long-distance traveling. The Appalachian Trail thru-hiker wanted all the comforts of home, from a cushy bed made of two sleeping pads to enough books to keep his mind busy from Georgia to Maine. Seymour, on the other hand, asked himself, "Do I want to strain under a heavy pack all day and risk being injured, or can I deal with being less than perfectly comfortable at night?" He opted for the lesser of two evils. During the day, Seymour was comfortable and happy with his basic load of twelve pounds. In the evening, he was still able to get a good night's sleep in all types of weather and terrain, and didn't have nightmares about having to put his pack back on the next morning.

Now, I'm not saying that the Appalachian Trail thru-hiker I met in Maine was wrong for bringing what he wanted to bring. We should all hike our own hike. That philosophy dates back to at least Myron Avery's time. In 1936, Avery found his impressive place in long-distance hiking history by becoming the first person to hike every mile of the Appalachian Trail (though not in one continuous trip), and from the 1920s to the 1950s he was an advocate for the formation, administration, and maintenance of the Appalachian Trail. In their book *Forest and Crag*, Guy and Laura Waterman remind us that Avery did not care for people "who take it upon themselves to closely monitor how others hike and to criticize them if they do not hike in a prescribed manner. What is important is that a hiker be true to his or her own goals. . . ." So again, the Appalachian Trail thru-hiker was not wrong, but the question remains, was the Appalachian Trail thru-hiker *enlightened*? Did he know he could have felt "fresh as a daisy" at the end of each day? Was he aware that he could have thru-hiked the entire Appalachian Trail without blisters, sore shoulders, bruised hip bones, tired legs, and an aching back? To know that it's possible to hike long distances quickly yet comfortably is to be enlightened. The way to become enlightened—to be smarter, not stronger—is no secret. It takes two steps to drop the extra weight.

STEP ONE: THE NEEDY

What do you *want* to bring but don't *need* to bring? Being infinitely comfortable in the woods comes at a cost: you have to carry all those creature comforts around with you all day. Let's compare the two tables (pages 8–10): the conventional Bring-It-All Gear List against the Smarter-Not-Stronger Gear List. Wow! We saved 21.7 pounds by cutting ounces here and there. Overall, we've dropped a weight equivalent to more than five 1,730-page Webster world dictionaries. Doesn't it make sense to not carry five dictionaries in your pack?

I know the The Smarter-Not-Stronger Gear List looks pretty spartan. You may wonder: is it enough? Well, it's what I bring for a thousand-mile, two-month adventure with temperatures ranging from 30 to 90° in nearly every conceivable type of terrain; and I've survived to tell the tale.

But, lightening up takes thoughtfulness, sacrifice, and discipline.

Keep in mind that buying a lightweight piece of equipment and putting it in a six-pound backpack doesn't do much good overall. Try to work on the three big things first: shelter, kitchen, and backpack. Although some people save weight by cutting the margins off topographic maps and sawing the handle off toothbrushes, each of these measures saves only 0.2 ounce.

In addition to what I carry, I usually wear nylon shorts, a long-sleeved polyester dress shirt, merino wool socks, and lightweight, nonwaterproof sneakers. (*Sneakers*—as in traditional Nike, Adidas, New Balance sneakers—not *lighthikers* made by boot companies.) You probably noticed that footwear isn't included in the lists below. No matter where the weight is—on your back or on your feet—it's still weight that you have to lift with each step. I devised a math formula to help hikers realize that the amount of weight on their feet is perhaps more detrimental than the amount of weight on their back.

Average stride on 1 mile of flat ground = 1,000 paces

Wearing a pair of boots weighing 4 pounds = lifting 4 pounds with each pace

4 pounds x 1,000 paces = lifting 4,000 pounds (2 tons) per mile

Now see what happens if you wear a pair of sneakers weighing two pounds.

2 pounds x 1,000 paces = lifting 2,000 pounds (1 ton) per mile

Okay, enough math. You get the point. Most dedicated thru-hikers I have met wear sneakers. Sneakers dry faster, are more comfortable, require less maintenance, cost less, and, of course, are much lighter than hiking boots. Sneakers that weigh less than two pounds but last more than 1,000 miles are not difficult to find. I had a pair of $120 sneakers that lasted less than 200 miles, and I had a pair of $85 sneakers that survived 1,700 miles. It's best to ask accomplished long-distance hikers what brands and models they recommend or hold in contempt.

Can you switch fully from the Bring-It-All Gear List to the Smarter-Not-Stronger Gear List? Try things out on a short practice trip or on day hikes. For example, I have permanently damaged, weak ankles, but I'm less likely to sprain my ankle while wearing sneakers than while wearing boots because I can "feel the trail" better. I find that boots tend to teeter-totter over roots, rocks, and other trail debris. But I didn't know this until I gave sneakers a chance on some day hikes and liked the results. From there, I started wearing them on long-distance hikes, and I'm now a happy sneaker-wearing hiker.

STEP TWO: ECONOMICS

A lighter pack does not need to result in a lighter wallet. Many companies that now sell lightweight gear are circling like buzzards over herds of hikers straining under heavy packs. Before you make any gear purchase, think about what you're getting in return. Put away for a moment the hype of "new technology," "top-of-the-line

(continued on page 10)

BRING-IT-ALL GEAR LIST

SHELTER		WEIGHT IN OUNCES
1.	THREE-SEASON, ONE-PERSON TENT, ALUMINUM POLES, STAKES, STUFF SACK	57.0
2.	20° SYNTHETIC MUMMY-STYLE SLEEPING BAG, STUFF SACK	47.4
3.	SELF-INFLATING AIR MATTRESS, 6 FEET BY 2 FEET BY 2 INCHES	42.2
KITCHEN		
4.	1- AND 2-QUART POTS, LIDS, ONE BOWL, ONE MUG, TWO METAL SPOONS, STUFF SACK	28.9
5.	WHITE-GAS STOVE, FUEL BOTTLE, 20 DAYS OF LIQUID FUEL, STUFF SACK	31.2
6.	TWO 1-LITER LEXAN WATER BOTTLES	10.4
7.	WATER FILTER	11.8
CLOTHING		
8.	WATERPROOF/BREATHABLE JACKET	29.1
9.	WATERPROOF/BREATHABLE PANTS	20.4
10.	SUN/RAIN HAT	3.4
11.	FLEECE HAT	1.6
12.	FLEECE JACKET	23.5
13.	MIDWEIGHT POLYPROPYLENE TOP	8.6
14.	MIDWEIGHT FLEECE PANTS	13.0
15.	TWO COTTON T-SHIRTS	15.4
16.	TWO PAIRS CARGO SHORTS	22.8
17.	LIGHTWEIGHT FLEECE GLOVES	1.8
18.	THREE PAIRS WOOL SOCKS	9.8
EXTRAS		
19.	CANDLE LANTERN, FOUR CANDLES, STUFF SACK	11.3
20.	HEADLAMP, FOUR AA BATTERIES	13.0
21.	LARGE DITTY BAG (MAPS, FIRST AID, IDENTIFICATION, TOOTHBRUSH, ETC.)	18.8
22.	BATTERY-POWERED 35MM CAMERA, ZOOM LENS, ONE ROLL FILM	14.2
23.	INTERNAL-FRAME BACKPACK, 5,500 CUBIC INCHES, SIZE MEDIUM	97.0

TOTAL WEIGHT: 533 OUNCES (33.3 POUNDS). 20.8 PERCENT OF A 160-POUND HIKER

SMARTER-NOT-STRONGER GEAR LIST

SHELTER	WEIGHT IN OUNCES	(OUNCES SAVED)
1. TARP (7 SQUARE FEET), 25 FEET OF CORD, BUG HEAD NET	18.6	(38.4)
2. 40° DOWN MUMMY-STYLE SLEEPING BAG, WATERPROOF GROCERY BAG	22.0	(25.4)
3. FOAM PAD IN PACK, 2-FOOT BY 6-FOOT SECTION OF HOUSE WRAP	5.3	(36.9)
KITCHEN		
4. 1-QUART POT, HOMEMADE LID, TWO LEXAN SPOONS	4.8	(24.1)
5. TUNA-CAN POT SUPPORTER, 20 DAYS OF SOLID FUEL TABLETS	11.1	(20.1)
6. TWO 1-LITER SODA BOTTLES	3.2	(7.2)
7. 20-OUNCE WATER BOTTLE WITH FILTER, BOTTLE OF IODINE TABLETS	5.5	(6.3)
CLOTHING		
8. WATERPROOF/BREATHABLE SHELL	12.5	(16.6)
9. NO WATERPROOF/BREATHABLE PANTS	0.0	(20.4)
10. SUN/RAIN HAT	3.4	(NONE)
11. FLEECE HAT	1.6	(NONE)
12. SYNTHETIC VEST	12.1	(11.4)
13. MIDWEIGHT POLYPROPYLENE TOP	8.6	(NONE)
14. LIGHTWEIGHT POLYPROPYLENE BOTTOMS	6.5	(6.5)
15. ONE SHORT-SLEEVED POLYESTER DRESS SHIRT	4.6	(10.8)
16. ONE PAIR NYLON SHORTS	4.3	(18.5)
17. NO LIGHTWEIGHT FLEECE GLOVES	0.0	(1.8)
18. TWO PAIRS WOOL SOCKS	6.6	(3.2)
EXTRAS		
19. NO CANDLE LANTERN	0.0	(11.3)
20. SMALL LED HEADLAMP WITH BATTERY	1.7	(11.3)

(continued)

EXTRAS (CONTINUED)	WEIGHT IN OUNCES	(OUNCES SAVED)
21. SMALL DITTY BAG (MAPS, FIRST AID, IDENTIFICATION, TOOTHBRUSH, ETC.)	9.4	(9.4)
22. MANUAL-WIND 35MM CAMERA (NO BATTERIES), ONE ROLL FILM	5.3	(8.9)
23. DAY PACK, 3,000 CUBIC INCHES, SIZE MEDIUM	38.0	(59.0)

TOTAL WEIGHT: 185 OUNCES (11.6 POUNDS). 7.2 PERCENT OF A 160-POUND HIKER

(continued from page 8)
materials," and "state-of-the-art design" propagated by outdoor magazines and manufacturers with near religious fervor. Take a Gear Hype Time-Out (GHTO) with the following examples.

1. The pitch: "Lightweight tricked-out guide pack" and "H_2O-compatible tech pack."

   You and I call it a *backpack*.

2. The pitch: "Highly breathable, multisport, low cut designed for fast-paced outdoor performance activities."

   You and I call them *sneakers*.

3. The pitch: "Omni-Grip rubber sole with multi-directional lug tread."

   You and I call it *the bottom of a sneaker*.

4. The pitch: "High-aerobic activity," "fast-forward sport," "performance-oriented sport," and "high-output activity."

   You and I call it *hiking*.

When I started hiking, I thought the gear made the hiker, but that's not the case. Hikers—the people who spend their days off out there in the mud—make themselves. Unfortunately, it's easy to fall prey to all the product hype.

For example, a man we'll call Nick needed a new mug to bring on his hiking trips. He decided to buy a $30 1.9-ounce titanium mug because the salesperson assured him that the cup had a "cutting-edge design" and was made of "high-tech material." If Nick had taken a GHTO (a Gear Hype Time-Out), he could have used his 1.6-ounce water bottle as a makeshift mug. A water bottle holds more liquid and is about as efficient as a titanium mug at keeping the contents hot or cold. And this water bottle can be used as a mug in the evening as well as a water bottle all day. The water bottle wears two hats, so to speak. Unfortunately, Nick was swooned by the gear hype. On top of this, he was talked into purchasing a six-pound backpack to carry his $30 mug in.

Shelters—a key piece of equipment—are often surrounded by gear hype. You can buy a lightweight four-season single-wall tent with 7,000-series aluminum poles and titanium stakes for $500. It weighs four pounds. Or you can buy a $40 tarp plus some cord and a bug head net. This costs $50 and weighs one pound. Now that's economics.

TIPS AND SKILLS

Humans tend to create plenty of problems on their own. Known as *subjective hazards*, many of these problems can be avoided with planning and skill. Many hiking clubs, guide services, gear shops, and colleges offer introductory mountaineering and hiking classes for those new to backpacking. Beyond learning the hard skills of outdoor life, I would recommend gaining certifications in wilderness first aid and CPR for the professional rescuer. With medical talent you can assist an injured member of your group, a complete stranger, or yourself in an outdoor emergency. Remember, even after contacting help outside of the woods, it will be several hours, perhaps a full day, before help actually arrives. Only in the movies can you phone a wilderness-oriented 911 operator who will formulate a militarily precise search-and-rescue mission to whisk you away in a helicopter.

There are many books and magazines on how-to backpacking and endurance sports, and all hikers are encouraged to seek more knowledge through these media. Below is a very modest list of subjective hazards that may lead to a backcountry disaster.

IMPROPER GEAR

No winter gear in April, no rain gear on a cloudy day, or no flashlight on a supposed day hike? Bad idea. What's the best rule for packing? Expect the unexpected—to a reasonable degree. For example, I wouldn't bring a down parka on a summer day hike, but I would bring a rain jacket, no matter what the forecast.

NEW GEAR

The first day of a hundred-mile hike is not the best time to see if your tent doesn't leak, the stove truly works, your pack is comfortable, and your boots actually fit. Take a practice trip of reasonable length before tackling a long-distance hike. During this practice trip you'll answer such questions as, does the tent have all the poles, and do they actually fit? Is my pack adjusted to fit my torso properly? Will one quart of fuel last two weeks? Will my new 30° sleeping bag keep me warm only in temperatures of 40° and above? And will those chintzy plastic spoons I stole from the college cafeteria break with the first stir of my noodles? Remember, in the woods there are no items for sale, and no returns counters.

THE WRONG PEOPLE FOR THE WRONG JOB

Many people, like me, hike solo for a good reason: a compatible long-distance hiking partner is hard to find. I once took a chance and hiked for a week with a stranger described as a "great partner" by a friend. The trip was a disaster. I found my "great partner" to be a know-it-all. He told me how to cook. He refused to take breaks. He became annoyed when I asked him to take my picture. He asked for one bite of my macaroni and cheese and ended up finishing it all. I learned my lesson the hard way. He was a jerk, and he may have thought the same of me.

Good partners are hard to find. A good partner from the normal world of going to work and running errands may not be the best partner in the wilderness world of hiking up mountains and cooking in the dark. Conflict on the trail is simply unavoidable and is usually a necessary part of a relationship, but sometimes it can spiral out of control. Husbands and wives who loved each other at mile ten of a long-distance hike may want to get divorced by mile two hundred. Fiancées throw their engagement rings into privies. Families break apart. If a long-distance hike can end a close relationship, hiking with someone you don't know at all, regardless of the recommendation, is chancy to say the least. In fact, I would avoid any long-distance hiking partner with whom I had not survived a bloody insurrection or a natural disaster.

Having a partner you can trust, though, is a wonderful thing. Emergencies arise, motivation plummets, and some decisions are hard to make along the trail. A partner can be your link to much-needed help, motivation boosts, and decisiveness. Before you head out on a long trek with your partner, you may want to define your goals. Will you hike fast or slow? Will you hike in the rain? In a snowstorm? How much hiking experience has each of you had? Will you cook pesto-spiced organic pasta with fresh veggies for dinner, or two packs of ramen noodles? Will dessert be homemade pudding topped with dark chocolate shavings, or a package of Twinkies? Why do you hike? Once these and a host of other questions are answered, you can move forward with the planning stage. You can choose a trail that's as easy or rugged as you both want, a trail that's as long or short as you desire, located in a place you think you'll both enjoy.

PHYSICAL PREPAREDNESS

A busy schedule makes it difficult to be in top physical condition prior to a long-distance hike. But increasing your strength and endurance prior to your trip, even at a minimal level, will make life much more enjoyable when you are out in the wilds. Starting your hike in marginal physical and mental shape can lead to soreness, injuries, unnecessary mental stress, and, yes, even death. People do die while hiking. All mountain ranges have the potential to kill, from the Presidential Range of New Hampshire, where nearly 150 people have died in the last 150 years, to the Japan Alps, where more than 500 people have died in only the past 30 years. Raising your level of physical endurance and strength is a good first step toward ensuring your survival. The approach I used before entering the military back in my youth is a good way to get into shape before heading out on a long-distance hike. For months prior to my first day of basic training, I ran. I did push-ups. I did sit-ups. I was ready when I got there. While all the drill sergeants watched the out-of-shape recruits (whom they called maggots) flounder on the hot Georgia pavement, out of breath, begging for mercy, they saw me merrily doing fifty push-ups. I was finally reaping the benefits of my months of hard work, established prior to my first day of basic training. (Nonetheless, the Drill Sergeants still called me names.)

To get ready for a long-distance hike, get active. Ride your bike to work instead of driving. Take the stairway to your office instead of the elevator. Day-hike each week with a heavy pack. Go running or skiing twice a week. Intending to get in shape on the trail may sound good while you munch on snacks, watching *SpongeBob SquarePants* all day, but your first day out will be a real wake-up call.

POSSIBLE PERILS

Lions? Tigers? Bears? Bears and a handful of other powerful critters are out there, but there are more hazards than ornery mammals. To make sure you get from one end of a long-distance trail to the other, it would be best to first read backcountry how-to books and learn the ropes with experienced hikers. In the meantime, here are the basics.

BUGS

Wasps, hornets, bees, fire ants, velvet ants, spiders, and a host of other stinging and biting creatures can cause physical ailments ranging from a swollen wound to death. Be on the lookout for possible tree or ground nests. Trails with a host of stinging and biting creatures include the Arizona Trail, Florida Trail, Mountains-to-Sea Trail, and Ouachita Trail. Blackflies, no-see-ums, deerflies, horseflies, and mosquitoes are more mental obstacles than physical threats, but they can ruin a trip nonetheless. Blackfly populations are legendary on the International Appalachian Trail, Cohos Trail, Northville-Placid Trail, and Long Trail, among others.

CRITTERS

Bears, mountain lions, moose, venomous snakes, rabid animals, and wounded or cornered animals can be dangerous, although confrontations are extremely rare. Being able to identify venomous snakes, making sure you are not crowding wildlife, and having a basic understanding of human–wild animal interactions may provide you with a near guarantee to be free from harm. All trails in this guide host large mammals or venomous snakes. Overall, education and respect, not fear and aggression, are safeguards to bring with you into the woods.

SUN

Bringing proper defenses against the sun and heat, such as sunblock, lip balm, light-colored clothing, and a sun hat can make your trip an enjoyable challenge rather than a disaster in an environmental broiler. Long shadeless sections can be found on the Arizona Trail, Colorado Trail, Florida Trail, John Muir Trail, and Tahoe Rim Trail. These sunny areas can be gravel and sand deserts, hundred-mile elevated levees, or alpine terrain at the 13,000-foot level.

HEAT

Summertime temperatures on some trails in this guide exceed 110° F. When it's oppressively hot, it's a good idea to get an early start before the day heats up, hike in the evening after the sun has set, and take afternoon siestas. Some days it may be best to not hike at all. Trails located near towns that meet or exceed an average high temperature of 95° for the month of July are the Arizona Trail, John Muir Trail, Lone Star Hiking Trail, Ouachita Trail, and Ozark Highlands Trail. On these trails you should carry several water containers, know the location of the next water source, and be prepared to carry up to two gallons of water or cache water prior to the trip. Some of these trails are generally not hiked in the middle of summer.

SNOW

Snow is not just a winter thing. In April 2003, the southern terminus of the Northville-Placid Trail in New York received twenty-four inches of fresh snow on top of the 36-inch base already on the ground. That same week, the highpoint of the Mountains-to-Sea Trail—North Carolina's Mount Mitchell—received 22 inches of fresh snow, which clearly did not make for ideal spring hiking conditions. The Cohos Trail, Colorado Trail, International Appalachian Trail, John Muir Trail, Long Trail, and Wonderland Trail usually hold significant amounts of snow well beyond the first calendar day of spring, and these trails can see snowfall in nearly every month, too.

COLD

Many trails in this guide are full-on winter trips from December to March, where winter lows can dip to –35°. Brrr! Trails located near towns that meet or drop below an average low temperature of 10° for the month of January are the Cohos Trail, Colorado Trail, Ice Age Trail, International Appalachian Trail, Metacomet-Monadnock Trail, Long Trail, Northville-Placid Trail, and Superior Hiking Trail. Many trails in this guide can harbor dangerously cold conditions even in summer. The Cohos Trail, for example, climbs over central New Hampshire's Presidential Range. According to the Appalachian Mountain Club's *Mountain Deaths in the Presidential Range*, at least ten people have died from hypothermia during the months of June, July, or August. Some instances resulted from summer snowstorms. Hypothermia results when your body's core temperature drops below 95 degrees. Initial symptoms can include intense shivering, while more severe symptoms progress to uncoordinated movements and irrational behavior. Stay alert to initial signs and take measures to warm yourself, such as changing out of wet clothes and drinking something hot.

LIGHTNING

The combination of mountainous terrain and treeless areas equal a setting ripe for afternoon lightning storms. Getting to know local weather trends, staying informed of incoming fronts, and learning basic skills to predict the weather will help keep you from having a truly electrifying experience. If caught in a lightning storm, stay out of shallow caves or rock overhangs, and get off summits or ridgelines. Try to find a clump of trees to hide in and hope for the best. Trails most prone to electrical storms in exposed terrain include the Arizona Trail, Colorado Trail, Florida Trail, John Muir Trail, and Tahoe Rim Trail.

LEAVE NO TRACE

Heading out on an extended trip can be a great experience for you, but what about the next hikers? They don't want to sleep amid used toilet paper, half-burned logs, and commando squirrels. Leave No Trace (LNT) principles are guides for having a responsible and ethical long- or short-distance journey. You can greatly reduce environmental damage by diligently following LNT guidelines.

PLANNING

Learn the rules and regulations of the areas you'll pass through. Bring in less potential trash, keep the group size to fewer than six people, do not cut or build new trails, and be prepared for any type of weather and terrain. Have an experienced outdoors person lead the hike, and make sure the group is aware of its LNT obligations.

HIKE AND CAMP ON A DURABLE SURFACE

Try to walk on gravel, compacted soil, and established trails, and do not cut switchbacks or go around mud holes in the trail. Cook, sleep, and camp at least 200 feet from all water sources. Stay at preexisting campsites. Remember: a good campsite is found, not made.

GET RID OF YOUR WASTE PROPERLY

If you packed it in, you can surely pack it out. Do not attempt to burn food, foil, plastic, or metal in fires, and do not bury these items. Use only biodegradable soap, and use it at least 200 feet from all water sources. Pack out or burn to ash your toilet paper; bury human and dog waste six inches in the ground's duff layer, or use the provided facilities. In some instances—such as the Wonderland Trail and John Muir Trail—you may be encouraged or required to pack out all human waste.

WHAT NOT TO PACK OUT

Don't be a wilderness shopper. If you like the look of something that doesn't grow near your home, take a picture of it; it will live forever. This includes geological features and cultural objects, too. If someone took all the neat things before you arrived, it wouldn't be fair to you, right?

MINIMIZE CAMPFIRE USE AND DAMAGE

A stove will cook your meals better than a campfire, and calories will keep you warmer throughout a cold night than a fire. Some areas have outlawed fires because of overuse or misuse in the past. If fires are allowed, use only dead and downed wood no bigger than the diameter of your wrist; use established fire rings, and make sure the fire is dead out when you leave. Many areas, especially in the West, enact fire bans during times of extreme fire danger. Before you set out, find out whether fires are allowed where you'll be camping.

RESPECT ALL CRITTERS

Do not harass wild animals, and keep your distance. Never feed wild animals; it only does them harm. As the old saying goes, "A fed animal is a dead animal."

BE CONSIDERATE

Hikers yield to horses; mountain bikers yield to hikers and horses. Usually, whoever is hiking uphill, or the rougher, more dangerous side of the trail has the right-of-way. Keep your noise level down, especially when traveling in groups. Say hello to everyone. Be nice. Remember, as Ralph Nader once said, "Love, in the United States, is not in surplus."

Dogs have become a consistent problem on trails. Nowadays they are not allowed in many national and state parks and they're required to be leashed in many wilderness areas. Polluting water sources, terrifying two- and four-legged animals, stomping on rare plants, and keeping campers up all night with incessant barking are just some of the charges lodged against many canines out there. Not all dogs are cut out for hiking. If this is the case with your dog, please leave Fido at home. Unfortunately, bringing your dog into the woods has become a privilege, not a right. Don't blow it for all the responsible dog owners.

WHAT YOU'LL FIND IN THIS GUIDE

As I've said, this guide is meant to broaden your horizons when it comes to choosing a long-distance hike. To find these gems, you won't get buried under an avalanche of maps and assorted trail guides, or go blind surfing the web. I've done all the grueling initial research for you! You just have to curl up and dream about your next adventure.

Each trail chapter gives you the basics. The Vitals section tells you distance and how long a trail might take to hike, the hiking season, water availability, resupply opportunities, who to contact for trail updates, when the trail was first thru-hiked, and how many annual thru-hikers generally complete the trail. The Don't Leave Home without It sidebars feature items you'll want especially for that trail. The Weather section provides a month-by-month profile of each trail's average temperatures. The Terrain section describes some key features you can expect to see, and what kind of route the trail follows—whether on trail or on roads. Next, the Water section tells you how to tank up on a trail. The Wildness section tells you how much solitude you might expect and what permit and regulation issues you might encounter. The Wildlife section lists animals to see (or avoid), even on the most "front-country" of trails. Points of Interest are just that: noteworthy places along the trail or nearby.

Each trail chapter winds down with In Their Own Words—descriptions of the trail from the people who know it best, whether they are thru-hikers or dedicated trail volunteers. Finally, check out each chapter's Recommended Resources, which appear at the end of the book. This is your next stop for research after you've chosen a trail.

A NOTE ON TRAIL DISTANCES

You may notice that trail distances on eight hikes have been slightly rounded off. For example, the 117.7-mile Metacomet-Monadnock Trail is listed as 120 miles. This was done to make things clearer. With simplified mileage, lengths are more straightforward and comparable. Besides, if you were to push a measuring wheel the entire length of the Metacomet-Monadnock Trail, or any other long path for that matter, you would not get the same exact reading every time.

A NOTE ON PACE

The estimations for daily mileage and days needed to complete each trail assume that you're an experienced long-distance hiker with a lightweight pack and that you're traveling during the normal hiking season. Many of the miles-per-day figures represent my personal thru-hiking experiences with roughly 20 percent of my daily mileage subtracted. Along those lines, many of the total-days figures represent my personal thru-hiking experiences with approximately 20 percent of my total days added. Each hiker is expected to set his or her own pace.

ARE YOU READY?

All right! You've packed your gear, the neighbors are going to check the mail while you're gone, and you reviewed the guidebooks and maps for the trail you intend to hike. You even earned wilderness first-aid certification. You are ready! But wait a minute. *Are* you ready? Hiking a long-distance trail is the combination of living in an unfamiliar environment, eating repetitive rations, finding yourself alone in the middle of nowhere, and tolerating all kinds of nasty weather with only a damp sleeping bag to look forward to at the end of the day. Trust me, a long-distance adventure will resemble nothing like the deceitful photos of overjoyed, squeaky-clean people featured in magazines and gear catalogs, where it never rains and blackflies don't exist. In reality, tents leak, knees scrape, snow falls in May, boots fall apart, swarms of bugs resemble clouds, and you start to smell really, really bad. You'll begin to detest trail life when you learn that all these things can happen to you before 9:00 a.m. You may even find yourself saying these things once you're on your way (I have said most of them):

> "I haven't taken off my bug net in a week."
>
> "According to the map, we have more than six thousand vertical feet of climbing to do today."
>
> "I know it's really hot, honey, but there's a tiny spot of shade seven miles ahead."
>
> "Oh, this bandage? Yeah, I got attacked by a dog yesterday."
>
> "At least it wasn't a *steep* forty-mile road walk."

"This feels like a scene from *Deliverance*."

"Did you see where the alligator went?"

"I thought there was a limit to how gross an outhouse could be."

"Apart from the chunks of ice, it shouldn't be *too* hard to cross the river."

"Does this look like poison ivy to you?"

"They're calling for another two weeks of rain."

"I never want to be that close to a moose again."

"It's supposed to drop down into the eighties tonight."

"Having the runs for two weeks just can't be good for you."

"I can't eat this; I had the same thing for breakfast *and* lunch already."

"This is not what I thought it would be."

. . . you are warned.

GET PACKING

Long-distance hiking is a unique experience that I encourage you to try at least once in your life. Being deep in nature's arms, self-sufficient, and visiting areas that are beyond beautiful are the things that keep the animal within us alive. After completing a long-distance hike, you'll probably be a different person. You'll see the world differently. You'll appreciate natural areas and notice ones that are being threatened or exploited. You'll be in better physical and mental condition. Your senses will be sharp, and noise will seem like . . . noise. You will think a two-mile walk to the store is pretty short. You'll meet wonderful people on your trip and remember the outrageous stories they told you. Your trip will be good for the environment, too: your unused car will release zero emissions, you will use no electricity, you will buy only what you can carry, and you'll produce a limited amount of garbage. And when you do your "business" out there, you won't flush a tree and waste a gallon of water.

E. SCHLIMMER

You can leave behind the material-based world we have created. Jerry Mander's book *In the Absence of the Sacred* describes this human-altered, unnatural world of ours.

From morning to night we walk through a world that is totally manufactured, a creation of human invention. We are surrounded by pavement, machinery, gigantic concrete structures. Automobiles, airplanes, television, electric lights, artificial air have become the physical universe with which our senses interact.

Through a long-distance trail, you can leave most of these things behind. During an extended stay in the natural environment, you will possess the power to remove what has been slowly forced into your daily existence: domestication, complacency, and unobtainable, unrewarding goals. Renew your relationship with the natural world, and yourself, today. Get outside, and happy hiking to all!

arizona trail

790 MILES | ARIZONA

TO GO . . .

- great chances for solitude
- guaranteed sunshine
- possible thru-bike route
- state highpoint as a side trip

OR NOT TO GO?

- gets very hot in summer
- few reliable water sources
- limited thru-hiker support system
- possible heavy snow in winter, especially north of Payson

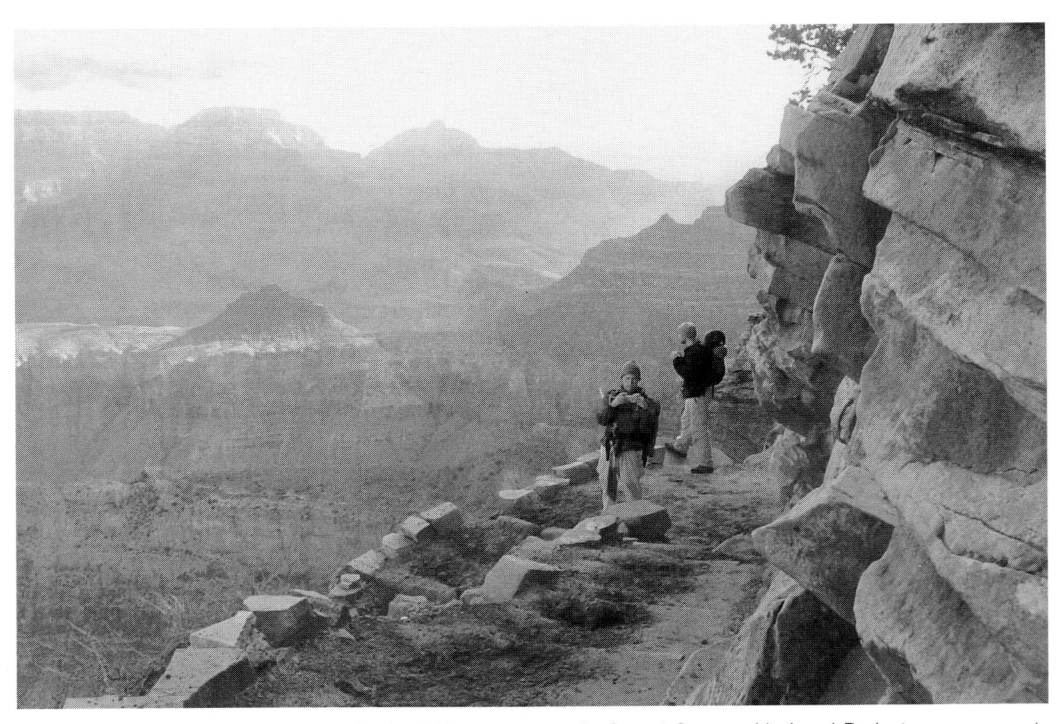

The South Kaibab Trail above the Cedar Ridge rest area in Grand Canyon National Park. (DORI PEDERSON)

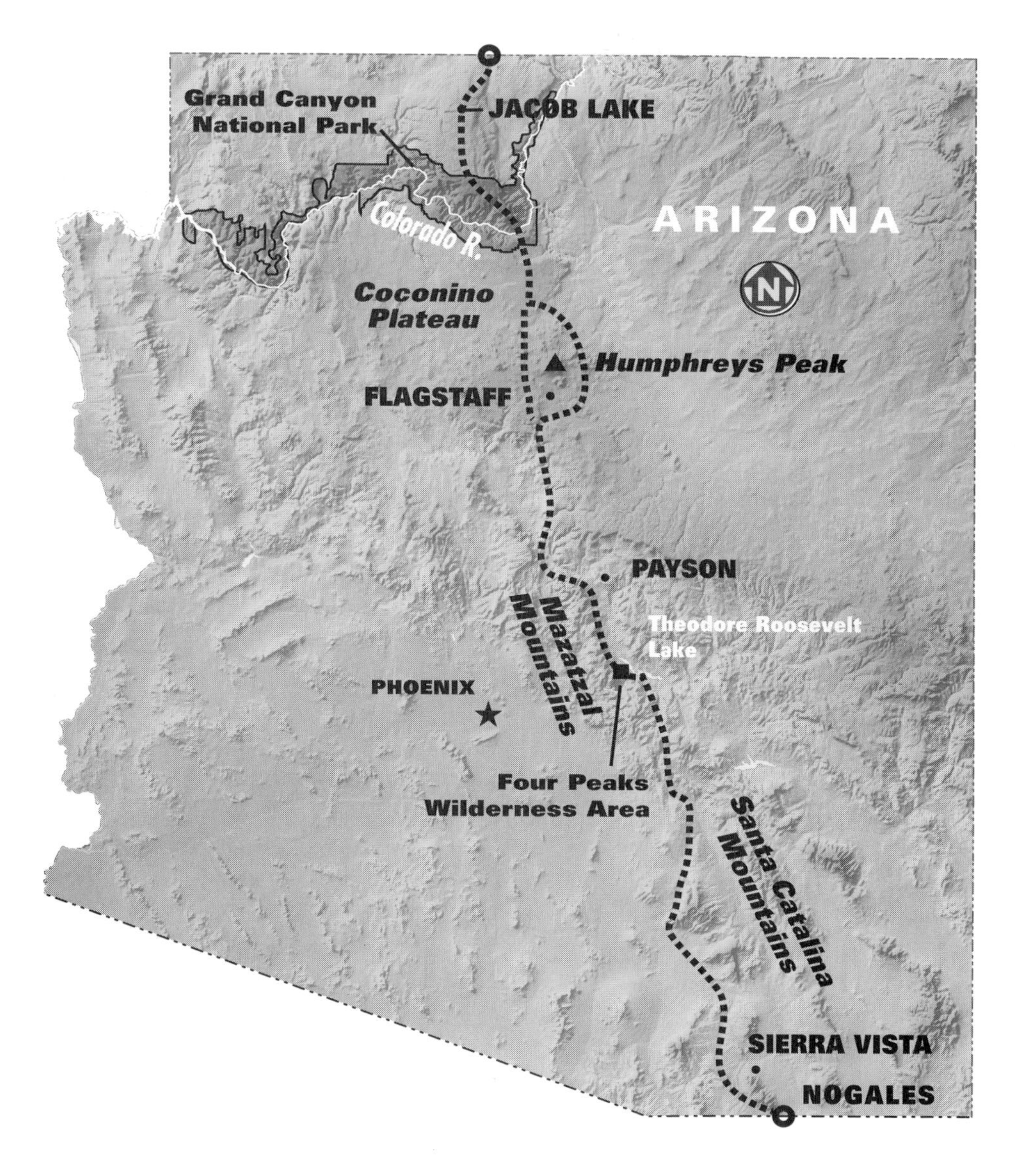

- Towns near or on the trail
- ★ State capital
- Trail terminus
- Trail route
- Wilderness area

The Arizona Trail (AZT) is the fifth-longest trail in the guide, clocking in at just less than 800 miles in length. When fully completed, it will wind its way from the northern terminus at the Utah border all the way to the Coronado National Memorial, near the United States–Mexico border town Nogales. It will take you deep into desert territory, a landscape unfamiliar to most of us.

People sometimes imagine the Southwest as a barren land, mostly composed of sand, minor hills, and flat desert. Although the AZT travels through these types of terrain, this trail throws in major mountain ranges (with major climbing) more reminiscent of California's Sierra Nevada or Utah's Uinta Mountains.

The AZT has not been completely marked as of yet, and sections of unmarked terrain, especially south of Flagstaff, can be confusing. But this trail is thru-hikeable, if you examine maps carefully and don't mind some road walking. The trail is also "thru-bikeable"; see Andrea Lankford's well-researched book listed under Recommended Resources.

Concerning desert environments, some claim the AZT course through the Grand Canyon traverses "three of the four deserts in North America." However, no one can seem to agree on two things: (1) how many deserts there are in North America and (2) which ones are in the Grand Canyon. At least three separate legitimate lists can be found in regard to how many deserts are in North America and an equal amount theorize which ones are in the canyon. After crossing the entire U.S.-Mexico border by bike, biking the Arizona Trail, spending a month in the Mojave Desert, and doing some computer-based research, I conclude that there are five deserts in North America: The Chihuahuan, Colorado Plateau, Great Basin, Mojave, and Sonoran deserts. I also think the Colorado Plateau, Mojave, and Sonoran Deserts are in the Grand Canyon.

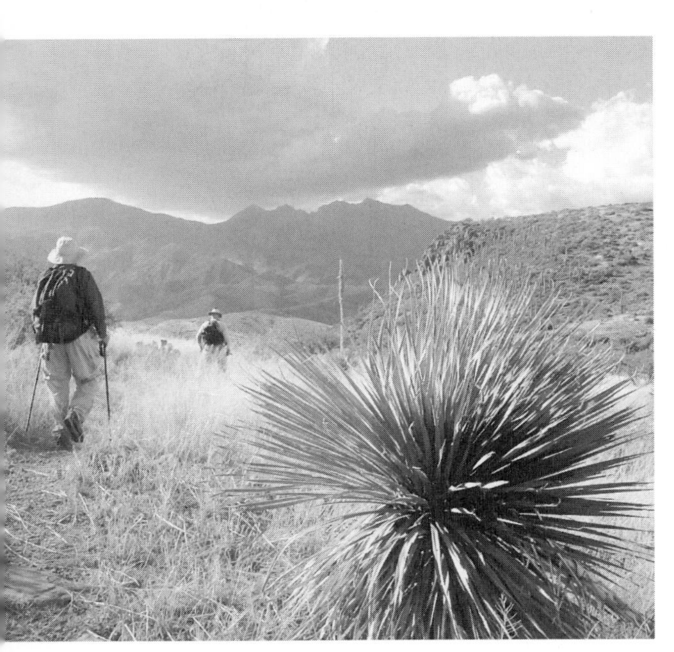

Hikers make their way north on the Arizona Trail while Four Peaks Wilderness Area looms in the background. (DORI PEDERSON)

Desert walking makes for some serious alone time. In a past issue of *Backpacker* magazine, readers voted the Arizona Trail number four in the best solitude category. Dale Shewalter surely knows this. Dale is a schoolteacher who first covered the AZT's basic route in 1985 and since then has dedicated himself to getting this trail built. Today, Shewalter serves on the Arizona Trail Association's Board of Directors.

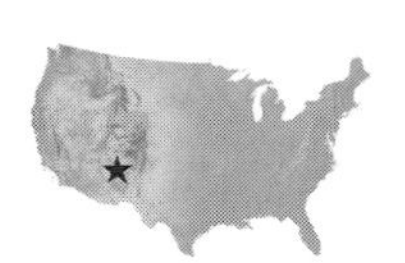

GRAND CANYON NATIONAL PARK

No, Richard Nixon didn't visit this park and say, "Wow, this really is a grand canyon!" But it is. Really. Covering nearly 2,000 square miles, with 277 miles of the Colorado River at the bottom, the canyon is as wide as 18 miles and as narrow as 4 miles, and is roughly one mile deep. The highpoint in the park is Lookout Tower, at 9,165 feet; the low point is the Colorado River, at around 2,400 feet. The Grand Canyon is estimated to be five million years old, with some rocks on the very bottom dating back two billion years. This national park is a jackpot for those seeking a

SCHLIMMER'S SIDE TRAIL

HIGHPOINTERS TAKE NOTE

Towering 12,633 feet above sea level and more than 5,000 feet above the nearby town of Flagstaff, Humphreys Peak (Arizona's highest summit) is a day hike away from the AZT itself (a "day hike" once you get used to the elevation). The AZT travels to the Snow Bowl trailhead, located at 9,450 feet at the base of a ski area on the west side of the mountain. Hikers reach this starting point by driving up a steep, winding seven-mile-long road; from which you can pull off for a night of camping above 7,000 feet to help get acclimated. A 4.5-mile walk brings you to Humphreys's narrow summit, but only after tiptoeing through loose rock above 12,000 feet. The immediate area surrounding Humphreys lacks any other major mountain ranges, but nearby Agassiz Peak (12,356 feet), Freemont Peak (11,969 feet), Humphreys's ancient volcanic crater, and the flat desert far below constitute a satisfying view. Nearby Agassiz Peak and most areas above the 11,500-foot level are closed to foot traffic due to fragile vegetation. If you get caught in these areas, you just had yourself a $500 off-trail hike. Also, Humphreys Peak is located in the Kachina Peaks Wilderness Area, where bikes are not allowed. AZT thru-bikers can ride on the wilderness-area boundary, following Forest Road 522 south of the San Francisco Peaks and Forest Road 151 on the west side of the wilderness area.

The view of Agassiz Peak from atop Humphreys is worth the detour. (E. SCHLIMMER)

The first recorded ascent of Humphreys Peak was before 1900, but it's certain that Native Americans reached the top long before that time, because the Sinagua Indians lived in present-day Flagstaff prior to the year 1000. Going back further to its prehistoric state, Humphreys and the rest of the San Francisco Peaks comprised one huge mountain that may have been as tall as 20,000 feet. More recently, the peak was named for A. A. Humphrey, of the U.S. Army Engineers. ■

The Arizona Trail crosses the Gila River numerous times. Saguaro cacti stand tall here in Whitford Canyon. (DORI PEDERSON)

variety of natural wonders. If you look hard enough and long enough, you could spot more than fifty species of reptiles, nearly ninety different mammals, hundreds of flowering plant varieties, and more than three hundred types of birds. This canyon certainly deserves its ranking as one of the natural wonders of the world. Traces of humans living in and around the canyon date back to 2,000 BC; the first Europeans to see the canyon were probably the Spanish Conquistadors, led by García López de Cárdenas, who conducted expeditions in the Southwest around 1540.

In 1869, John Wesley Powell, a one-armed U.S. Army major, ran the Colorado River during a near-hundred-day expedition in 1869. During this trip Powell and his team named the main canyon and many of its features. From that point forward, many developments took place within the Grand Canyon; the first hiking trail was built in 1891, and the area gained national park status in 1919. Today, AZT thru-hikers descend the North Rim on the North Kaibab Trail (~14 miles long, descends ~6,000 vertical feet) and climb the South Rim on the Bright Angel Trail (~8 miles long, climbs ~4,000 vertical feet).

During non-winter months in the Grand Canyon you will most likely need to secure a backcountry camping permit. For more information, surf the trip planning section of the National Park Service's website at www.nps.gov/grca/ grandcanyon/index/htm. You can also call the park's backcountry office at 928-638-7875.

If you decide to thru-bike the AZT, there's bad news: biking (that is, *riding* bikes) is not allowed below the canyon rim. If you're coming from the north, you'll have to carry and push your bike down approximately 6,000 vertical feet, cross the twenty-four-mile thru-canyon route, and climb 4,500 vertical feet to the South Rim. As an Arizona Trail thru-biker in 2002, I pushed and carried my bike through the entire canyon rather than riding all the way around it. I'll share my plan of attack with you.

First, I took off the pedals, seat, and seat post so my intentions were clear. (The park's real beef with bikes is people riding them, not pushing them.)

At the Colorado River—the topographical low point of my cross-canyon trek—I walked my bike across a stunning suspension bridge, then through a tunnel. At this point I had to get my bike up to the South Rim, which stood 4,500 vertical feet above me. The Bright Angel Trail leading up the South Rim was too rough to even push my bike up, so I had to carry it and its panniers nearly the whole way out. The trail up to

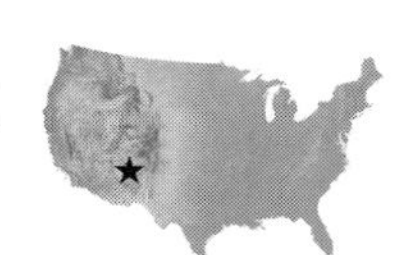

VITALS

- Expect to cover 16 miles a day
- Expect a thru-hike to take 49 days
- Hiking season: September to November, March to May
- Water availability: Seldom
- Resupply opportunities: Sometimes
- First year thru-hiked: 1985
- Approximate yearly thru-hikers: Fewer than 20
- Primary contact: Arizona Trail Association

the South Rim was an eroded mess of dust, slick stone, rock steps, water bars, more dust, and a tiny bit of pack-stock poop. The morning was frigid and the afternoon broiling. There was little shade. On top of this, everyone looked at me as though I was an idiot. Needless to say, pushing and carrying a mountain bike down, across, up, and out of the Grand Canyon was not fun.

If you want to avoid a similar travesty, you can attempt to have your bike shuttled around the canyon using local services, then hike the canyon. Expect to pay at least $75 for a one-way bike transport. You also have the option of biking an eastern route around the canyon on Route 89, but this route is more than 200 miles long. Plus if you take Route 89 you will miss walking through the Grand Canyon, one of the most interesting natural features in the United States. And many people I spoke to who worked in the Grand Canyon told me that I was not the first fool to bring a bike from rim to rim. If you do attempt to thru-bike the entire Arizona Trail, I suggest you stick with your bike, be a rebel, and carry your bike through. Besides, once you explain to people that, yes, you *do* know what you're doing, they'll think you're really tough.

WEATHER

Well, there's no way around it: Arizona can get mighty hot. And the part about it being a dry heat? Actually, the lack of humidity *is* noticeable. A humid 80-degree day of hiking in the Catskills of New York will seem much, much hotter than hiking in 80° on the AZT. However, the intense Southwest sun can fry you if you are not properly prepared. Many savvy Arizona Trail hikers choose to take afternoon siestas. If you're on the AZT in the warm months, getting an early-morning start on this hot-weather trail will save you a lot of frustration and energy later in the day. Hiking at dusk may be a good idea, too.

On the other hand, my experiences proved that it can get pretty cold on the AZT. On my north-to-south trip, the weather was quite cool and sometimes downright cold, because I traversed the trail in the middle of November. In fact, by the time I got to the North Rim of the Grand Canyon, there was an inch of snow on the ground and all facilities were closed. The solitude was great, but I froze!

The nighttime hours are tough, too. If you've been hiking or biking in sunny, 80-degree heat all day, when the sun finally sets and the thermometer drops to 50,

DON'T LEAVE HOME WITHOUT IT

WATER AND MORE WATER

The AZT may be the driest of all 25 trails in this guide. To keep search-and-rescue personnel from finding your dead, dehydrated body (which, by the time they find you, may resemble a handbag more than a human body) be sure to carry plenty of H_2O and always know where the next source is.

---

you're going to feel pretty cold. No more solar radiation and a sudden 30-degree temperature drop? Brrr! In the minds of some well-traveled Southwesterners, there's nothing colder than the desert at night. In addition to those chilly nights, enough snow falls in northern Arizona to support a fully operational ski center in Flagstaff from mid-December to April. And as I personally learned, snow closes the facilities and some roads on the North Rim of the Grand Canyon from November to April. Entering Arizona's higher elevations can mean encountering significant snow and ice, but generally, AZT sections south of the town of Payson are doable year-round.

As for temperatures, the AZT tied with the Cohos Trail and the Ice Age Trail for the widest temperature range: 85° between July's average highs and January's average lows (as recorded in settlements near the trails). On the AZT, the average high for July was 100° in the Grand Canyon, and the average low for January was 15° on the North Rim.

TERRAIN

Terrain ranges from high peaks and plateaus to low canyons. Vegetation can take the shape of forty-foot-tall saguaro cacti to vast mature conifer forests to the low scrub growth of deserts. The AZT passes through the seven life zones of North America on its journey from Utah to our big neighbor to the south, Mexico. The tread is mostly composed of hard-sand-and-pine-needle-based singletrack, forest roads, loose rock and sand, and bedrock.

Basically, the AZT's terrain has two distinct qualities. North of Payson (roughly the halfway point of the AZT), you'll consistently be above 5,000 feet on plateaus among ponderosa pines and aspens. The major areas of high elevation, starting from Utah and heading south, include the Paria Plateau, with a low point of about 5,000 feet, and the Kaibab Plateau that meanders near the 9,000-foot level. After crossing the Grand Canyon you'll be on the Coconino Plateau, which hovers around 7,000 feet for extended distances, and finally, the Mogollon Plateau and Mogollon Rim are ascended. Both rise to more than 7,000 feet.

South of Payson, you'll spend a lot of time in a desert environment mostly below 4,000 feet. You will climb out of the desert, if traveling on foot, among the Mazatzal Mountains, which exceed 7,900 feet, the Santa Catalina Mountains, which reach upward of 9,000 feet, and the Santa Rita Mountains, which also exceed 9,000 feet. Finally, you'll hike (but not bike) in the Miller Peak Wilderness Area of the

AVERAGE HIGHS AND LOWS IN DEGREES FAHRENHEIT	JAN	MAR	MAY	JUL	SEPT	NOV
JACOB LAKE, AZ (7,920 FT.)	25–40	40–60	55–80	70–85	60–85	35–55
PAYSON, AZ (4,890 FT.)	25–55	30–65	40–80	60–95	50–85	30–65
SIERRA VISTA, AZ (4,640 FT.)	35–60	40–70	55–85	65–95	60–90	40–70
GRAND CANYON NATIONAL PARK						
NORTH RIM (8,800 FT.)	15–40	35–55	50–75	65–90	55–80	30–50
COLORADO RIVER (2,400 FT.)	35–55	40–65	60–95	80–100	70–95	30–60
SOUTH RIM (7,000 FT.)	20–40	40–55	55–80	70–90	60–85	30–55

Huachuca Mountains, also exceeding 9,000 feet. End to end, the trail also comes within a series of one- to two-day hikes to the high points of six of Arizona's fifteen counties. The highest points in Coconino, Gila, Maricopa, Pinal, Pima, and Santa Cruz counties can be reached as extended side trips. All of these peaks exceed 7,000 feet in height.

WATER

The AZT deserves respect when it comes to finding ample water. In the hot and dry season from May to September, water is nearly nonexistent for long stretches. All four major river systems that meet the AZT may be completely dry. Almost all of the reliable sources I found on my three-week ride of the AZT in November 2002 were reservoirs and towns; the only natural water source was a stream near the Mexico border. There were sections of my trip where the next reliable water source was more than thirty-five miles away; that would have meant an eleven-hour walk if I hadn't had a bike.

So how do people hike this trail? Well, I didn't say there's *no* water on this long-distance trail; there just isn't as much water to be found here as on the other twenty-four trails discussed in this guide. You have the option of caching water along remote sections of the trail, but the difficult part would be getting to your cache areas prior to your actual thru-hike. Contacting the Arizona Trail Association is a good way to meet "trail angels," people who can cache water for you or help you with

TERRAIN HIGHLIGHTS

- Plateaus over 7,000 feet
- River systems (sometimes dry)
- Deserts
- Conifer and aspen forests
- Vast grasslands
- Canyons
- 9,000-foot peaks
- Washes

Looking southeast into Mexico from the flanks of Miller Peak in southern Arizona. Miller Peak is the highpoint of the Arizona Trail. (DORI PEDERSON)

transportation to and from caches prior to your trip. In my opinion, the best idea is to fill up at all available water sites and pay attention to all informational sources. I never ran out of water on my thru-ride, but, then again, I could carry up to 196 ounces of water and cover 40 miles a day. Carrying one gallon of water in the north seems to be the norm; in the south I carried at least six liters. Remember, that was six liters on a bike. If I had run out of water, I could probably have ridden into town with a few hours of pedaling. If traveling the Arizona Trail on foot, you could be a day's walk away from water.

Another thing to remember is that during the winter and late fall, the water sources at many campgrounds are shut off and unavailable for use. What I mean is, the water faucet is not just turned off; it is made inoperable. Even with a government-style water key, I wouldn't have been able to get water from campground systems. To top off the bleak water situation, on central sections of the Arizona Trail, many lakes were completely dry, including Lower Mary Lake and Upper Mary Lake. As Andrea Lankford reminds us in *Biking the Arizona Trail*, "It will surprise some of you to see what passes for a 'lake' in Arizona."

There are also "tanks" listed in Andrea Lankford's guide, but I would not rely on these; nor would I use most of them even if they were full of water. A tank can be a human-made aboveground holding tank or simply a hole dug in the mid-

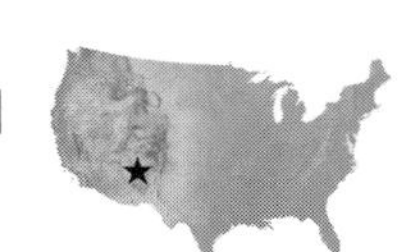

dle of a pasture. Unless I had really good health insurance and happened to be traveling with a gastroenterologist, I wouldn't drink water from these tanks, even if I filtered it. Some of the water sources are really gross. Cows standing in the water. Feathers on the surface. Bad smells. Bad news. Besides, in the fall of 2002, I found half of these tanks empty. Needless to say, good water planning on the Arizona Trail is of the utmost importance.

WILDNESS

For wildness in an open setting, the Arizona Trail is hard to beat. Though a legitimate long-distance trail, it is not as well known as its similar alpine neighbor in California, the John Muir Trail. This is good; you will see fewer people than you would on the John Muir Trail. Although nearly all sections of the AZT are within half a day's drive of Phoenix, Tucson, and Flagstaff—with a collective population exceeding 1.8 million people—most of those people are not going to find you on the desolate parts of the AZT. I saw few other mountain cyclists and hikers on my end-to-end trek—maybe a dozen hikers or bikers overall. However, there is a section near Flagstaff where thru-hikers can choose between a more urban or wilderness route.

Concerning roads near the AZT, most likely you'll find major throughways heading only to the bigger cities, away from the AZT. Most roads clearly avoid the state's more remote desert areas.

The Arizona Trail is designed for multiple uses, allowing mountain bikes, in addition to llamas, horses, and other pack stock, for most of the route. Along the way, you'll encounter lands administered by the Bureau of Land Management, National Park Service, Arizona State Land Department, United States Forest Service, and Arizona State Park. Grand Canyon National Park requires backcountry permits for camping. Throughout the trip, resupply points for food and water, and a cool shower, will only be a few days apart, but be prepared to carry up to six days' worth of food and, of course, a lot of water (at 8.3 pounds per gallon). I found the most northern- and southernmost sections of the AZT to be the most remote. At these locations you'll walk perhaps an entire week between sources of food and water.

WILDLIFE

The thought of hiking among only snakes and lizards on the Arizona Trail should be put aside. Expect to see a lot of different critters, from little reptiles to large mammals. The AZT's elevation ranges from a low point of approximately a thousand feet all the way up to 9,000 feet, creating different life zones. (If you decide to take the

CRITTERS

- California condor
- Coyotes
- Elk
- Mountain lions
- Pronghorn antelope
- Ringtail cats
- Scorpions
- Spotted skunks
- Venomous snakes

side trail to Humphreys Peak, then the upper range of your trip will top 12,600 feet.) In many sections of the trail, the increased elevation creates "sky islands," which support different ecosystems. Some of these sky islands stand 5,000 feet above the surrounding deserts.

POINTS OF INTEREST

ON EACH END

The AZT's northern terminus is set among gorgeous red peaks and ridges that rise from the rugged Paria Plateau and flow into Utah. The southern terminus is located only a few miles south of Miller Peak, which reaches more than 9,000 feet above sea level, with views into Mexico's desert-and-mountain wonderland.

FOUR PEAKS WILDERNESS

The Four Peaks Wilderness Area, located inside Tonto National Forest and near the small town of Punkin Center, is home to black bears, as well as the distinctive mountain range this area is named for.

DAM IT!

In central Arizona's arid Tonto Basin sits a lake of such enormous proportions it looks like a mirage. This body of water, Roosevelt Lake, is human made and quite popular with those who love water sports. You'll cross blue-painted Roosevelt Bridge, which provides grand views of the lake and surrounding mesas. Below this bridge is the largest masonry dam in the world. In 1995, Roosevelt Bridge was voted onto the top-twelve list of most outstanding bridges in the United States.

TOWERING OVER TUSCON

Located northeast of Tucson, the Santa Catalina Mountains are popular with local valley residents attempting to escape the desert heat. If you are thru-biking the Arizona Trail south, you'll savor the 10-mile descent on the Catalina Highway as you coast down 3,000 vertical feet into downtown Tucson. The Catalina Ridge hosts picnic areas and at least one campground, too.

CANYON HIKING

The Grand Canyon, albeit the biggest and most grand, is just one of the many beautiful canyons and washes of the Arizona Trail. Places like Alamo Canyon, Coyote Wash, Fish Canyon, and Cottonwood Canyon give the thru-hiker all they could imagine: sand and rock walls, culturally significant historic sites, and a grand scale that may make you feel relatively insignificant. Water is sometimes available at the bottom of major canyons, and there is shade down there when the sun is not at its apex.

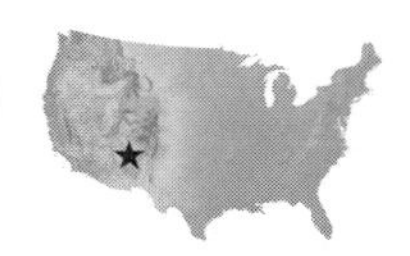

In Their Own Words . . .

Greetings from Nogales, Arizona, everyone. I made it! The hardest part of my Arizona Trail Ride was trying to buy a bus ticket here in Nogales. No one in the entire town except me, a Border Patrol guy, and one bus driver speaks English. My bike is way more tired than I am. It has a leaky front tube, shredded sidewall on the rear tire, broken front and rear shifters, and bare-bones brake pads.

Overall the trip was good, and a great learning experience for another (?) bike trip. The 800 miles included six flat tires, well over 25,000 vertical feet of climbing, washboard dirt roads, and challenging singletrack. I met one spotted skunk, seven mule deer, many roadrunners, vacationing and resident birds, squirrels, and four coyotes, with packs of coyotes around me every other night. I averaged forty miles a day. My shortest day was six miles in the Grand Canyon, and my longest day was approximately fifty-two miles. At one point, in Tortilla Flats, AZ, I bombed a road where I hit fifty miles per hour, at the same time covering one mile in only ninety-four seconds! Wow!

I rode by locales such as Mad as Hell Ranch, Punkin Center, The Butcher Hook, Bar X Road, and I biked through Ed Abbey's old hometown, as well as a section of road maintained by the fine people from the Metallica Club of Tucson. I traversed three national forests and one national park, with this entire bike route being about half dirt and half pavement.

Temperatures ranged from 20° to 70°, with snow, freezing rain, gorgeous sunsets and sunrises, rainbows, rain, wind (mostly headwinds, of course), clouds, fog, sun, sandstorms, and lightning storms. On the entire route I encountered just one stream and one marsh. The flora included ponderosa pine, cacti, scrub oak, and Saguaro cacti. The terrain was great—three of the five deserts in the U.S., the seven life zones of the U.S., the highest peak in Arizona—and I rode at over 8,000 feet for seven days on four major plateaus.

—Blake McDonnel, 2002 Arizona Trail thru-biker

baker trail

140 MILES | PENNSYLVANIA

TO GO . . .

- interesting geology and rugged terrain
- small, rural towns with nearby Amish culture
- crowd factor is low
- additional 4,200 miles of hiking available beyond the northern terminus

OR NOT TO GO?

- 55 miles of road walking
- lack of true wilderness
- some shelters in rough shape
- obvious human impact

Crooked Creek shelter, a classic Adirondack-style lean-to, is one of ten shelters along the 140-mile Baker Trail. (JIM RITCHIE)

The Baker Trail (BT), in western Pennsylvania, is the first of four trails described in this guide that are located in the Keystone State. The BT was established in the early 1950s, as were many long-distance trails throughout the United States. The trail's southern terminus is located just northeast of Pittsburgh, near Freeport. The trail heads a basic course of north-northeast to its northern terminus near the small town of Marienville, approximately 60 miles from the New York State border. If the 140 miles are just not enough for you, the BT hooks up with the North Country National Scenic Trail (NCT), which continues north to the New York border ninety-five trail miles to the north. And if you *really* want to keep walking, the North Country National Scenic Trail will cover roughly 4,200 miles total, stretching from Lake Champlain, in New York, all the way to North Dakota, when complete. Currently, the North Country National Scenic Trail and Baker Trail share 16 miles of tread

After decades of stewardship, the Pittsburgh chapter of Hostelling International (formerly AYH) elected to relinquish the Baker Trail and the Rachel Carson Trail to

SCHLIMMER'S SIDE TRAIL

THE NORTH COUNTRY NATIONAL SCENIC TRAIL (NCT)

At nearly double the length of the legendary Appalachian Trail, the NCT is the longest of America's eight national scenic trails. Starting from Crown Point on the shore of Lake Champlain in Upstate New York, the NCT travels west through New York, Pennsylvania, Ohio, Michigan, Wisconsin, and Minnesota, to end in Lake Sakakawea State Park in the middle of North Dakota. Though the current NCT route has literally thousands of miles of road walking and is insanely long, about five people have actually covered the current route end to end. The good news is that there are 1,700 off-road miles waiting for you and the great news is that this figure increases annually. The NCT certainly has a relationship with many trails featured in this guide. The Baker Trail, Buckeye Trail, Shore-to-Shore Trail, and Superior Hiking Trail each tie into the North Country Trail and sometimes these shorter trails are actually overrun by extended sections of the NCT. ■

The Rachel Carson Trails Conservancy—an all-volunteer organization dedicated to the development, protection, and promotion of hiking, biking, and walking trails throughout western Pennsylvania.

Founded in 1994 (as the Harmony Trails Council), its mission was to develop, promote, establish, and maintain a multi-use public trail system as an alternate transportation and recreation facility serving the residents of Pittsburgh's North Hills, focusing on the railbed of the former Harmony inter-urban rail line. The Harmony Trails Council chose to adopt the BT and RCT thereby expanding its mission. At the same time, the Council voted to change its name to the Rachel Carson Trails Conservancy to better reflect its broader mission.

Wilder than Pennsylvania's 190-mile Mason-Dixon Trail but more civilized than its 260-mile Mid State Trail, the Baker Trail winds its way among countless hills, ridges, and drainages, complete with rocky ascents and descents. When comparing shortest hiking times from end to end, the Baker Trail ties for third place with the Metacomet-Monadnock Trail and the Northville-Placid Trail. At sixteen miles a day, you can hike the BT in fewer than ten days.

The BT is one of the older long-distance trails in this guide. It was officially opened way back in 1951. An early edition of Jim Ritchie's *Baker Trail Guide Book*, published to celebrate the twenty-fifth anniversary of the trail, tells of the trail's creators and first thru-hikers.

Betty Bierer and Wes Bunnelle hiked the entire length of the trail and arrived just in time to attend the official opening ceremony held in Cook Forest State Park on August 18, 1951.

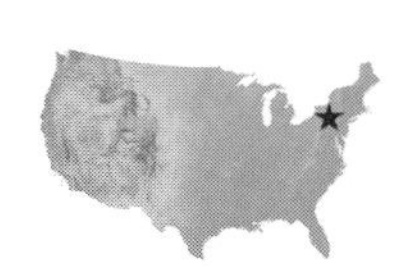

VITALS

- Expect to cover 16 miles a day
- Expect a thru-hike to take 9 days
- Hiking season: April to October
- Water availability: Frequent
- Resupply opportunities: Frequent
- First year thru-hiked: 1951
- Approximate yearly thru-hikers: Fewer than 20
- Primary contact: Rachel Carson Trails Conservancy

Betty Bierer is notable in that she and Tony Pranses (first Chairman of the Pittsburgh AYH [American Youth Hostels], 1948–1950), while on an AYH canoe trip on the Allegheny River from Freeport to the Point in Pittsburgh, conceived the idea of the Baker Trail. Tony writes in his journal, "Betty and I were paddling slowly and pleasantly down the river somewhere between Freeport and Tarentum when it occurred to us that it would be equally special to be on top of those scenic cliffs looking down on the river as it would be where we were looking up."

WEATHER

Northwestern Pennsylvania can see major amounts of lake effect snow thanks to nearby Lake Erie, so unless you're looking for a full-on winter trip, you'll have to wait for the white stuff to melt from the Baker Trail, especially on the northern sections. Parts of the Baker Trail north of I-80 have held snow until mid April, whereas the southern sections had no significant snow at that time. If you're getting ready to head out in late April, a south-to-north trek is the natural choice.

Late spring may be the best time of the year for hiking. There will be no bugs (yet), you'll find plenty of water, and the springtime blooms of early May are wonderful to hike through.

Summers can be humid and hot, with daytime highs sometimes reaching the upper eighties. The hiking season can last into mid November, which will bring cool temperatures, the possibility of some light flurries, and gorgeous fall foliage, which starts to peak in early October. You should be aware that hunting seasons start at this time of year; please note that many folks will be out there with guns. But, your chances of encountering a problem are extremely low. Use common-sense tactics, such as making a little bit of noise and wearing bright colors. (Fur coats are *not* OK.) Heading south to north, expect to hike in the temperatures listed.

AVERAGE HIGHS AND LOWS IN DEGREES FAHRENHEIT

	JAN	MAR	MAY	JUL	SEPT	NOV
FREEPORT, PA (780 FT.)	20–35	25–50	45–75	60–85	50–80	30–55
MARIENVILLE, PA (1,740 FT.)	15–30	25–45	45–70	55–80	50–70	30–50

A swimming hole awaits you under this old iron bridge at Mill Creek in Jefferson County. (JIM RITCHIE)

TERRAIN

Hiking in Pennsylvania means hiking over, under, and around a plentiful selection of rocks, boulders, cliffs, scree, gravel, cobble, and talus. Surely this is why many Appalachian Trail thru-hikers have affectionately dubbed Pennsylvania "Rocksylvania."

Of course, there's more to this route than just rocks. The BT takes you on paved and dirt roads, fields, farmland, clearcuts, gas lines, singletrack, and doubletrack jeep trails. Parts of the Baker Trail, especially the singletrack portions, can be quite overgrown due to the trail's limited use. In addition, this part of Pennsylvania is home to Japanese knotweed that can overwhelm a trail by growing up to eight feet tall.

You'll encounter many short, steep, and rough climbs on the BT. A pace that slows to one mile per hour will allow you to notice the up-close intricacies of Pennsylvania's geology, only to reach a macro view at the top of your hard-earned climb. Half of the seventeen BT maps included in Jim Ritchie's *Baker Trail Guide Book* have a highpoint exceeding 1,500 feet, and all of these maps contain a highpoint reaching upward of 1,000 feet in elevation. No ascents on the Baker Trail exceed 1,000 vertical feet. Most of the climbs, which are sometimes very rough, rarely exceed 400 vertical feet.

WATER

Finding water is not a challenge on the BT. A quick look at any of the seventeen maps in the *Guide Book* reveals numerous drainages (although some are seasonal) that will bring you water each day. Most of the shelters along the BT usually have a reliable water source, too, and the trail passes major river systems (most notably the Allegheny and Clarion rivers) and several small lakes and ponds. In addition to skirt-

TERRAIN HIGHLIGHTS

- Rocky climbs and scree fields
- Oak forests
- Allegheny River valley
- Historical landmarks
- Mountain views
- Amish culture
- Spring-fed streams

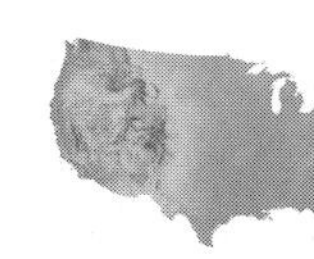

DON'T LEAVE HOME WITHOUT IT

PEPPER SPRAY

If those Baker Trail lean-to "beer heads" can't find anything better to do than harass you for being a "tree hugger," you'll be well prepared with a canister of good ol' oleoresin capsicum.

---

ing natural sources, the trail passes through many small settlements, where the polite hiker can request a couple of quarts of water from local residents.

WILDNESS

Like Pennsylvania's Mid State Trail, the Baker Trail gives you the feeling you're in the middle of nowhere, when in reality the nearest road is only one to two miles away and the nearest town is less than a day's hike. Simply put, the Baker Trail feels wilder than it actually is. It sees few thru-hikers and little other hiking traffic, so you can expect to find periods of solitude from one end of the trail to the other.

You'll make your way through private land, state forest, state game lands, state parks, national forest, and Christmas tree farms (no fires whatsoever are allowed on Christmas tree farms or state game lands). You will walk through several settlements, although many of these towns don't even show up on a road atlas. Of the BT's 140 miles, approximately 85 miles are located off road, with the remaining 55 miles of road walking being pretty much in the middle of nowhere on paved or dirt country roads. A typical Baker Trail section may be like this one described by Jim Ritchie:

You will come to some nice (unofficial) campsites overlooking the creek. After this, the trail goes on rural backroads for a long ways. Interesting, but not wilderness. Amish country. The Idaho Shelter (#4) is ok; it's about a mile off the trail to get there. Back off the road. Back on the road. The Atwood Shelter (#5) is ok. On backroads. The Milo Weaver Shelter (#6) is ok. On backroads. Off-road, along Little Mahoning Creek. On road past Milton. Off roads, down to Mahoning Reservoir.

So do not fear: you'll never find yourself hiking among intense traffic or in the breakdown lane of I-80 (although horse traffic is allowed on most of the trail). If you hike from end to end, you'll pass ten shelters, most with a fire pit in front and a water source close by, in addition to a privy. Some of the lean-tos are in poor condition due to their old age (some date back to the 1950s) and vandalism by people whom Ritchie calls "beer heads." These absinthe-minded recreationists have been a consistent concern. Therefore, it would be wise to avoid these shelters on Friday or Saturday nights (aka beer nights). Cautious hikers would not stay at roadside lean-tos no matter what night of the week, no matter what trail. In general, shelters nearest roads are the ones you'll most likely find trashed prior to you getting there. Or you can witness a trash-

CRITTERS

- Black bears
- Coyotes
- Farm animals
- Rattlesnakes
- Red foxes
- Skunks
- Wild turkeys

ing firsthand if you stay there on a beer night. You'll find many primitive tent sites, both official and unofficial, near the BT as well. Other human-made features that you'll encounter are gas lines, gas wells, modest mining operations, neighborhoods, small towns, roads, and farmland.

WILDLIFE

You should see an assortment of Pennsylvania residents that climb in the trees, hide among the rocks, run through the woods, and swim in the water—and those are just the humans. The second-most common mammal you'll see will likely be the white-tailed deer. Anyone who has hiked in Pennsylvania has probably had the luck to see one of these animals; some drivers have been unlucky enough to literally run into one. If you keep your eyes peeled and ears open, you also have a chance of spotting other critters, from as small as a vole to as large as a black bear.

POINTS OF INTEREST

SOUTHERN TERMINUS

The south end of the Baker Trail is a real gem. Starting at the bridge that crosses the Allegheny River in Freeport, you climb a bluff for a view of this small town and big river. After this climb you'll shortly cross the Kiskiminetas River. (This area, especially the bridge over "the Kiski," is prone to closures by landowners. Check with Rachel Carson Trails Conservancy before heading to the southern terminus.)

THE ALLEGHENY

From some of the high bluffs and ridges near the southern terminus of the BT, you can see the Allegheny River. This waterway, which drains more than 10,000 square miles of terrain, cuts a 300-mile course through southwestern New York, northwestern Pennsylvania, and eventually into the Ohio River. In the past, and now to a lesser extent, this river was used mainly to haul oil, gas, and coal.

A RIVER RUNS OVER IT

Cherry Run, located at the far southern section of the BT, can become gnarly enough in spring to flood a section of the trail. You may have to slab against the steep slopes that confine Cherry Run, which flows south. This area is loaded with wildflowers in spring. A proposed cable bridge may soon be built nearby.

The Baker Trail's path skirts the southwestern edge of Allegheny National Forest near its northern junction with the North Country Trail. (JIM RITCHIE)

WHERE ARE WE?

The Baker Trail passes by or through many small rural settlements such as Langsville, Cochrans Mills, Cooksburg, Heathville, and North Freedom, many of which are steeped in Amish culture and surrounded by gorgeous farmland.

OLD VIRGINS

Cook Forest State Park, near the northern terminus, has stands of virgin pine, hemlock, and hardwoods growing up to 175 feet tall. If you don't feel like climbing to the top of one of these for a view, there's a fire tower nearby, which you can safely scale.

In Their Own Words . . .

Most backpacking trails take one to the backcountry. Most hikers enjoy solitude and their day might be ruined if they see another hiker on the trail. But, you don't have to be a misanthropist to be a hiker. Some trails keep you in the frontcountry, the American Discovery Trail being the most publicized and prominent of those. The Baker Trail is Western Pennsylvania's version of a frontcountry backpacking trail.

About forty percent of the Baker Trail winds along remote rural dirt roads, past the farms of the Amish and the English, and in spite of itself, takes about sixty percent of its 140 miles through forests and farmlands. You will see people on this hike, you will have a chance to say "hello," and you will see this part of America from a footpath perspective. You might meet Mr. Himes, who gladly makes water available to hikers and allows backpackers to camp in his yard near Heathville. Amos Duck is another Baker Trail personality you may meet, who keeps a logbook of passing thru hikers north of Summerville, just past your route on Todd Town Road.

In spite of the pretence of gentility, the Baker Trail is a tough trail and requires advanced backpacking skills. The trail goes where it can, sometimes up very steep hills. The Baker Trail's ten backpacking shelters are an average of twelve to fifteen miles apart. You need to be trail savvy to hike this trail. It is primitive and mostly unimproved off-road. There are few bridges and once or twice you'll get your feet wet. And although it is generally well blazed in yellow (off-road), you need the map! Try it—you might like it.

—Jim Ritchie, *Baker Trail Guide Book* editor

buckeye trail

1,280 MILES | OHIO

TO GO . . .

- > longest loop hike in the United States
- > you'll see every corner of Ohio
- > enormous variety of terrain, both natural and unnatural
- > possible thru-bike route

OR NOT TO GO?

- > not a true wilderness setting overall
- > limited options for backcountry camping
- > urbanized terrain
- > extensive sections of private land to traverse

The inviting waters of Cedar Falls. (RICHARD PFEIFFER)

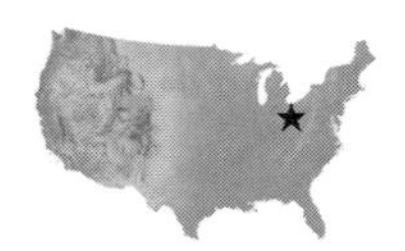

Some contend that the Buckeye Trail (BT) is the longest trail contained within a single state, but I'd say the 1,300-mile Florida Trail beats that claim by twenty miles. If you were to thru-hike the Buckeye Trail, though, I doubt it would seem any shorter; 1,280 miles is a formidable distance. The BT takes the longest to traverse of all the trails in this guide. On both the Buckeye Trail and Florida Trail you will perhaps average the same daily mileage, but an end-to-end hike of the Florida Trail can be completed by hiking only 1,180 of its total 1,300 miles due to two loop sections. When it comes to highest projected daily mileage, the BT ties the Florida Trail and the Lone Star Hiking Trail. Because of the BT's relatively smooth terrain, an experienced backpacker with a lightweight pack may be able to average eighteen or more miles a day.

It matters very little where you start your thru-hike because the BT is a giant loop trail. Therefore, if you make it all the way to the other end, you'll eliminate any frustrating post-trip logistics. (There are two other loops included in this guide: the Tahoe Rim Trail and Wonderland Trail.)

Traveling through forty of Ohio's eighty-eight counties, the BT crosses a mix of private, state, and federal land ranging from cornfields to historic sites along the Miami and Erie canals to national park land. On what other long-distance trail can you walk past 2,000-year-old Native American ceremonial mounds, Civil War camps, a zoo, Victorian homes, settlements more than 200 years old, and a chocolate factory?

According to the trail association's website, the seed for this trail was sown by a wildlife biologist for the Ohio Department of Natural Resources:

> *In 1958, Merrill Gilfillan wrote an article for the* Columbus Dispatch *proposing a trail from Cincinnati to Lake Erie. One of his hopes was that the trail would serve as an encouragement to young people to slow down and learn about their native land. Spurred on by the article, several people, including Merrill, met in Columbus in February 1959, to discuss building such a trail. In June, they formed a non-profit organization—The Buckeye Trail Association. The first 20 miles were dedicated on September 19, 1959, in Hocking County.*

A nearly 500-mile section of the Buckeye Trail is part of the 4,200-mile North Country National Scenic Trail and parts of the BT also coincide with the 6,800-mile coast-to-coast American Discovery Trail. The Ohio section of the American Discovery Trail (ADT) is 510 miles long and follows the extreme southern section of the BT for most of its cross-Ohio route.

WEATHER

Well, I must admit, I didn't think that Ohio got that cold, but winters get "pretty wicked" (as North Country residents say). But the plus side of winter in Ohio is that you can do a lot of cross-country skiing on the Buckeye Trail, although sections of the trail through towns are nearly impossible to ski, or at least not much fun. But someday this entire trail could be pieced together each winter for its whole length, to reward the hard-charging cross-country skier with an end-to-end ski of 1,280 miles! Come on, somebody's got to be up for this . . . it just isn't me. It does sound like a fun challenge.

AVERAGE HIGHS AND LOWS IN DEGREES FAHRENHEIT

	JAN	MAR	MAY	JUL	SEPT	NOV
TOLEDO, OH (620 FT.)	20–35	33–50	55–75	70–90	60–80	40–50
GREENVILLE, OH (1,040 FT.)	15–30	30–50	50–70	60–85	50–75	30–50
PORTSMOUTH, OH (540 FT.)	20–40	30–55	50–75	65–85	55–80	35–55
EAST LIVERPOOL, OH (690 FT.)	20–35	20–50	50–70	60–80	55–75	30–50

VITALS

- > Expect to cover 18 miles a day
- > Expect a thru-hike to take 71 days
- > Hiking season: April to November
- > Water availability: Frequent
- > Resupply opportunities: Frequent
- > First year thru-hiked: Unknown
- > Approximate yearly thru-hikers: Fewer than 5
- > Primary contact: Buckeye Trail Association

More snow falls in the northern part of the state than the south due to Lake Erie and, naturally, increased latitude. In the north, a seasonal average of sixty inches of snow falls, whereas the south receives about half that amount. But those thirty inches are surely enough to have hikers hole up until April.

The hiking season generally lasts from April to early November. April may be the best time to hike. Spring brings many water sources and wildflowers in bloom. Plus, the bugs have not yet emerged to pursue their purpose in life—bothering you and me. In summer, heat waves can be brutally hot, with both the temperature and humidity rising into the upper eighties—perhaps not the best time to tackle more than 500 miles of road walking.

TERRAIN

The terrain on the Buckeye Trail is relatively smooth, so expect to cruise through many sections, covering more than twenty miles a day. You'll mostly be walking on rail beds (either on operating systems of tracks, or rails-to-trails initiatives), bike paths, singletrack hiking trails, and desolate dirt roads. The BT doesn't try to avoid communities. In fact, it seems to gravitate to them; so expect some hiking on sidewalks, pavement, and farmer's fields.

All the same, the BT has cliffs, extensive cave systems, and consistent, yet mellow, climbing; surprisingly rugged terrain considering that it's not a mountain trail. For scenic areas, you'll travel on lakeshores, deep-woods hiking trails, and canal towpaths.

WATER

Finding water should not be a concern on the BT. Each day you'll pass by houses, stores, and farms, which can provide you with water for free or otherwise. If using

TERRAIN HIGHLIGHTS

- > Waterfalls
- > Caves
- > Hardwood forests
- > Human-made features
- > Short climbs
- > Agricultural fields
- > Historical sites
- > Small settlements

DON'T LEAVE HOME WITHOUT IT

PLASTIC

Since the Buckeye Trail is a frontcountry trail, you may find yourself staying in motel after motel. Since we thru-hikers are a stinky, grimy lot, your platinum card may hold some sway with an otherwise skeptical innkeeper.

---

water from streams, lakes, and so forth, be sure to treat all of it by boiling, filtering, or treating with chemicals.

WILDNESS

A word of caution to potential thru-hikers: the BT is not as wild as most other trails in this guide. Due to long walks on bike paths, sidewalks, and roads, it may be better to make this a biking trip instead of a hiking trip. This trail is also shared with mountain bikers and horseback riders for extended lengths. The Buckeye Trail Association states that 35 percent of the BT is currently off road. That's 450 off-road miles as of this writing.

Because the BT is still on roads for 65 percent of its around-the-state route, you cannot expect to find substantial lengths of solitude on this hike. The BT does go through many beautiful natural areas. You'll travel on remote back roads and hiking trails, over hills, and through grasslands, hardwood forests, national forests, state parks, and the Cuyahoga Valley National Park, near Cleveland. As opposed to many other trails that just show you the woods of their state, the Buckeye Trail takes you through all of Ohio, from the farms to the streets to the woods.

There is much private land along the Buckeye Trail. When dusk approaches you will have to make a decision. You can (1) keep hiking until you reach a town and stay in a motel or hostel, (2) attempt to find federal or state land to camp on, or (3) approach a private landowner and ask them if you can camp on their land. If employing the third option, it would be best to tell the land owners that you're hiking across Ohio on the Buckeye Trail by your lonesome, you won't litter or build a campfire, you'll be gone by first light, and you're a really nice person.

WILDLIFE

You might say, "By the sound of this frontcountry Buckeye Trail, I'm only going to see barn cats and old ladies' poodles, right?" Oh, come on. Sure, Ohio is one of the

CRITTERS

- Black bears*
- Diamondback rattlesnakes*
- Eastern cottontail rabbits
- River otters
- Turkeys

*Listed as endangered species in Ohio

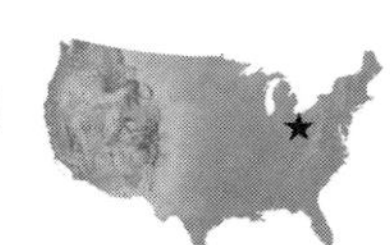

most developed states out of the fifty, but it does have a wide assortment of critters. It also has a problem that comes with its enormous human population—many of its animals are listed as threatened or endangered. This is mostly the result of poor water quality, pollution, and the division and reduction of natural habitats.

Snakes have been particularly affected. Many people feel threatened by snakes, and when they see a snake they pick up a shovel or a hoe and . . . well, you know the rest. Usually, snakes won't bother you if you use common sense rather than a hoe. Innumerable snakes are killed each year because people "thought" they were venomous when it turns out they were not. Even if they are venomous, don't be the aggressor. Simply avoid them.

You'll have to walk single file across this narrow, yet handsome bridge above Cedar Falls. (RICHARD PFEIFFER)

POINTS OF INTEREST

WAYNE'S WORLD

Besides a lot of hiking trails, Wayne National Forest, in southeastern Ohio, has one of the state's few remaining fire towers. At 100 feet tall, this tower provides grand views of the "foothills of the Appalachians."

SEPTUAGENARIAN PEDESTRIAN

One of Hocking Hills State Park's more than twenty-five miles of hiking trails is the five-mile Grandma Gatewood Trail. This path is a memorial to Emma R. Gatewood, Ohio resident and mother of eleven children, who in 1958, at age seventy, became the first woman to hike the 2,170-mile Appalachian Trail (AT). In 1960 and 1963, she completed two more thru-hikes of the AT, each time carrying a lightweight duffel bag and wearing tennis shoes. In 1959, Gatewood also hiked 2,000 miles from Missouri to Oregon on the Oregon Trail. When Grandma Gatewood died in 1973 at age eighty-five, she left behind an outlook that "anything's possible."

In Their Own Words . . .

The purpose of the Buckeye Trail is to connect a number of state scenic and historic spots by a marked, hiking route. Preference is given to footpath, however, the trail comprises little used country roads, urban alleys, improved rail to trail conversions, footpaths hand built by volunteers, and even some state and federal highways. The trail visits all five physiographic zones that exist in Ohio: the lake plains, till plains, glaciated Appalachian plateau, non-glaciated Appalachian plateau, and bluegrass country. . . . The result is a mix of experience that reflects the Ohio scene.

—James Sprague, Buckeye Trail state trail coordinator

cohos trail

160 MILES | NEW HAMPSHIRE

TO GO . . .

> excellent chances to see moose
> wilderness setting
> well-written guidebook and great map set
> state's highpoint as a side trip

OR NOT TO GO?

> heavy use on the southern peaks
> limited resupply points near the trail
> middle of nowhere northern terminus
> muddy, rough, eroded, and ill-marked-northern track

Looking south to Franconia Ridge and the Twin Mountains from the summit of Mount Martha. *(E.SCHLIMMER)*

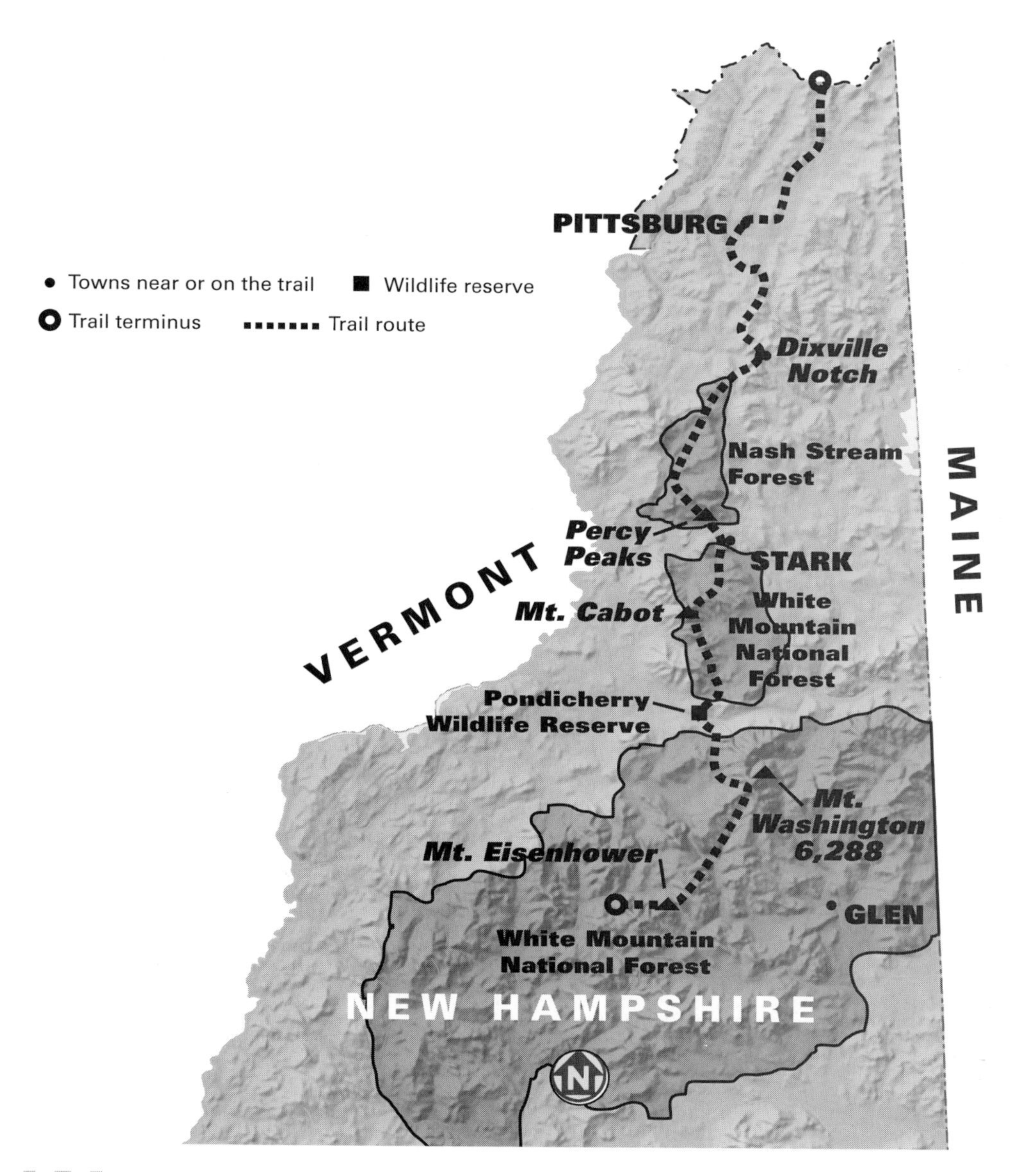

While throngs of people eat chili dogs and buy matching T-shirts atop Mount Washington, or Appalachian Trail thru-hikers sleep shoulder to shoulder-to-shoulder in the dark, dank basement of an expensive Appalachian Mountain Club hut, the Cohos Trail (CT) hiker can quietly enjoy a peanut butter and jelly sandwich at a remote campsite in a New Hampshire region where few others venture. Starting south of the White Mountains' Presidential Range near the town of Glen and meandering north to the Canadian border, this trail is more of a mountain trail than an easygoing lowland route, crossing several peaks that exceed 3,500 feet in elevation.

When the prime mover behind this trail, Kim Robert Nilsen, envisioned a wild

Things are considerably quieter north of White Mountain National Forest, as evidenced by this lonely dirt road beneath the Percy Peaks. (E. SCHLIMMER)

trail in New Hampshire, he pictured it in a place called Coos (pronounced COE-aas) County, the largest and most northern county in New Hampshire. Now a reality, the Cohos Trail leads hikers to see the *other* side of the White Mountains. Instead of heading deep into the popular Presidential, Franconia, and Carter ranges, the CT climbs only one peak in the Presidential Range—Mount Eisenhower (4,780 feet)—Satisfied, the trail then heads off to lesser-known points.

There are more than 140 trail miles already established for the hiker who wants to enjoy northern New Hampshire, and with a little luck, the rest of the CT's projected route should be fully in place and off road by 2010. Trail relocations, particularly in the Presidential Range's Dry River Wilderness Area, will follow. Recently, a new second-edition guidebook has been released, six information kiosks are being installed, and a CT data book is being worked on, too. In addition to these improvements, more campsites with moldering latrines will soon be in place in the far north.

The first person to thru-hike the Cohos Trail was Susan Kenn, of Lincoln, New Hampshire. Kenn spent the first three days of her 2000 thru-hike with some partners but then blazed the rest of her hike solo.

WEATHER

When temperatures are in the sixties in Boston or in the coastal city of Portsmouth, New Hampshire, you can figure it's about half as warm to the north in the White Mountains. There's usually a dramatic difference in temperature, snowpack, and wind speed between the sheltered valleys of the Whites (let alone a coastal city) and the wind-torn summits high above. After all, Mount Washington is only three miles from a section of the CT. Mount Washington, among other summits in the Presidentials, has seen snow fall in every month, has recorded winds in excess of a hundred miles per hour every month, and reportedly recorded a wind speed in excess of 230 miles per hour in April 1934. If this reading was correct, then Mount Washington measured the highest wind speed ever recorded on the surface of the Earth.

AVERAGE HIGHS AND LOWS IN DEGREES FAHRENHEIT

	JAN	MAR	MAY	JUL	SEPT	NOV
GLEN, NH (540 FT.)	10–30	20–40	40–70	60–80	45–70	30–45
STARK, NH (960 FT.)	0–20	15–40	40–60	55–75	45–70	25–40
PITTSBURG, NH (1,330 FT.)	-5–20	10–35	35–60	50–75	40–65	20–40

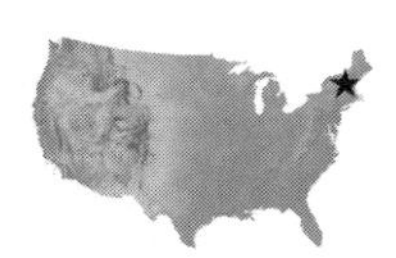

VITALS

- > Expect to cover 14 miles a day
- > Expect a thru-hike to take 11 days
- > Hiking season: June to September (Hiking is discouraged in April and May due to a surface that easily erodes.)
- > Water availability: Frequent
- > Resupply opportunities: Sometimes
- > First year thru-hiked: 2000
- > Approximate yearly thru-hikers: Fewer than 20
- > Primary contact: Cohos Trail Association

Luckily one doesn't have to worry too much about being blown off the CT. Only small stretches of the CT reach above tree line, and these are in the southern sections. However, it's important to remember that ambient temperature drops approximately 3.5° for every thousand feet of elevation gain. In addition, the larger ranges, such as the Presidentials and the nearby Carter Range, influence weather patterns.

Regarding temperature, the Cohos Trail tied the Arizona and the Ice Age trails for having the widest temperature range. Between July's average high and January's average low (as found in nearby settlements), the CT's temperature range was 85°. In Glen, New Hampshire, the average high in July was 80°, and the average low in January was –5° in Pittsburg).

TERRAIN

The CT is a climber's trail; the 160-mile trip takes you over at least twenty peaks that exceed 3,000 feet in elevation, the highest of them being Mount Eisenhower (4,780 feet), ranked the twentieth-highest peak in the Northeast. Summits higher than 3,500 feet have a boreal forest of wind-tolerant spruce, paper birch, and fir, sometimes giving way to bald summits with excellent views. When starting down from a high summit, it is easy to notice the change to hardwoods near the 2,500-foot level. This forest is composed of maple, American beech, yellow birch, and expansive stands of paper birch. When the trail descends lower into major drainages, the slopes are lined with softwoods including pine, fir, and hemlock.

The CT's tread consists mostly of hard-packed soil, mud, more mud, and rock. Sections range from hundred-year-old established trails to nothing more than a moose path with some faded-paint blazes on the trees. Rock hopping is the approach used by many veteran New England hikers to get down the trail. Hopping from

TERRAIN HIGHLIGHTS

- > Remote summits
- > Balsam fir, red spruce forests
- > Stands of paper and yellow birch
- > Connecting road walks
- > Boulder-strewn streams
- > Rocky climbs
- > Swamps
- > Rare alpine plants
- > Remote, recovering logging areas

durable surface to durable surface saves you from getting stuck in the mud, and it leaves zero impact.

WATER

If you're looking for somewhere to hike for a couple of weeks and you don't want to worry about finding water, look no farther than northern New England. I have come across reliable springs above 3,500 feet many times on the CT, and these sources are accurately portrayed on the Cohos Trail Association's maps. Upon descending to any peak's base, I have nearly always found water of some kind, be it a stream, river, or pond.

After August, smaller drainages, especially near cols (high mountain passes), can be dry, so if you are going on any extended ridgeline hike—such as on the Presidential Range or the peaks of the Kilkenny region—you may want to carry two quarts of water. Also keep your eyes peeled for more water as the day progresses. Peaks above 3,500 feet usually hold snow until mid May, sometimes June, and feed the lower drainages that provide communities with ample water. You will usually be able to find snowfields near the highpoint of the CT as late as mid June.

This premier long trail in New Hampshire's northern forest doesn't have as many bodies of water as the Northville-Placid Trail in New York, so if you like to swim, you may find yourself taking a dip in a quite cold (I mean *refreshing*, yeah, refreshing) mountain stream. On the CT, not finding water should be a concern only on the taller peaks that rise above tree line into the full heat of the sun.

WILDNESS

When I was living in New Hampshire, my hiking and climbing friends would always ask me what mountains I climbed over the weekend. I would tell them about my treks on Percy Peaks, Long Mountain, Sugarloaf Mountain, and Mount Muise (all of which are on or near northern sections of the CT.) "Mounts *what*?" was the usual response. To put it mildly, this part of New Hampshire is off the beaten track. And as you travel farther and farther north, you can expect to see fewer cars at the trailheads, fewer people on the trail, and more critters in the wild. Plus, you'll hear more of my favorite sound.

Silence.

The trail travels through state and private land, and of course crosses White Mountain National Forest. In the south, below the town of Jefferson, there are only two Adirondack-style shelters near or on the CT. You'll find only three more from north of Jefferson all the way to the Canadian border. More of these three-sided structures may be built, but for now the Cohos Trail Association is concentrating on hardening the tread and installing primitive campsites and kiosks.

Interest in the Cohos Trail has increased due to articles in regional and national publications, from the *Boston Globe* to *Backpacker* magazine. So you may see hikers from as far away as Alaska in addition to the more common Northeast-based hikers.

WILDLIFE

The CT is home to the largest member of the deer family: the moose. Moose can weigh up to 1,500 pounds and their racks can exceed six feet in width. Once CT hikers cross U.S. Route 2 north of the Presidential Range, they'll hike near moose nearly

SCHLIMMER'S SIDE TRAIL

HIGHPOINTERS TAKE NOTE

One of the most popular peaks in the East, Mount Washington (home of the "world's worst weather") is truly the president of New Hampshire's Presidential Range. It's a worthy detour about a two-day hike from the CT's southern start near the town of Glen. Rising 6,288 feet above the Atlantic Ocean, a hundred miles to the southeast, and its uppermost 2,000 feet extending beyond the tree line, this mountain was the first 4,000-foot peak in the Northeast to be summited. Darby Field and his Native American guides reached the top way back in 1642, a full 195 years before the highest point in New York was reached. The mountain was named much later, in honor of General George Washington, probably during a New Hampshire scientific expedition led by Dr. Jeremy Belknap in 1784.

But things have changed since those early days. For those seeking peace and quiet, Mount Washington is not the place to go, as Bruce Scofield notes in *High Peaks of the Northeast*.

The crowds in the summer, the inexperienced and weary hikers who didn't know what they were getting themselves into, the cars and the whistle-blowing of the train all make Mt. Washington's summit a great destination for the contemporary anthropologist, though not for the hiker seeking solitude.

Currently the summit can be reached via a cog railway, innumerable hiking trails, and an auto road. The auto road, on the east side of Mount Washington, hosts a bicycle race, a foot race, and an auto race to the top each summer. The cog railway, on the west side of the mountain, is now open year-round to tote alpine skiers and tourists to the upper reaches of the mountain. But all this activity doesn't make the peak any less cold, steep, or dangerous. More than 140 people have died in the Presidential Range (famous for its above-tree-line terrain).

The distant peak of Mount Washington peers over the foothills. (ED ROLFE)

From the CT to the top of Mount Washington, it's a three-mile hike along the Crawford Path-Appalachian Trail. Nearly all of it is above tree line. This side trip to the pinnacle of New Hampshire involves more than 1,500 vertical feet of climbing from the CT proper. ■

CRITTERS

- Black bears
- Bobcats
- Coyotes
- Moose
- Mountain lions
- Porcupines
- Red foxes
- Snowshoe hares

every day, with a little luck. While day-hiking sections of the Cohos Trail around the midway point, I've spotted as many as six moose a day. Although their massiveness can be intimidating, there's no reason to worry about a moose hurting you. Use common sense: keep your distance. The only times you need be wary are when you see a protective mother with her calf, or a bull moose during the rutting season. In these instances, pay close attention to the moose's body language. Some basic research on moose before your trip to the Granite State will provide you with some interesting facts and an increased sense of safety.

POINTS OF INTEREST

GETTING HIGH

At 4,780 feet, Mount Eisenhower (the highest point on the Cohos Trail) gives hikers a view of the surrounding ranges stretching in endless folds toward the horizon. Because the summit supports fragile and rare alpine vegetation, please do not step on plants—or soil! Step on bare rock or trail only.

BIRD'S-EYE VIEW

Located near the town of Jefferson, the Pondicherry Wildlife Reserve is home to more than sixty species of birds. Black-capped chickadees, boreal chickadees, Canada jays, hermit thrush, and wood thrush are just a few of the winged creatures that are attracted to the shallow waters of Cherry Pond. Hikers, too, love the view across Cherry Pond to Mount Washington. On my 2003 thru-hike, I spotted three moose in the area, and you have a good chance to see 'em, too.

HIGH POINT OF THE FAR NORTH

Of New Hampshire's forty-eight peaks that exceed 4,000 feet, Mount Cabot (4,170 feet) is the only one to offer free, improved accommodations above the 4,000-foot

DON'T LEAVE HOME WITHOUT IT

GAITERS

True, they'll make you look like an old-schooler, but function beats fashion on this remote, muddy trail. On the CT you'll tramp through moose wallows, flooded logging roads, countless streams, and tons of New England mud. In terms of muckiness, the CT may be the sloppiest trail in this book. A pair of gaiters might be the only way to keep the slick stuff from seeping into your socks.

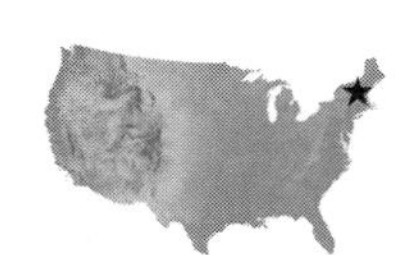

level. The Cabot Cabin, a green and white wooden structure near the summit, is the former fire warden's cabin. It has bunk room for eight, a porch, and a fine view; best of all, it's free. In the past this cabin has been trashed. Pack out all your garbage and leave the cabin in better condition than you find it, please.

THAT FIRST STEP IS A DOOZY

Located in the north, Table Rock—a ledge above Dixville Notch—offers a great view. Perched seven hundred vertical feet above Route 26, this is not a place for the faint of heart.

PERCY PEAKS

The CT symbol is modeled after these two distinct mountains located in the Nash Stream area. North Percy (3,400 feet) offers a 360-degree view; South Percy (3,234 feet) has expansive views to the west and northwest.

THIS LAND IS OUR LAND

Nash Stream Forest, which was owned by a paper company but was recently acquired by the state of New Hampshire, is unruly and rugged. Besides hiking trails, only a few dirt roads penetrate the area.

WE'RE NOT IN KANSAS ANYMORE

The far-north section of the state (near the town of Pittsburg) is so remote it sees only the local old codger out hunting, or people who enjoy bushwhacking heinous, trailless, viewless 3,000-foot peaks all day. You know, weirdos.

In Their Own Words . . .

At 5:30 a.m., when the ground fog covers the Connecticut River Valley 2,000 feet below as if it were an inland sea, and when two hours earlier the eight-hundred-pound bull moose that had been standing twelve feet from your sleeping bag finally decides to leave, you know you really are in a most special place along a most unusual trail. On the Cohos Trail you lose the T-shirt-and-sneaker crowds, and even most of the earnest day hikers. This is a long-distance trek for people with stout packs and experience. The Cohos Trail is quirky. It reaches only one true town (population 700). Otherwise, you're on your own for 160 miles (the first person to hike the whole thing was a woman going solo). Moose do visit you in the night. Coyotes howl near your camp. Barred Owls will shadow you through the forest. Peregrines streak above and scream. You can stand with your feet on both sides of the Connecticut River. You can get a massage in a natural Jacuzzi. You can get snowed on in September or June. If drifting over thirty unknown peaks, skirting 2,000-acre lakes, tiptoeing around moose bogs, showering under eight waterfalls, and ending up in nowhere land on the border of another country is your idea of a wild time, then the Cohos Trail is your pathway to heaven.

—Kim Robert Nilsen, Cohos Trail president and author of *The Cohos Trail: The Guidebook to New Hampshire's Great Unknown*

colorado trail

470 MILES | COLORADO

TO GO . . .

- incredible views
- high-elevation hiking
- gorgeous wildflower blooms and good weather overall
- possible thru-bike route

OR NOT TO GO?

- multiple-use trail can get busy
- high elevation requires time to acclimate
- afternoon lightning storms
- short thru-hiking season

The long shadows in Lost Trail Creek spell the end of another rewarding day on the Colorado Trail. (AARON LOCANDER)

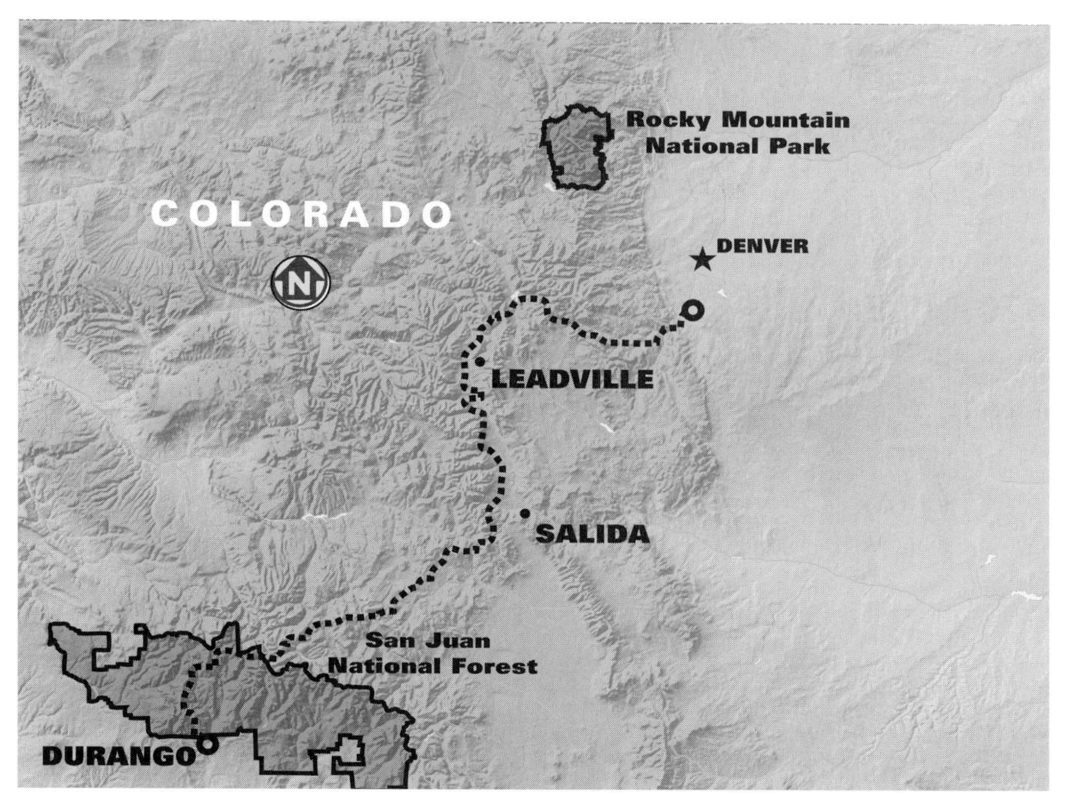

● Towns near or on the trail ★ State capital

○ Trail terminus ▪▪▪▪▪▪▪ Trail route

Colorado. The name rolls off the tongue and evokes images of snow-covered mountains soaring above fertile, wildflower-covered valleys. Colorado is home to an impressive number of the Lower Forty-Eight's high peaks—fifty-four 14,000-footers. The highest point in the state is Mount Elbert (14,433 feet), which is second in height only to Mount Whitney (14,494 feet), on the John Muir Trail. Even with more land area, California has only fifteen 14,000-footers. Even Alaska, with the highest peak in North America (Denali, at 20,320 feet), does not contain anywhere near as many "fourteeners" as Colorado. Wildflowers explode throughout these mountains once the snows are gone in early summer. Entire hills can be covered in a red, yellow, orange, and purple tapestry.

If you have ever wanted to see the Rocky Mountains, the Colorado Trail (CT) is the perfect choice, as is the Continental Divide Trail, which overruns 200 miles of the CT. Taking a southwest route from the state capital of Denver and heading to Durango, the CT is literally a mile-high journey from end to end. Completed in September 1987, mostly by the Colorado Trail Foundation and the U.S. Forest Service, this non-motorized use trail is open to hikers, mountain bikers, horse packers, and pack stock. You can bike nearly the entire CT thanks to a gentle tread and alternate routes around the half dozen wilderness areas. Readers of *Backpacker* magazine once voted the Colorado Trail number five in best scenery, number five in best wildlife, and number six for best overall long-distance trail.

If you attempt to hike the CT end to end, it's highly recommended you start at the northern terminus and hike south. This enables you to gradually climb a seventy-mile piece of trail up to timberline. If you start at the southern terminus, you have only a twenty-mile distance to reach timberline, a much steeper grade. In fact, if you start from the southern terminus, you'll encounter the biggest climb of the entire trip right off the bat: a 6,960-foot ascent to Kennebec Pass (11,760 feet). If you are acclimated to the high elevations, this initial climb will be merely a lousy introduction to the CT. However, if you are not acclimated properly, this initial major ascent could spell disaster, bringing acute mountain sickness (AMS), which can escalate to high-altitude pulmonary edema (HAPE) or high-altitude cerebral edema (HACE), both life-threatening conditions that require an immediate descent and medical attention. Before heading out on the Colorado Trail, it's highly suggested that you educate yourself about hiking at altitude.

WEATHER

The very high elevation of the CT can mean nasty weather—including snow—at any time of year, but perhaps the most important thing to watch out for are afternoon lightning storms. Areas that extend above tree line can become dangerous places when storms roll in, usually during summer afternoons. Stay alert to the weather and avoid travel above timberline if thunderstorms are approaching.

The CT hiking season begins in July, because snowfields, especially on the northern slopes of mountains and along northern sections of the trail, can last well into June. If you want to avoid traversing giant snowfields, it's highly recommended you wait until nearly the beginning of the calendar summer, June 21. And if you start this late in summer, you better get walking fast, because snow starts falling steadily again in early October. In fact, the Colorado Trail is the only trail in this guide with a nearby town (Durango) that reaches a monthly average high of 90° in July (what I use to gauge a trail as "hot") and an average low of 10° in January (what I use to gauge a trail as "cold").

VITALS

- Expect to cover 14 miles a day
- Expect a thru-hike to take 34 days
- Hiking season: July to September
- Water availability: Seldom to frequent, depending on trail section
- Resupply opportunities: Sometimes
- First year thru-hiked: Unknown
- Approximate yearly thru-hikers: Fewer than 100
- Primary contact: Colorado Trail Foundation

AVERAGE HIGHS AND LOWS IN DEGREES FAHRENHEIT	JAN	MAR	MAY	JUL	SEPT	NOV
DENVER, CO (5,260 FT.)	15–45	25–55	45–70	60–90	50–80	25–50
SALIDA, CO (7,080 FT.)	10–40	20–50	35–70	50–85	40–75	20–50
DURANGO, CO (6,520 FT.)	10–40	25–55	35–70	50–90	40–80	20–50

Expect most of your days to be sunny on this five-week walk. The combination of being above tree line and at altitude leaves you at the mercy of the sun, so be sure to bring defenses against that great ball of fire in the sky.

TERRAIN

Plains and mountains, then more mountains. The trail ranges from 5,520 feet on the South Platte River at the northern terminus to 13,240 feet near Coney Summit (13,334 feet), a little more than 110 miles north of the southern terminus. The Colorado Trail Foundation's guidebook *The Colorado Trail* breaks the CT into twenty-eight segments, each averaging approximately seventeen miles. Each section is high enough to induce at least mild acute mountain sickness (AMS) symptoms in anyone coming from low elevations.

- All twenty-eight sections have a highpoint that exceeds 7,000 feet.
- Twenty-five sections have a highpoint that exceeds 9,000 feet.
- Nineteen sections have a highpoint that exceeds 11,000 feet.
- One section has a highpoint that exceeds 13,000 feet.

You'll break above tree line on nearly every section of the CT. Tree line ranges from roughly 11,000 feet in the far northern ranges to approximately 12,000 feet on the New Mexico border. The average elevation of the Colorado Trail exceeds 10,000 feet as it traverses eight major mountain ranges. More than 25 percent of Colorado's fifty-four 14,000-foot peaks are within twenty miles of any part of the CT. Overall, the CT could be called a "double-mile-high" adventure. This trail is the highest hike in this guide.

Believe it or not, the terrain of the CT is easier to get through than the thin air. To help you get from one end of this path to the other, there is a gentle, graded surface that hikers, horse packers, and mountain bikers can enjoy. There are few steep climbs end to end, only gentle climbs that seem endless. Countless switchbacks (we Northeast hikers have seen switchbacks only in pictures) make the Colorado Trail an undulating, snaking path through the most glorious peaks in the United States rather than a trail that slams up and down among precipitous ledges and knee-popping grinds.

You won't have to worry about clamoring over blowdown, wading through gigantic mud holes, or tiptoeing through tedious scree fields on your way to the other end of the CT. Tread consists of double-track jeep roads, some short road walks,

TERRAIN HIGHLIGHTS

- > Alpine terrain
- > Mountain steams
- > Apline lakes
- > Snowfields
- > Major river systems
- > Canyons
- > 14,000-foot peaks
- > Conifer and aspen forests

Forest Service dirt roads, and smooth singletrack. Hikers should cruise the CT's surface at a good pace once they get acclimated.

Despite the mild-mannered tread, this won't be a cakewalk. Of all the trails in this guide, the Colorado Trail is ranked number five for the most vertical feet climbed per average mile. At 162 vertical feet per mile, you'll truly earn each awe-inspiring view. (See page 112 for a complete listing of the five toughest trails.)

WATER

Being so high up in the Rockies doesn't mean you'll have to go to the bottom of the mountains to get water, though there are some dry sections. The hiking season on the CT is a damned if you do, damned if you don't timeline. Starting a thru-hike prior to June will ensure that you'll have to cross many large snowfields; you'll post-hole, get soaked, get cold, and have a miserable time. To bring this point home, it should be mentioned that twenty-one (39 percent) of Lou Dawson's fifty-four summit-to-base ski descents of Colorado's 14,000-footers took place in May, and six (11 percent) more descents took place in June.

However, if you start your thru-hike after July, you will encounter long waterless sections. If you start from the northern terminus of the CT, you'll soon hit a section that can be dry for as long as thirteen miles. At least two other sections of the CT can be dry for up to twenty miles. If you check out *The Colorado Trail*'s twenty-eight segments, you'll see that the water situation can be bleak in many sections. On five sections totaling nearly 195 miles, "water is difficult to obtain." On eleven sections totaling more than 181 miles, there are "scattered water sources."

No better place to pop a squat than at the alpine meadows in La Garita Wilderness Area. (AARON LOCANDER)

The remaining ninety-five miles of trail have lots of water sources. On these wet sections, the word *cache* will never even cross your mind. From end to end you'll come across five major river sys-

tems as well as smaller perennial drainages and stable bodies of water at higher elevations. The CT goes directly through one resupply point and comes within ten miles of eleven more resupply points. These are usually in the form of towns and are located at (if heading north to south) mile 0, 25, 38, 69, 101, 114, 152, 170, 211, 331, 395, and 470. In these locations hikers can stock up on potable water. Many of the water sources on the CT are shared by pack animals or are near grazing lands, so be sure to treat all water, including water from springs and wells. Though it may waste fuel and time, in a pinch you could always melt snow to supplement any dwindling water supplies.

WILDNESS

Colorado is legendary for its natural beauty, and its appeal draws crowds. For the most part, you'll run into other CT users only in areas near trailheads, towns, and popular scenic climbs. Once you get into the backcountry proper, your experience will be similar to the rest of the trails in this guide; weekends are busy, especially around holidays, and perfect, sunny afternoons will suck everyone out of their cubicles and into the hills, especially on Fridays.

Mountain bike use is regarded as "heavy" on many sections of the trail, especially the northernmost forty miles. When you enter a wilderness area, the wildness and quiet should noticeably increase, because mountain bikers are not allowed in federally designated wilderness areas, pack animals are restricted from being tethered near water sources, and leashing pets may be required.

Nearly the entire course of the CT is on forest service land, and it crosses six wilderness areas. The national forests crossed are Pike, White River, San Isabel, Gunnison, Rio Grande, and San Juan. Small connecting sections exist on private land. At times these private sections have been in jeopardy of being shut down due to misuse, and other sections have been closed permanently due to landowner-hiker disputes. Many sections on long-distance trails precariously remain open due to good-natured hikers and selfless landowners. Be sure to always behave, no matter whose land you are on. There is no established series of shelters on the CT, so be prepared to set up camp nearly every night. As stated in the section on Water, above, the CT goes directly through one resupply point and comes within ten miles of eleven more resupply points. Some other resupply points are located farther than ten miles off the trail. According to the Colorado Trail Foundation, the longest stretch of concern to thru-hikers is from Salida to Creede, about a hundred miles with no close resupply points.

DON'T LEAVE HOME WITHOUT IT

EXTRA LUNG CAPACITY

With an average elevation exceeding 10,000 feet and plenty of side-trip options up intimidating 14,000-footers, I suggest you start training for the Colorado Trail long before you take those first breathless steps at altitude.

CRITTERS

- > Bighorn sheep
- > Black bears
- > Lynx*
- > Marmots
- > Mountain lions
- > Picas
- > Wolverines*

*Listed as endangered species in Colorado

Even the resupply points on the north and sound ends of this section are thirteen and ten miles off the CT, respectively.

WILDLIFE

To go along with the big mountains and big views are big animals. You'll see a large assortment of mammals and other critters on your CT hike. Some are found only in this particular part of the United States, so keep your eyes peeled.

POINTS OF INTEREST

A GOOD PLACE TO GET LOST

Located approximately fifty-five miles south of Denver, the 120,000-acre Lost Creek Wilderness Area has rare rock formations, including underground watercourses, deep canyons, granite arches, and bald, domed summits.

PART OF THE SKY

The Sky Line Trail, which the Colorado Trail overruns near the town of Creede, is aptly named. Ambling well above the 11,000-foot level, this section of the CT is the closest you will get to a 14,000-foot peak. San Luis Peak (14,014 feet) stands about a thousand vertical feet above, and less than two miles from, the CT.

THIS AIN'T MISSOURI

A side trip off the CT in Collegiate Peaks Wilderness Area takes you into Missouri Basin, a vast drainage that is flanked on the north by Mount Belford, on the west by Missouri Mountain, and on the south by Mount Harvard—all of which are fourteeners. Bedrock Falls is in this area, too.

SOMETHING'S FISHY

Though this is not a natural feature, many in-the-know hikers recommend you get off the CT and see the Leadville National Fish Hatchery, located six miles west of Leadville (elevation 10,152 feet) in a beautiful building. It is the second-oldest federal fish hatchery in the United States.

TOP OF THE WORLD

No, I'm not describing Mount Elbert, the highest peak in Colorado, but a campground. Top of the World Campground was closed as of 2002 because a wildfire swept through the area, but the site has a great view of Pikes Peak (14,110 feet).

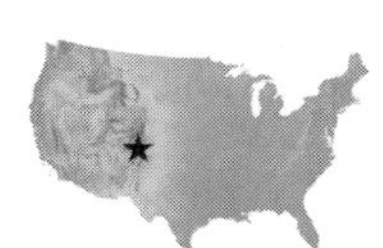

SCHLIMMER'S SIDE TRAIL

14 AND UP

There are no fourteeners on the CT, but twelve such monsters are within five miles of the trail. In all, Colorado has fifty-four 14,000+-foot mountains. To bag each one you'd need to hoof a total of 300 trail miles and ascend more than 130,000 vertical feet.

Here are some stats:

- In 1923, Carl Blaurock and William Irvin became the first people to climb all of Colorado's fourteeners.
- In 1937, Carl Melzer and Bob Melzer—a father-and-son mountaineering team—became the first people to hike all of Colorado's fourteeners in a single summer. (A year earlier, the Melzers, along with Julius Johnson, hiked Colorado's Continental Divide; a route somewhat similar to today's Colorado Trail. And, in 1939, the Melzers were the first to hike all the 14,000-foot peaks in the Lower Forty-Eight.)
- Ted Keizer currently holds the speed record for ascending all fifty-four, touching each of these summits in less than eleven days.
- On May 9, 1991, Lou Dawson became the first (and still the only) person to ski down all the 14,000-footers from summit to base, when he shot down the Coles Couloir with his partner, Glen Randall, on Kit Carson Mountain (14,165 feet).
- Since 1923, more than a thousand people have ascended all fifty-four peaks. ■

WATCH YOUR STEP

Ten miles north of Leadville, you'll find one of the most well-known ghost towns near the Colorado Trail is Camp Hale. This legendary World War II compound was used by the U.S. Army's 10th Mountain Division for training in skiing, snowshoeing, and overall cold-weather, mountainous combat. Please do not stray from the Colorado Trail here; you may find unexploded munitions.

I'm serious.

In Their Own Words . . .

It's the third week of August and the mountain flowers that were blooming so fresh and beautifully just one month ago are beginning to wither. Only the columbine still looks vibrant. It's been four days since I've seen anyone on this remote portion of the Colorado Trail, and that was at a distance of two miles across a cirque well above tree line. Now, as I hike along Indian Trail Ridge, there is a grand panoramic view over mountains in all directions.

Tomorrow the trail will lead me down into Durango and this dream hike will come to an end. It has been a wonderfully exhilarating two months through spectacular mountains, along the Continental Divide, and across the headwaters of major rivers: the Rio Grande, Colorado, South Platte, Arkansas, and others. The hike will end, but the memory of this majestic mountain trail will live on.

—Chuck Wilson, 1997 Colorado Trail thru-hiker

florida trail

1,300 MILES | FLORIDA

TO GO . . .

- a warm, sunny place to spend the winter
- excellent chances for solitude
- possible thru-bike route
- state highpoint as a side trip

OR NOT TO GO?

- limited thru-hiker support system
- nearly 300 miles of road walking
- southern sections prone to extensive flooding
- middle of nowhere southern terminus

The Florida Trail crosses many creeks through Eglin Air Force Base in Florida's panhandle. (FLORIDA TRAIL ASSOCIATION/DEB BLICK)

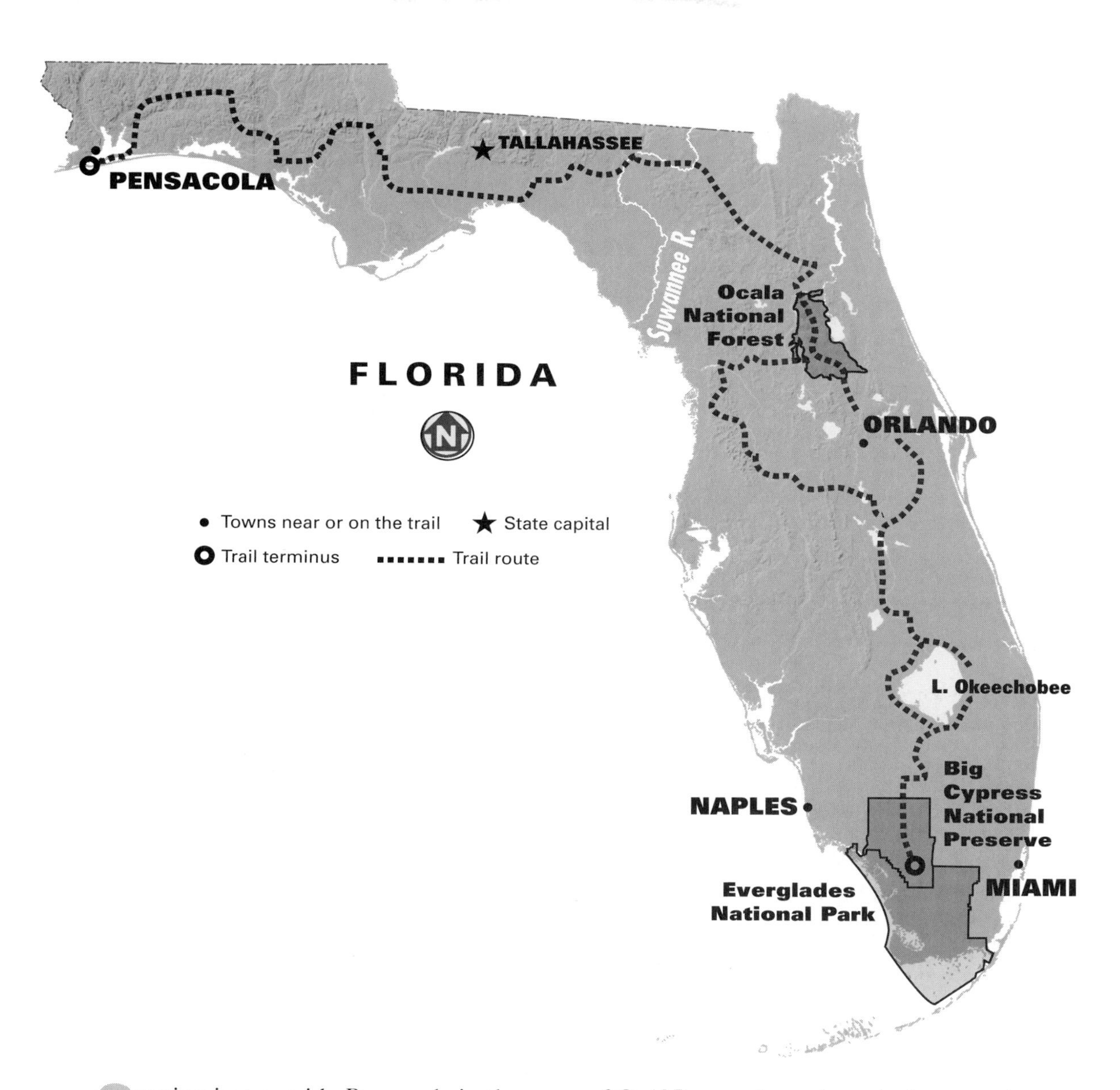

Starting just outside Pensacola in the town of Gulf Breeze (now doesn't that sound like a nice place?), then following the Panhandle east, and turning due south for the long journey to Big Cypress National Preserve, the Florida National Scenic Trail (FT) is one of eight national scenic trails in the United States. Of the twenty-five trails in this guide, the FT is probably the flattest one, but that certainly doesn't mean that this trail does not have its share of challenges. It's estimated that only 25 percent of those who start an intended thru-hike on the FT actually complete it. However, this figure includes Eastern Continental Trail hikers who leave the FT early (near the town of Crestview), to head north toward the Appalachian Trail in Georgia.

VITALS

- Expect to cover 18 miles a day
- Expect a thru-hike to take 66 days
- Hiking season: October to April
- Water availability: Sometimes
- Resupply opportunities: Sometimes
- First year thru-hiked: 1989
- Approximate yearly thru-hikers: Fewer than 10
- Primary contact: Florida Trail Association

The entire FT system totals 1,300 miles, but this includes east and west routes around both Orlando and Lake Okeechobee. A thru-hike requires only about 1,180 miles, because you'll be taking only one side of these two loop routes. I took the western side of the Orlando area loop. This option may be the wilder of the two because the trail meanders through the Cross Florida Greenway, Withlacoochee State Forest, and Green Swamp West Wildlife Management Area. It matters little what route you take around Lake Okeechobee because both halves are on levees.

When it comes to highest projected daily mileage, the Florida Trail ties with the Buckeye Trail and the Lone Star Hiking Trail. The smooth terrain should enable an experienced backpacker with a lightweight pack to average eighteen miles a day.

The first person to hike the basic route of the FT was Florida Trail Association founder Jim Kern. Hiking the Florida Trail in sections, Kern traversed the final stretch in 1964. The first person to thru-hike the FT was Steve Sheridan between February and April 1989, followed closely by a second thru-hiker, Chet Fromm, who started his Florida Trail hike in March 1989.

WEATHER

October through April is the most pleasant time for hiking in Florida, especially considering that by the end of March the waters in the southern swamps generally drop enough to permit wading; arrive any earlier and you might have to swim.

The summer brings very hot weather ("hot enough to boil yer brain," a Florida Trail thru-hiker was told), and many water sources dry up. On my southbound end-to-end trek in February and March 2002, temperatures ranged from 20° on the Panhandle to near 90° around Lake Okeechobee, in the south.

Most of my time on the FT the weather was beautifully sunny, with rain falling on only 10 percent of the days. Nights were mostly clear and cool, but humidity did

AVERAGE HIGHS AND LOWS IN DEGREES FAHRENHEIT

	JAN	MAR	MAY	JUL	SEPT	NOV
PENSACOLA, FL (30 FT.)	45–60	50–70	65–85	75–90	70–90	50–70
SALT SPRINGS, FL (20 FT.)	45–70	50–80	65–90	70–90	70–90	55–80
NAPLES, FL (10 FT.)	55–75	60–80	70–90	75–90	75–90	60–80

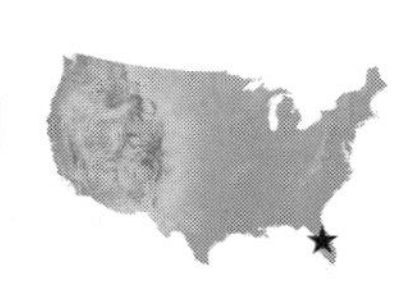

increase as I hiked south. However, despite all the rumors I'd heard before heading to Florida to hike, the humidity did not become unbearable at any point. Quite the opposite; the Florida Trail proved to be much colder than I expected. Granted, the temperatures I encountered were colder than normal. Day after day on the Panhandle it was colder than the weather on the same days in Lake Placid, New York, more than 2,000 miles north. So keep in mind that winter does exist in Florida.

Other weather hazards on the Florida Trail include tropical storms and hurricanes. Three successive hurricanes in fall 2004 caused extensive damage and involved the evacuation of millions of people. During such storms, wind gusts have been clocked at ninety-five miles an hour on the levees of Lake Okeechobee, which the Florida Trail travels on. Trust me, you do not want to be hiking the Florida Trail during a hurricane.

TERRAIN

Terrain along the FT is mostly flat, with elevations ranging from sea level along the Gulf of Mexico to about 160 feet in the north-central area. All FT thru-hikers find themselves walking on hiking trails composed of pine needles and hard sand, dirt-and-sand forest roads, levees, ranchers' fields, bike paths, or levees in the central and northern sections. Muddied or flooded swamp paths are par for the course near the southern terminus. What the FT doesn't have in dramatic elevation gain it certainly makes up for with beautiful scenery. Starting on the Gulf of Mexico and ending in the Cypress swamps of the Everglades, the FT is an ecological adventure.

The Florida Trail Association has broken down the FT into forty-two map sections. Trail descriptions for maps 41 and 42 (the southernmost sections, including Big Cypress National Preserve), which cover more than 60 miles of trail, say that "wading should be expected, even with average rainfall. . . ." In March and April 2002 ("the drier months," according to the maps), I found at least five miles of the trail in this area to be under one to almost four feet of water, which was pretty spooky to say the least. Another five to ten miles in this area was ankle-deep mud. Unfortunately, there's no way around flooded sections, because basically the entire southern part of Florida is one big swamp. Wear your pack a little higher than normal, watch out for the alligators, and hope for the best.

WATER

Water quality in Florida is often poor due to heavy polluting by agriculture and industry, a problem that the southwestern United States and Texas share. Overall,

TERRAIN HIGHLIGHTS

- Cypress swamps
- Hardwood swamps
- Pine and palmetto stands
- Freshwater streams and lakes
- Gulf of Mexico coastline
- Giant limestone sinkholes

water quality in the northern sections is usually okay, the central sections marginal, and the southern sections lousy.

The Panhandle has the best water quality, with many swiftly flowing streams and rivers. With a little searching or asking around in the central sections of the FT, you should be able to find some natural water sources that aren't bad, but any section of the FT below Ocala National Forest is where I would rely only on bottled water.

In a few southern trail sections, even household wells are polluted, forcing residents to purchase all their drinking and cooking water from nearby stores. From end to end, except for the longer roadless sections, the FT passes through dozens of small towns, where bottled water is for sale at reasonable prices. Basically, the northern sections of the FT have fine water in wells and city systems; treat all water in the woods. The central sections of the FT have fine city system water, but some wells are polluted; treat all water in the woods and out of wells. On the southern section of the FT nearly all sources are polluted; treat all water in the woods and out of wells. Some city supplies are bad, too.

WILDNESS

You may ask, "There are woods in Florida?" Yes, there are woods in Florida. No one believes me, but Florida is indeed the most beautiful place I have ever hiked. The 200-year-old live oaks, the largest remaining stand of sand pines in the world, magnolias that encompass whole houses, and the expansive hardwood swamps of the Everglades region combine to make this a wonderful and unique experience. And did I mention the Fruit trees? On some sections of the Florida Trail you'll come across sweet orange, sour orange, and grapefruit trees; perfect for your afternoon siesta or morning breakfast. Currently the FT is routed on roads for 250 to 300 miles, but the Florida Trail Association is trying to relocate this young trail to more pristine areas. There are already two FT sections that exceed a hundred off-road miles. Only rarely used paper company roads cross these two remote stretches in the Panhandle, with no close resupply points nearby.

The most civilized sections of the FT seem to be in the westernmost extent of the Panhandle and around Orlando, whereas the sections that travel through the three national forests of Florida (Apalachicola, Ocala, and Osceola) provide true backcoun-

DON'T LEAVE HOME WITHOUT IT

INFLATABLE KAYAK

True, if you're trying your best to be a disciplined lightweight hiker then an IK will really blow your diet. Even today's lightest, most packable solo models weigh in at a cumbersome 17 pounds (but they're getting lighter every year). Nonetheless, the extra bulk may seem tolerable when you consider that southern sections of the FT are often flooded with waist-deep water and sludge for stretches of five or more miles. To stay above pesky man-eating critters and venomous snakes, and to keep your feet dry, the FT may be the best place for a thru-hike/thru-paddle.

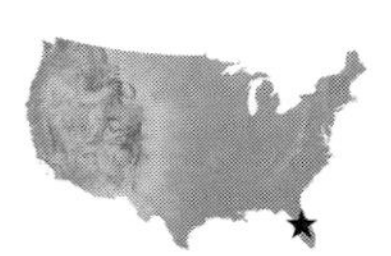

CRITTERS

- > Alligators
- > Bobcats
- > Coyotes
- > Feral hogs
- > Fox squirrels
- > Pelicans, storks, and cranes
- > Tortoises
- > Water moccasins, coral snakes, rattlesnakes

try settings. Once you enter the Everglades region of the far south, you can expect to see no one else. On my FT thru-hike, I think I ran into eleven backpackers. That's one hiker for every 108 miles. Needless to say, the crowd factor on the FT is low.

The FT is getting a bit of use though. Chuck Wilson, the Florida Trail Association's long-distance-hiker information analyst, lists more than thirty total successful Florida Trail end-to-end hikers as of 2002. Away from the road walks, Lake Okeechobee, and the national forest campgrounds, you'll have great chances of finding solitude. There are basically no established shelters along the Florida Trail. I encountered one shelter on my entire 1,180-mile trip. Of course I stayed in it!

WILDLIFE

Florida may conjure up visions of hiking through thigh-deep water in swamps among alligators and venomous snakes . . . and it should! Luckily, the parts that look like something out of a horror film constitute only short sections of the FT. With some basic research before your intended FT hike, you'll learn that common sense will keep you safe from the critters in most situations. Sometimes bad luck can have its way, though, and you may find yourself having several run-ins with the large-bodied, mean-spirited water moccasin, as I did in 2002. At times the FT can seem more like a zoo than a hiking trail. A highlight during the winter is seeing many different vacationing birds.

Beneath the oaks in northern Florida. (FLORIDA TRAIL ASSOCIATION/SANDRA FRIEND)

POINTS OF INTEREST

BEACHCOMBING

If you're starting a hike of the FT from the northern terminus, the first twenty miles of hiking will be on the beaches of the Gulf of Mexico. No other long-distance trail in the United States travels extensively along such warm waters. The area is developed, but there are some trail sections in the palm and palmetto woods and among high sand dunes and wild miniature crabs.

SCHLIMMER'S SIDE TRAIL

HIGHPOINTERS TAKE NOTE

If you wish to tackle Florida's highest point, Lakewood (also called Britton Hill), at a nose-bleeding 345 feet, it can be reached via a twenty-five-mile road walk from a trail section near DeFuniak Springs. But don't expect a dramatic ending to your twenty-five-mile pilgrimage; the highest point in Florida is a modest rise. A granite marker, a picnic area, latrines, and a kiosk mark the area, and there are some nice walking trails through a large pine forest. There is a slight view of the surrounding rolling terrain, but it's really not much of a Kodak moment. ■

ROLLIN' ON THE RIVER

The Florida Trail meanders along the banks of the Suwannee River, which in some spots can loom more than a hundred feet above the water. Most homes in this area are on twenty-foot stilts in anticipation of the hundred-year floods.

OCALA NATIONAL FOREST

Regarded by some as "the crown jewel" of the FT, Ocala, the oldest national forest east of the Mississippi River, offers remote scenery even though it's just north of Orlando. It also contains the largest stand of sand pines in the world.

LAKE OKEECHOBEE

At 705 square miles, Lake Okeechobee is the second-largest freshwater lake entirely within the United States. Florida Trail hikers hike on the large levee that circumnavigates the lake. These elevated walkways provide sweeping views of the lake and surrounding communities. This area is great for viewing birds and alligators.

BIG CYPRESS SEMINOLE RESERVATION

The community on this reservation, just north of the Big Cypress National Preserve, is inquisitive and friendly toward long-distance hikers. A visit to the new Ah-Tah-Thi-Ki Museum is highly recommended.

In Their Own Words . . .

Although the Florida Trail is flat, your heart rate can still increase. Seven miles from the southern terminus I had a huge water moccasin open wide and try to bite me when I was just two feet from him. Luckily I jumped high enough and quick enough to just be missed. On that same day I saw no less than twenty alligators. The farther south I ventured on this trail the more and more I thought they would never find my body. But obviously I did make it, becoming one of less than forty people to traverse Florida's National Scenic Trail.

In the Panhandle I traveled through vacant and expansive pine and palmetto stands,

as well as hardwood forests. In the south, the terrain was either very hot with little to no shade among sugar cane fields, or I found myself in thigh-deep Cypress swamps teeming with critters on land, in the water, and in the sky. Miles and miles of ankle-deep mud had to be slogged through in the south, but the beaches on the Gulf of Mexico in the north were a breeze, although the high rise hotels and retirees in white Cadillacs detracted from the wildness. As a consolation, I got to use the free shower facilities on the beach.

The Florida Trail also throws out its fair share of monotony. Both desolate and busy roads had to be walked, as well as Forest Service roads, levees, canals, power lines, and all-terrain-vehicle paths. But these civilities extended the Florida Trail's variety and gave me a chance to meet people from all over the state, from Pensacola to Miami. But if thru-hiking the Florida Trail you must get ready to have the same conversation over and over again: "Where ya' headed?" "I'm hiking the Florida Trail." "The what?" "The Florida Trail . . . it's a long-distance trail . . . in Florida . . . I'm hiking it." (blank stares . . . sound of wind . . . tumbleweed . . .). Most people have never heard of this thing.

Public lands consisted of National Forests, a National Seashore, National Wildlife Refuges, National Wildlife Areas, Water Management Areas, and State Parks. I saw a bobcat, alligators, poisonous snakes, armadillos, tortoises, fire ants, wild hogs, deer, raccoons, foxes, crabs, gigantic spiders, fox squirrels, and about thirty different kinds of birds. At times I felt like I was hiking through the Dagobah System where Yoda lived in Star Wars more so than hiking inside the United States.

The Florida Trail was a great trip overall, and I would recommend this path to my best of friends . . . and worst of enemies.

—Stewart MacNaughton, 2002
Florida Trail thru-hiker

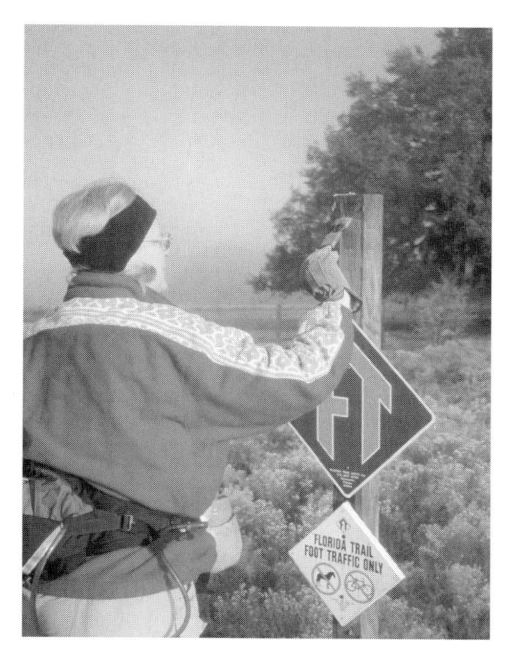

Painting a fresh blaze along the Florida Trail.
(FLORIDA TRAIL ASSOCIATION/SANDRA FRIEND)

ice age trail

1,100 MILES | WISCONSIN

TO GO . . .

- complete tour of glacial history
- possible thru-bike route
- state highpoint as a side trip
- crowd factor is low

OR NOT TO GO?

- approximately 275 miles of road walking
- not a wilderness setting in some sections
- lack of detailed guidebook
- bug season can be bad

The National Shrine of Mary tops Holy Hill, the highest point of the Kettle Moraine area in southeastern Wisconsin. The Ice Age Trail passes close to these dramatic spires in Holy Hill woods, a 650-acre hardwood forest. (PAUL G. HAYES)

Wisconsin's Ice Age Trail (IAT) is one of two national scenic trails in this guide; the other one being the slightly longer Florida Trail. Starting at Potawatomi State Park on Green Bay, the IAT travels southwest, then north, then west, to end inside the Interstate State Park Ice Age Reserve Unit on the St. Croix River. The Ice Age Trail is still in development, with more than half of its route now in place. The expected length of the IAT when completed is between 1,000 and 1,200 miles, traveling through thirty-one Wisconsin counties.

Formed by Raymond Zillmer, a lawyer and explorer of northern Wisconsin and Minnesota, the Ice Age Park and Trail Foundation (IAPTF) is the main group of volunteers behind the construction and maintenance of this long trail. The trail was origi-

VITALS

- > Expect to cover 16 miles a day
- > Expect a thru-hike to take 69 days
- > Hiking season: May to October
- > Water availability: Frequent
- > Resupply opportunities: Sometimes
- > First year thru-hiked: 1979
- > Primary Contact: Ice Age Park and Trail Foundation

nally intended by Zillmer to be a national park that would wind its way across the state, but it was argued that too many interests and landholdings were involved. So instead there's a long-distance trail. The IAPTF's ambitious mission statement is "to create, support and protect a thousand-mile foot trail tracing the Ice Age formations across Wisconsin."

The trail is thru-hikeable, but at least 25 percent (275 miles) of the walking is currently on roads. If you want to thru-hike the IAT, you should contact the IAPTF beforehand. They'll be more than happy to help you piece together county road walks to get you to the next established section of trail. As of 2002, only 4,000 acres of the IAT were secured and fully protected. A loop trail makes up part of the IAT. Near Devil's Lake State Park you can take the more westerly route among sandstone cliffs, or take the eastern branch, which crosses extensive moraines.

A year before it gained National Scenic Trail status, the Ice Age Trail was first thru-hiked by Jim Staudacher in 1979. Staudacher, then a twenty-year-old man attending Marquette University, took eighty-one days to hike all of the IAT (an average of thirteen and a half miles a day).

WEATHER

You should expect the weather on the IAT to be similar to nearby trails such as the Shore-to-Shore Trail to the east and the Superior Hiking Trail to the north. The hiking season generally lasts from May to October. Starting your hike prior to May will mean that you will most likely encounter a consistent snowpack, especially if you are in areas prone to lake effect snow, in the far northern sections of the IAT, or on north-facing slopes. Temperatures in winter can be C-O-L-D, cold with temperatures dipping well below –20°. Any thru-hike beginning beyond the first of September will ensure a taste of flurries and perhaps significant snowfall by the time you get

AVERAGE HIGHS AND LOWS IN DEGREES FAHRENHEIT

	JAN	MAR	MAY	JUL	SEPT	NOV
KEWAUNEE, WI (700 FT.)	10–25	24–40	45–60	60–80	50–70	30–45
MADISON, WI (860 FT.)	5–30	20–45	45–70	60–85	50–75	25–45
STEVENS POINT, WI (1,090 FT.)	5–25	20–40	45–70	60–80	50–70	25–40
SAINT CROIX FALLS, WI (850 FT.)	0–25	20–40	45–70	60–85	50–70	25–40

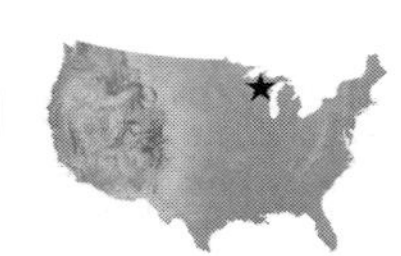

to the other end of this 1,000+-mile path. Many parts of the IAT are popular for cross-country skiing; the Badger State receives a good amount of snow each winter.

Elevations never exceed 2,000 feet, but being just west of Lake Michigan and south of Lake Superior, the area can get wicked winds and fluctuating temperatures anytime of the year. The Ice Age Trail tied with the Arizona Trail and the Cohos Trail for having the widest temperature range between July's average high and January's average low as recorded in nearby settlements. On the Ice Age Trail, the average high for July was 85° in both Madison and Saint Croix Falls, and the average low for January was 0° in Saint Croix Falls.

Wildlife revelers take a mid-summer stroll along a meadow near Loews Lake. (PAUL G. HAYES)

TERRAIN

If you found that the terrain described in Ohio's Buckeye Trail doesn't sound incredibly remote, don't pack your bags for a thru-hike of the Ice Age Trail either. The IAT is not a true wilderness trail overall. But the trail takes you by beautiful features formed by the last glacial sheet, which covered the northern United States with two-mile-thick ice about 15,000 years ago. The basic route of the IAT follows the southern extension of the last glacial sheet. It left behind terminal moraines, which help us find its southern limit.

The IAT has nearly 300 miles of road walking at this point. When you're off road you'll be on hiking trails, bike paths, and rail trails (or active rail lines) that cross private, federal, and state-owned land made up of meadows, boreal or hardwood forests, hills, and plains. You'll walk by 300 separate bodies of water, too.

With at least three interpretive facilities along the IAT's route, you're going to get a grand self-guided tour of past glacial activity. Key signs of the past Ice Age include:

Eskers. These meandering hills are composed of rounded gravel and sand deposited by streams that flowed through tunnels at the bottom of a glacier.

Erratics. Oddly placed boulders sometimes weighing more than fifty tons can be found near the IAT. These giants have been moved from their "original" homes prior to glaciations and appear dramatically out of place. Some look like you can push them right over.

Gorges. Powerful runoff from melting glaciers or draining glacial lakes cut these small canyons, which can be dry or still have water flowing through them.

DON'T LEAVE HOME WITHOUT IT

YOUR STUFFED ANIMAL

The Ice Age Park and Trail Foundation is the only trail organization that sells a stuffed animal—Monty the Mammoth, the official IAT mascot. Wouldn't it be nice to cuddle up with Monty every night?

Kames. These cone-shaped hills are composed of rounded sand and cobble deposited by flowing water.

Moraines. These ridges are composed of boulders, silt, sand, and other material lost from a melting, retreating glacier. Depending on the location in Wisconsin, moraines can be dry ridges or separators of wet areas.

Striations. These gouges and scratches were made by debris at the bottom of a glacier being scraped along the ground. Striations are found on exposed bedrock and show which way the glacier traveled.

WATER

Land O'Lakes is not just the name of a stick of butter. It's also the description you could use to note the availability of water along the IAT. At least 300 of Wisconsin's nearly 14,000 bodies of water can be seen on this thousand-mile glacial adventure. Every day you'll pass ponds, lakes, swamps, bogs, streams, and seasonal runoff. Because the IAT comes close to many settlements, you can stock up on potable water again and again to ensure that your drinking supply is cootie-free. Of course, be certain to treat all water from woodland sources, especially near any kind of farmland.

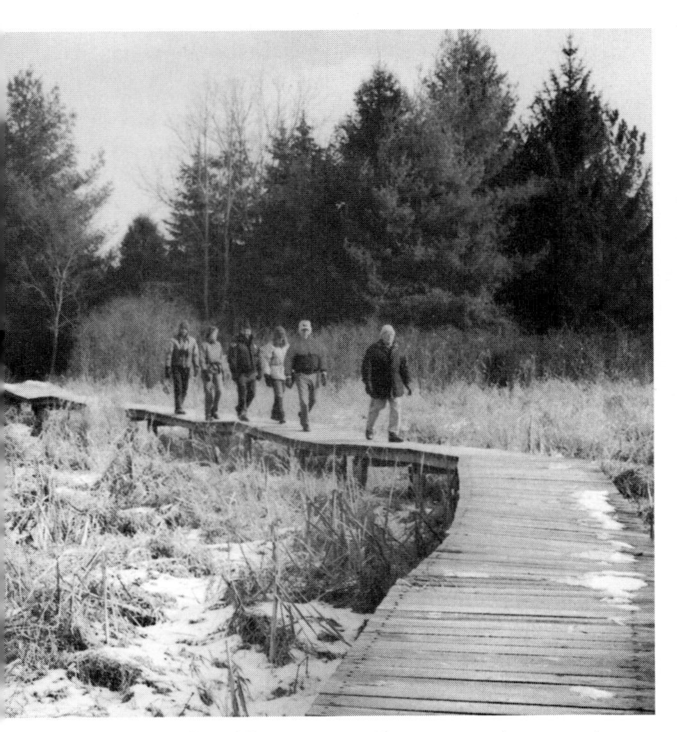

Day-hikers cross a frozen marsh on a volunteer-built boardwalk in Lapham Peak State Park. (PAUL G. HAYES)

WILDNESS

Road walking is sometimes part of the day's activities on the IAT, but the Ice Age Park and Trail Foundation is trying to reroute many sections into more pristine settings. They really have their work cut out for them, though; route proposals would direct the trail through

CRITTERS

- > Black bears
- > Bobcats
- > Coyotes
- > Snowshoe hares
- > Timber wolves
- > Turkeys
- > Voles
- > Wolverines

lands controlled by a collage of private citizens, the Wisconsin Department of Natural Resources, the U.S. Forest Service, county and town municipalities, and various forestry departments. But the IAPTF will not be deterred, and its members are optimistic that the Ice Age Trail will one day be complete. The IAPTF rightly reminds us that long-distance trails don't spring up overnight. The Florida Trail, Long Trail, and Appalachian Trail were on roads for considerable parts of their early routes. And newer trails, such as the Cohos Trail and Long Path, are still on roads but will eventually be located off road, too.

There are approximately 275 miles of road walking, 250 miles are cut and open for use, and 300 miles of the IAT have been recognized by the National Park Service to be developed and managed to meet certification requirements for National Scenic Trail status. These certified segments are marked with triangular Ice Age National Scenic Trail symbols, which feature a woolly mammoth. That leaves 275 miles in between all these categories. These remaining 275 miles are composed of bike paths, logging roads, and country dirt road walks. Currently, the longest roadless section is just less than ninety miles long. If you don't like all of the road walking, check on the IAT later. If everything has gone according to plan, it will be wilder. In the meantime, as reported by an IAPTF member, six hikers who just couldn't wait for the wildness to be extended have already hiked this cross-Wisconsin trail end to end in one continuous trip.

Parts of the trail are open to horses, snowmobiles, and bikes, though you will need to secure a state trail permit from the Wisconsin Department of Natural Resources to bike on five separate state trails that are part of the IAT.

The IAPTF states that about eighteen million people live within a hundred miles of any section of the Ice Age Trail, so you might run into people every other day while on the trail, but overall the crowds are limited to the most scenic, accessible areas. On remote or not particularly scenic parts of the IAT, you are ensured tranquility.

WILDLIFE

Once you're off the roads, you may see the kind of stuff that reminds you more of Alaska than Wisconsin. I was surprised to learn what you could see in this fairly developed state. Black bears? Wolverines? Really? Yup. And, according to Wisconsin's Department of Natural Resources website, "The sound of a howling timber wolf is becoming a more common event in Wisconsin. A growing population of wolves

SCHLIMMER'S SIDE TRAIL

HIGHPOINTERS TAKE NOTE

The highpoint of the trail is in the north-central part of the state, at 1,920 feet on a shoulder of Lookout Mountain. From here you can take the ten-mile Timms Hill National Trail to Timms Hill, the highest point in the state (1,952 feet). The wooden observation tower here provides great views of modest rolling hill after modest rolling hill. ■

---

now live in Wisconsin, one of about a dozen states in the country where timber wolves exist in the wild."

POINTS OF INTEREST

GREEN BAY BACKPACKERS

Backpackers starting on the Door Peninsula (located near the IAT's eastern terminus on Lake Michigan's Green Bay), will see beautiful limestone cliffs that drop into the water below.

HOT KETTLE

Broken into two large sections, Kettle Moraine State Forest's Northern Unit comprises nearly 30,000 acres of hills, lakes, and forest, and the Southern Unit, near the University of Wisconsin–Whitewater, exceeds 20,000 acres in size and offers IAT backcountry overnight shelters among the hills and pine forests. In some cases, moraines in Northern Unit jut 300 feet high.

SAY IT FIVE TIMES FAST

Chequamegon-Nicolet National Forest, located just west of Wisconsin's highest point (Timms Hill), is regarded by many Badger State hikers as the most primeval section of the IAT. Here, you'll walk atop elongated, meandering eskers. Major bodies of water in the area include the Yellow River, Mondeau Lake, and Miller Dam Flowage.

REC ROOM

The 3,063-acre Chippewa Moraine State Recreation Area north of Eau Claire is home to extensive hills and depressions. At the end of the last glacial period the area drained poorly, so we now are left with moraines interspersed with beautiful bogs and lakes. The visitor center is even on a hill that used to be the bottom of a glacial lake.

In Their Own Words . . .

A walk on the Ice Age Trail today has its challenges, but is considered leisurely by most amblers. The majority walk segments of the Trail for short periods of time—a day here, and a day

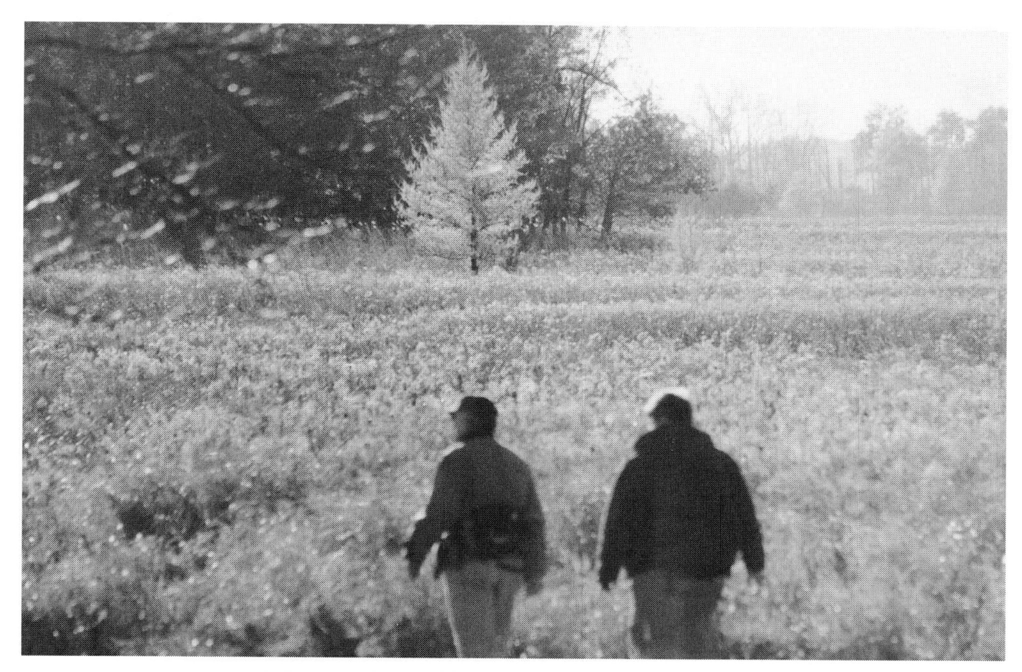

Day-hikers enter central Wisconsin's Fox River valley on a fine fall day. (PAUL G. HAYES)

there. Several people have hiked the entire Trail, and a few have thru-hiked it.

Perhaps the greatest challenge facing us today is actually finishing the Ice Age Trail. About half of the thousand-mile route is complete. Anyone thinking about hiking the entire Trail needs to plan on walking along a number of roads to connect the off-road segments. But the Ice Age Park and Trail Foundation and its partner organizations are acquiring lands, and volunteers are busy building the new segments necessary to fill in the gaps.

Like the eighty-year effort to finish the Appalachian Trail, we are confident that the Ice Age Trail will be completed.

The Route: The Ice Age Trail courses like a river for a thousand miles through a varied landscape. Walk the Ice Age Trail to witness hundreds of crystal lakes, thriving prairies, productive farmland, towering white pines, diverse wetlands, ancient Native American effigy mounds, remnant oak savannas, charming cities and many of the world's finest examples of the effects of continental glaciation.

—Ice Age Park and Trail Foundation's *Ice Age Trail: History of Wisconsin's Glacial Landscape*

international appalachian trail

700 MILES | MAINE
NEW BRUNSWICK
QUEBEC

TO GO . . .

> wilderness setting with big wildlife
> an international hike
> crowd factor is low
> one state highpoint and two provincial highpoints

OR NOT TO GO?

> red tape, Customs, Border Patrol, permits, rules and regulations, fees
> language barrier
> bugs can be of Biblical proportions
> difficult, muddy sections of trail

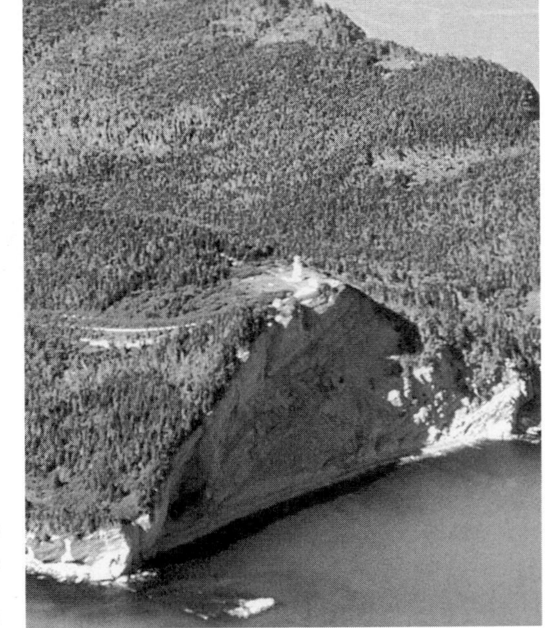

The northern terminus of the International Appalachian Trail is on breathtaking Cap Gaspé in Forillon National Park.
(WILL RICHARD WWW.WRICHPHOTO.COM)

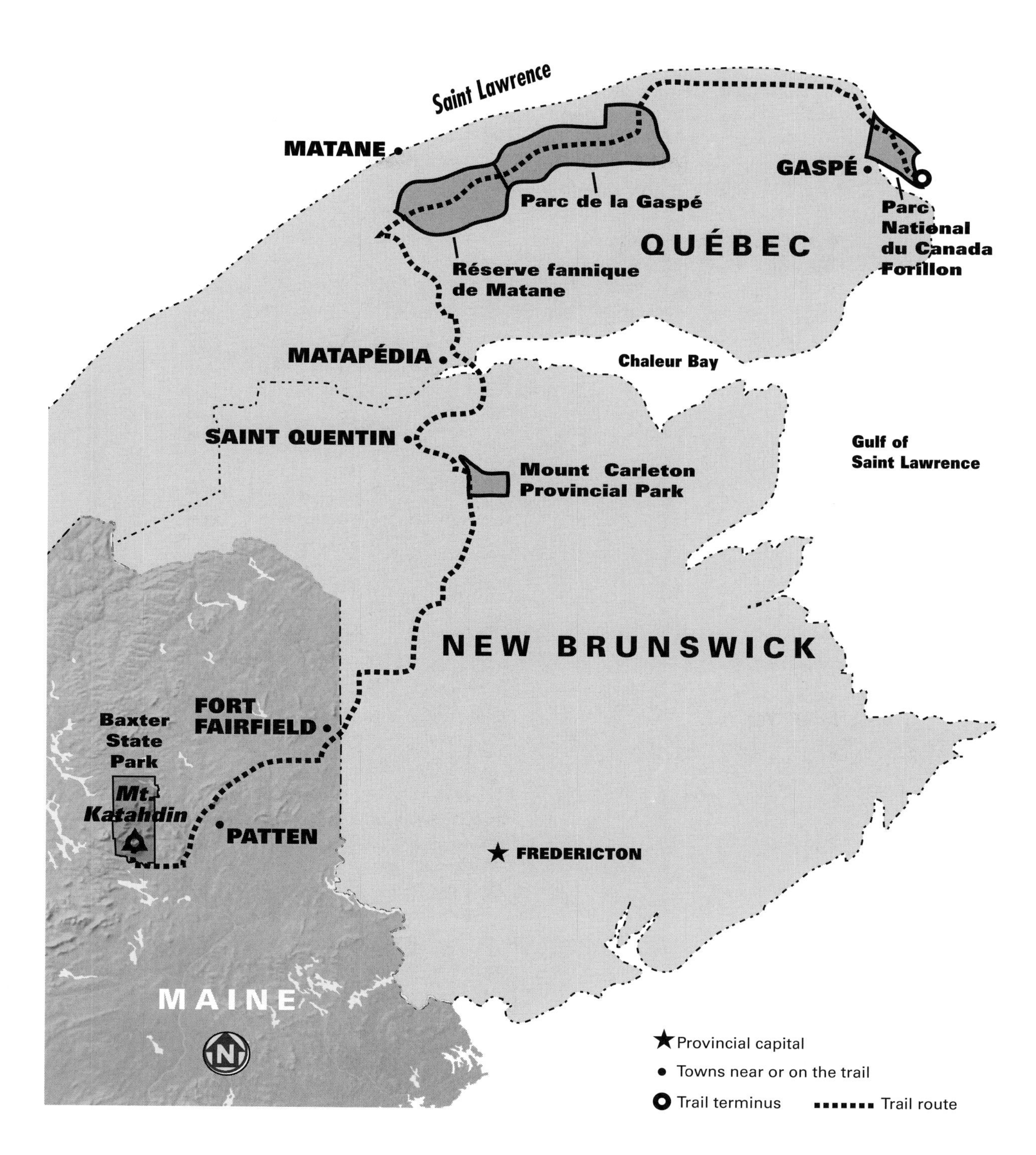
Saint Lawrence
MATANE
GASPÉ
Parc de la Gaspé
Parc National du Canada Forillon
QUÉBEC
Réserve fannique de Matane
MATAPÉDIA
Chaleur Bay
SAINT QUENTIN
Gulf of Saint Lawrence
Mount Carleton Provincial Park
NEW BRUNSWICK
FORT FAIRFIELD
Baxter State Park
Mt. Katahdin
PATTEN
FREDERICTON
MAINE
N
Provincial capital
Towns near or on the trail
Trail terminus
Trail route

The International Appalachian Trail—or Le Sentier International des Appalaches, to our neighbors in the north—is the only trail in this guide that travels out of the United States and the only trail in North America to have a bilingual trail patch. Starting on Mount Katahdin and ending on the Gaspé Peninsula of Quebec, this 700-mile trail is truly a walk on the wild side. In spring 2000, the trail was considered "done," with 75 percent of the route on footpaths that take you over the highest peak in New Brunswick (Mount Carleton, 2,690 feet [820 meters]) and the highest peak in mainland Quebec (Mount Jacques Cartier, 4,160 feet [1,268 meters]), in addition to Maine's Mount Katahdin.

The start of the IAT is where the Appalachian Trail ends: the highest point on Mount Katahdin (5,268 feet [1,606 meters]). From there you head south and retrace the Appalachian Trail's final 15 miles.

Because there are so many rules and regulations in Baxter State Park (see Wildness, below), some people choose to avoid the park. More still find themselves unable to get in because the park is "full." In these cases, you can opt to start on the southern border of the park at Abol Bridge and call it "close enough." From Abol Bridge the IAT skirts the southern and eastern borders of Baxter State Park. The other option, if you're feeling lucky, is to show up at the park gate around five in the morning and try to get in before everyone else. Reservations must be made to camp in Baxter State Park.

The first IAT thru-hiker was John Brinda in 1997. Brinda, who hailed from Washington state at the time, was completing the first thru-hike of the 4,400-mile Eastern Continental Trail. This unofficial path combines the Appalachian Trail, Florida Trail, and International Appalachian Trail, among a few other shorter paths, to take indefatigable trekkers from Key West all the way to Gaspé, Quebec. After this enormous expedition, Brinda stayed active in the long-distance hiking community, giving presentations on the International Appalachian Trail, the Sierra High Route, and the Tahoe-to-Yosemite Trail.

MOUNT KATAHDIN

Mount Katahdin is well known not only by Northeast 4,000-foot-peak climbers but by long-distance hikers as well. Mount Katahdin is the northern terminus of the most famous trail in the United States, the Appalachian National Scenic Trail. One

VITALS

- Expect to cover 14 miles a day
- Expect a thru-hike to take 50 days
- Hiking season: June to September
- Water availability: Frequent
- Resupply opportunities: Sometimes
- First year thru-hiked: 1997
- Approximate yearly thru-hikers: Fewer than 10
- Primary contact: IAT/SIA Maine Chapter

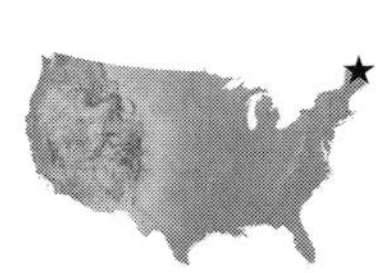

of the biggest motivating factors to complete your 2,170-mile walk from Springer Mountain, Georgia, is to set your eyes and feet upon one of the most dramatic mountains in the United States. A survey party led by Charles Turner, Jr., made the challenging first ascent of 5,268-foot Katahdin in 1804.

Mount Katahdin stretches far above tree line, which is around 3,000 feet on this massif. Baxter Peak is the highest point on the mountain and the seventh highest peak in the Northeast. There's also Pamola Peak, a narrow summit more than 4,900 feet tall with dramatic views. You can scramble on the Knife Edge, an arête as skinny as five feet wide in places, that drops 1,500 vertical feet on each side. There's also the Tableland, a flat area more than a square mile in size above tree line. Hamlin Peak (4,756 feet), the second-highest peak in Maine, is a quick half-hour jog from Baxter Peak. Below Baxter Peak is Chimney Pond, a beautiful glacial tarn with a ranger cabin nearby. This pond is located directly below the massive and intimidating cirque, the South Basin.

WEATHER

There's a short hiking season on the IAT due to the lingering snowpack, even in June. The other things waiting for you are billions of hungry biting insects that hatch

Mount Katahdin's South Basin, a glacial cirque that rises more than 2,000 vertical feet, holds residual snowfields in this early June photo. (E. SCHLIMMER)

AVERAGE HIGHS AND LOWS IN DEGREES FAHRENHEIT

	JAN	MAR	MAY	JUL	SEPT	NOV
PATTEN, ME (550 FT.)	0–25	15–40	40–65	60–80	45–70	25–40
KEDGWICK, NB (420 FT.)	0–15	10–35	35–60	55–80	40–70	20–40
GASPÉ, PQ (80 FT.)	5–15	15–35	35–60	60–80	45–65	25–40

from the thousands of lakes, bogs, and swamps of the Northeast. Most of these antagonistic entities start dying off by the last week in July.

Tree line is very low compared to that in more southern parts of New England, and you can experience nasty, windy storms while up in the hills on exposed terrain. The tree line in the high peaks of New Hampshire is around 4,500 feet, but in Baxter State Park drops to less than 3,500 feet. When nearing the northern terminus of the IAT, you can expect the tree line to be below 3,000 feet. Snow can fall in any month of the year on the IAT, though accumulations from April to September are minimal, and nighttime temperatures can dip to below freezing in any month. Expect temperatures to reach at least the fifties during the day, but be prepared to put on a down vest around dinnertime.

TERRAIN

The terrain you will cover on the IAT is rough. That's the only way to put it. Because glaciers raked this area more than 10,000 years ago, you'll now plod up climbs among disjointed rock for most of the day, and descend to areas composing major drainages or swamps. About 20 percent of the IAT is still not on a footpath, so you'll be hiking on roads, fields, the United States–Canada border swath, old railroad beds, and timber company land. When you're on a footpath, you may run into sections flooded by busy beavers. The terrain in Baxter State Park rises so dramatically into the nasty weather that trails above tree line are closed from late October to May. The easiest hiking is on the Gaspé Peninsula. At times the trail can be difficult to follow and may only be marked with some old surveyor's tape. Currently, Maine has more than 100 miles of trail, New Brunswick has 275 kilometers (about 160 miles), and Quebec has 635 kilometers (nearly 400 miles). Near more civilized areas, the IAT is a multiple-use trail that allows horse riders and mountain bikers to share this path.

TERRAIN HIGHLIGHTS

- Above-tree-line terrain
- Paper and yellow birch forests
- Spruce and fir forests
- Glacial erratics
- Atlantic coastline
- Bogs
- Pristine lakes
- Small settlements

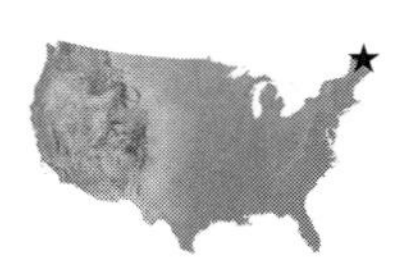

WATER

Even though that crystal clear stream in Middle of Nowhere, Maine, is running strong and looking good, don't be fooled; there are some little guys in that water looking for a new intestinal tract to call home. Remember, moose do more in the water than just wade. Keep the cooties homeless by treating all IAT water. Giardia is present in most regions of the United States, including on this remote trail. You'll have plenty of chances to filter out these tiny critters, because you'll be passing innumerable streams, lakes, and rivers. You'll pass a few settlements on your trek where you can ask the locals for some water (in French or English), or you can buy spring water at stores. The only place to be concerned about not finding water is on ridgelines.

WILDNESS

The IAT is one of the wildest trails, if not *the* wildest trail, in this guide. One thing that sets it apart from the twenty-four other trails is that you'll be crossing into another country and you'll see trail signs in the two respective languages. This alone can make the trail feel more removed from daily life than the other long trails. The trail's wildness is due not just to its dual citizenship; the IAT has a few sections that do not have any close resupply points. These sections may take more than a week to cross. Mailing food and equipment to Canada from the United States can be difficult, because it's international mail. Packages can be delayed or sent back or simply never arrive at their destination, eaten by the International Mail Monster, much like the Sock Monster that eats one of your socks when you do laundry.

In Maine you'll come across roughly eight lean-tos or campgrounds; New Brunswick has approximately six lean-tos or campgrounds. The Province of Quebec provides the most opportunities to have a roof over your head for the night, but reservations must be made in advance.

LOGISTICS

In Baxter State Park you may need to make reservations to ensure you'll have a place to sleep. People start making reservations for the summer on the second day of January of that year. No pristine camping or trailhead camping is allowed. You may not bring in radios, dogs, motorcycles, RVs, or trailers. You must be at least six years old to travel above tree line. Trails above tree line may be closed on nasty days. There's a fee to enter the park and additional fees to sleep in the park. Out-of-staters pay more than Mainers. Mountain bikes are not allowed in the park. Cell phones may not be operated. For winter trips, you must submit an application and solo trips are not permitted. Maybe Paul Petzoldt, founder of the National Outdoor Leadership School and the Wilderness Education Association, said it best when someone asked him how his trip to Baxter State Park went. He resentfully reported that the park felt like "a prison camp." I would agree with Petzoldt, but I'd add that it's a really pretty prison camp.

CRITTERS

- > Black bears
- > Caribou
- > Coyotes
- > Golden and bald eagles
- > Herons
- > Moose
- > Mountain lions
- > Whales

You'll hike along the U.S.-Canada border swath, and enter The Great White North via Customs near Fort Fairfield, Maine. Bring a photo ID. If you have warrants out for your arrest or have been arrested in the past, you will want to have that cleared up before your thru-hike.

Quebec has twenty-two shelters and twenty-four campsites, but reservations must be made ahead of time for the use of shelters and tent platforms. Shelters cost $15 Canadian and tent platforms are $7 Canadian. In Gaspé you need to secure permits to camp. From the Société des établissements de plein air du Québec (Sépaq) you can purchase a monthly pass to use the tent platforms or shelters of Quebec. Visit www.sepaq.com or call 800-665-6527.

WILDLIFE

On your 700-mile trek, you'll come across residents of the trail that you will not be able to find anywhere else in the East. Traveling on the more remote parts of the trail, you'll be the visitor in *their* woods, which can be a humbling experience for us usually-at-the-top-of-the-food-chain humans. But there's really nothing out there that's going to kill you. Stories about moose stomping on people and black bears tearing your face off are more fiction than fact. Simply give the wildlife the room they deserve and you shouldn't have any problems.

POINTS OF INTEREST

HIGHPOINTERS TAKE NOTE

Traveling over the highest points in Maine, New Brunswick, and mainland Quebec provides a great opportunity to hike above tree line to get a panoramic view of where you've been and where you're going.

LAKE MATANE

This long lake in Quebec is guarded on each side by tall mountains. The tent sites and the views from them are not to be missed.

FOR YOU, MY GOOD FRIEND

Located near the northern terminus in Forillon National Park, Cap Bon Ami has an observation tower, which provides extensive views of Newfoundland and the Cap Gaspé.

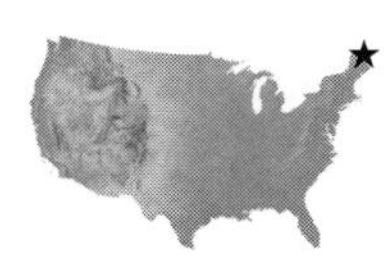

DON'T LEAVE HOME WITHOUT IT

ENGLISH-TO-FRENCH DICTIONARY

You can get around cities like Montreal and Quebec by speaking solely in English, but the Gaspé Peninsula has a much smaller bilingual population. To be understood by passersby on the final third of the IAT, you can either rely on your distant memories of high-school French class or pack a paperback.

"Monsieur, ou est le terminus?"

END OF THE LINE

It's not only home to the most northern portion of the trail, but Gaspé Peninsula may be the IAT's most scenic area, too. Your walk to the north terminates among tall cliffs that drop into the Atlantic among the whales and seals.

In Their Own Words . . .

The International Appalachian Trail/Sentier International des Appalaches (IAT/SIA) is a trail that connects two countries, two Canadian provinces, one state, and two cultures—French and English. The trail passes over the highest place in Maine, New Brunswick, and Quebec, and ends at the spectacular Cap Gaspé on the eastern end of Quebec's Gaspé Peninsula. Hikers can observe the great mammals of the north along the International Appalachian Trail—the majestic moose, the woodland caribou, and several species of whales. From the potato farmlands of Maine's Aroostook County to the northern forests of New Brunswick and Quebec, it is a wonderful trail through the northern Appalachian Mountain Chain.

The International Appalachian Trail is a relatively new trail and gives hikers new places to explore in the forests and mountains, and in the many towns and villages through which the trail passes. Wonderful people along the way will offer help and guidance, whether you speak French or English, and they may even invite you in for dinner. Thinking beyond borders is our theme. You will cross many borders on the trail, and even get to walk on the border swath between the United States and Canada, but you will find that the natural and cultural worlds transcend all borders.

—Dick Anderson, International Appalachian Trail president

john muir trail

220 MILES | CALIFORNIA

TO GO . . .

- expansive alpine terrain
- graded tread
- abundant wildlife
- state's highpoint included

OR NOT TO GO?

- true solitude a rarity; permits needed
- can't turn your back on your food
- time needed to acclimate
- difficult to resupply

Tarn located on the north side of Forester Pass. (AARON LOCANDER)

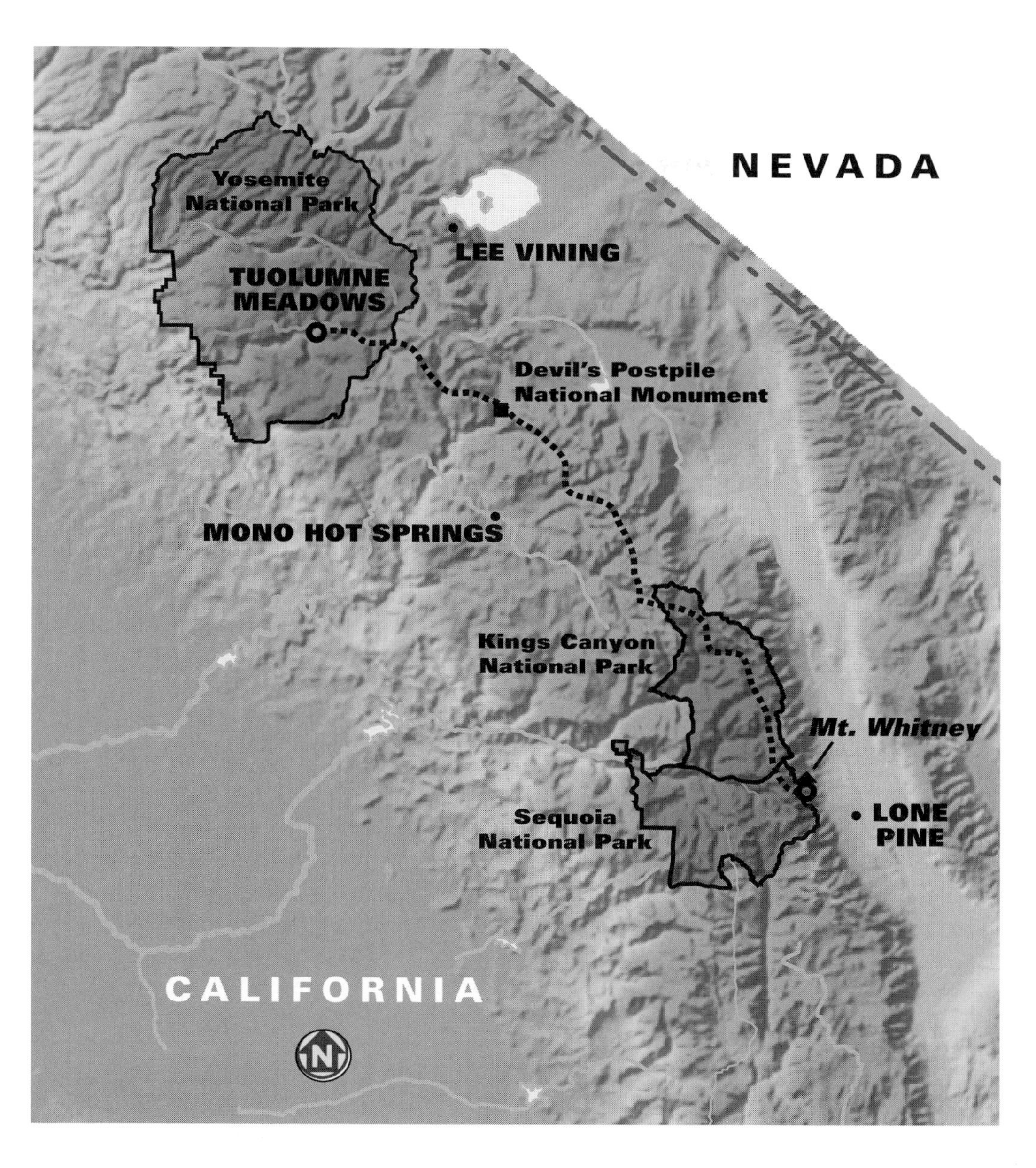

• Towns near or on the trail ■ National monument

O Trail terminus ■■■■■■■ Trail route

The John Muir Trail (JMT), which shares its tread with the Pacific Crest Trail for nearly its entire route, is perhaps the most popular trail in this guide besides the Long Trail of Vermont. Right off the bat I should tell you that if you're looking for solitude, you might not find it on this trail. Do not expect a solo, wilderness experience end to end, especially during popular summer months. But as with all the other trails, solitude seekers can find what they are looking for if they try hard enough.

Overall, the beauty of the JMT overrides any crowds. Readers of *Backpacker* magazine voted the John Muir Trail number four in best scenery and number four in difficulty. Concerning best signage/trail marking and best trail/camp/shelter conditions, the JMT was voted fifth best. Overall, the JMT was voted eighth greatest long-distance hiking trail in the United States.

From Yosemite Village in the north to the summit of Mount Whitney (14,494 feet) in the south, the JMT makes its way over passes, across snowfields, and among gorgeous tarns high in the Sierra Nevada. It's recommended that you start in the north, as most other JMT thru-hikers do, and make your way south, because starting in the south (perhaps with the most amount of weight in your pack for the whole trip) means you start off grinding up a 5,000-vertical-foot climb to Mount Whitney, the highest point in the Lower Forty-Eight. If you start in Yosemite National Park at the northern terminus, you can acclimate more steadily, with gentler climbing.

The JMT probably has the strongest thru-skiing history of any other long path in this guide, perhaps even surpassing the Colorado Trail in long-distance, high-elevation skiing. According to Lou Dawson, a ski mountaineering historian and accomplished skier in his own right (Dawson was the first and currently the only person to complete ski descents of all peaks in Colorado above 14,000 feet), the JMT has had winter devotees on its tread for more than seventy-five years. In 1928, Orlando Bartholomew became the first person to ski the JMT end to end and became one of the first, if not *the* first, to cover the entire JMT solo. During this time, Bartholomew also skied down the Sierra's Mount Tyndall and Mount Langley, two of California's fifteen 14,000-footers. In 1970, Carl McCoy and Doug Robinson made the second ski traverse of the John Muir Trail. In 1978, Pam Kelley and Bill Nicolai skied an extended version of the JMT, traveling from Carson Pass south to Whitney Portal. And in 1982, Brad and Randall Udall skied the entire JMT in only seven and a half days, using Nordic racing equipment.

VITALS

- Expect to cover 13 miles a day
- Expect a thru-hike to take 17 days
- Hiking season: July to October
- Water availability: Frequent to sometimes, depending on trail section
- Resupply opportunities: Seldom
- First year thru-hiked: 1928
- Approximate yearly thru-hikers: Fewer than 200
- Primary contact: Pacific Crest Trail Association

Forester Pass near the southern terminus of the John Muir Trail. (AARON LOCANDER)

MOUNT WHITNEY

This dramatic granite peak, described by early Sierra Nevada mountaineer Clarence King as looking "like the prow of an ocean steamer," had its first recorded ascent in 1873 by three fishermen, of all people. The first ski descent from the summit was made by Paul Arthur and Larry Yout in 1958. The mountain is named for Josiah Whitney, who was chief of the California State Geological Survey from 1860 to 1874.

Mount Whitney is one of the most climbed peaks in the state, and it's rumored that the United States Geological Survey's topographic map featuring Mount Whitney is the number-one-selling topographic map in the United States. Most climbers start at the Whitney Portal Trailhead (8,400 feet), which is actually the southern end of the JMT and is located thirteen miles outside the small town of Lone Pine (home to the best pancakes I have ever had).

Along your 10.7-mile hike toward the summit, you have the option of staying at Outpost Camp (10,300 feet, 3.5 miles from the trailhead) or Trail Camp (12,000 feet, 6 miles from the trailhead) before making your way up the rest of the route. Tons of switchbacks guide you to the top, and there's only one nasty spot where a slip would prove deadly. In summer, all you need to tackle this peak are a pair of sneakers and the time to acclimate; the colder months require crampons, an ice ax, and a helmet.

Certain logistics have to be dealt with to hike and camp near the Mount Whitney zone, at least from May to October (this zone is from Lone Pine Lake, 2.5 miles west of Whitney Portal, to Timberline Lake, near Crabtree Meadows). Prior to starting your hike, make sure you contact Sequoia and Kings Canyon National Parks and Inyo National Forest.

WEATHER

The John Muir Trail's short hiking season is due mainly to snow, which is still on the ground in early summer and starts again in early fall. Snowfields can last well into summer and on very high passes some actually ride out the entire season. Starting your end-to-end hike too early, perhaps in late May, means you will face snowfields and dangerous stream crossings. Most streams along the John Muir Trail are not bridged, and you may find what's usually a mild-mannered drainage has turned into a ripping brown torrent. Be aware that you may be delayed quite a bit if you attempt to traverse the JMT before the first of July.

The majority of days on the trail are beautifully sunny. Temperatures can range greatly, from the upper seventies and even the mid-eighties during the after-

AVERAGE HIGHS AND LOWS IN DEGREES FAHRENHEIT	JAN	MAR	MAY	JUL	SEPT	NOV
LEE VINING, CA (6,780 FT.)	20–40	25–50	40–65	55–85	45–75	25–55
LONE PINE, CA (3,750 FT.)	30–55	35–65	50–85	70–100	55–90	35–65

noon to below freezing at night. The numerous clear days combined with the high elevation means a thru-hiker can get fried pretty quickly by the sun. The dangerous stream fords and the sun are the biggest concerns on the JMT . . . okay, besides the lightning . . . all right, and the bears . . . and the possible summer snowstorms. But that's it. Really!

With the pleasant afternoon temperatures come intense lightning storms, as on the Colorado Trail in the Rockies. Keep your eyes peeled for cumulonimbus clouds, especially after noon, and retreat from ridgelines if you hear thunder.

Because much of the trail is 2,000 to 8,000 feet above surrounding towns, the average temperatures listed above may not be of much use to the JMT thru-hiker. For example, Lone Pine is located more than 10,000 vertical feet below the summit of Mount Whitney. You could estimate that the temperature on the summit of Mount Whitney is 35° cooler than that in the valleys below. Do your research concerning weather. The Pacific Crest Trail Association posts weather links on their website, including ones that give the Sierra Nevada snowpack from the previous winter.

JOHN MUIR

An inventor, sheepherder, naturalist, writer, and mountaineer, Muir, born in Scotland in 1838, was one of the legendary Sierra Nevada explorers of the late 1800s. Muir made several first ascents in the Sierras, many of them solo, including wonderful peaks such as Mount Ritter and Cathedral Peak. On Mount Whitney, Muir completed the first ascent of the class 3 Mountaineer's Route in 1873.

Citing his experiences among the gorgeous meadows, summits, and tarns of California, Muir became one of the leading individuals responsible for the formation of the national park system, at one point conferring with President Theodore Roosevelt about the importance of securing wild lands for future generations. During his lifetime, Muir wrote more than three hundred articles and at least ten books, and founded the Sierra Club in 1892. He also served as the American Alpine Club's councilor from 1902 to 1904, and gained presidency of the club from 1905 to 1910. Muir also completed a long-distance walk, covering a thousand-mile route from Indianapolis to Florida.

Recently, Muir was chosen to be featured on a coin: the California quarter. The John Muir-clad quarter was chosen by Governor Schwarzenegger over approximately 8,000 entries. The image shows Muir with his usual attire—walking stick, hat, and gentleman's coat—in front of Half Dome in Yosemite Valley, a land he helped preserve. ■

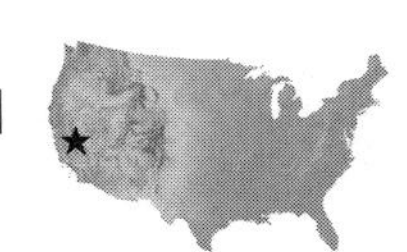

TERRAIN HIGHLIGHTS

- > Meadows
- > Glacial tarns
- > Sequoia groves
- > Waterfalls
- > Canyons
- > Alpine terrain
- > High passes
- > Scree fields

TERRAIN

The John Muir Trail has a relatively smooth tread compared to the rocky, rooty, steep, and muddy trails of the East. You can expect to make moderate progress on the JMT, once you get acclimated. The trail climbs across nine major passes above the 10,000-foot level and wanders above that elevation for approximately sixty-five miles. The tread is a graded surface of rock and sand for the most part, with tons of switchbacks to help you get up climbs that can exceed 2,500 vertical feet. On Mount Whitney alone, if you start from the south, you'll ascend a total of ninety-nine switchbacks from Whitney Portal to the summit. Forests in this area are mostly an assortment of pines, including Jeffrey, white, lodgepole, foxtail, and jack. You'll also see aspen, hemlock, and red fir.

WATER

Although the John Muir Trail is generally located at a high elevation, you'll come across countless tarns, lakes, streams, and springs. You shouldn't have to worry about finding water. However, as with any other mountainous trail, it can be dry in late summer and on ridgelines. Just keep your eyes peeled. There are no potable sources on the trail, and no nearby towns, but a long trip off the trail will lead you to folks who sell or give water to thirsty JMT thru-hikers.

WILDNESS

California is home to much wildness, some of evil proportions in certain people's opinions. I asked a friend what was new in Los Angeles, "just the usual dope, guns, murder, and mayhem?" I thought I would get a lighthearted answer, because she's a funny woman. Instead, things got ugly.

If I could go live with the aboriginals, or something, I would. That isn't very realistic though, so I'd more likely go to Spain, maybe Canada. So, in answer to your question, "How is Los Angeles?" You're right. Just the usual. Full-blown insanity. This is the Belly of the Beast. The future of the whole country. In due time, everywhere in the U.S. will be just like L.A. That is a sickening, horrifying thought.

Luckily the JMT avoids the most evil parts of the Golden State, but you won't avoid people. The JMT is well known, and unfortunately you cannot have a trip alone if you're heading from end to end. Many of the campsites are above tree line, so if you're not next to your nighttime neighbors, you will at least be within sight of

CRITTERS

- > Black bears
- > Coyotes
- > Fishers
- > Marmots
- > Mountain lions
- > Pikas

them. You can usually find solitude by heading farther from local water sources, but in many areas you'll be required to camp in designated sites only. Many older sites have been closed due to overuse. Seasonal rangers can be found along the JMT keeping an eye on the most heavily used areas and educating users on how to reduce the impacts of their visit by practicing LNT principles.

Resupply points cannot be found directly on the trail, but there are points where you can exit the JMT and head into towns. From the north, these are located between the 58- and 70-mile marks, between the 148- and 161-mile marks, and near mile 135. Two resort areas near mile 110 will hold any forwarded packages for a fee. It is recommended that you do not cache food because of bears. There are only two shelters on the trail, and these are for emergency use only. One is on the summit of Mount Whitney, and the other is in Muir Pass. Be aware that lightning has killed at least one person inside the Mount Whitney shelter, which has an elevated wooden floor.

WILDLIFE

I'd bet my life savings that anyone hiking the JMT end to end will see our buddies, the bears. Bears have developed into a major problem on the trail thanks to people who have voluntarily and involuntarily fed them. Bears in this area have gotten smarter than, say, the average bear. There was a time when you could simply hang your food without a lot of fuss, and bears couldn't get to it. Then you had to do a fancy counterbalance hang on a cable, and they *probably* wouldn't get it down. But now, it is highly recommended that you carry a bear canister, which can be purchased or rented near the JMT. It is also prudent to use the bear boxes located at many of the established campsites.

When leaving your car at a trailhead, be sure to use the provided bear boxes. Any food left inside your car may result in your car being opened like a can of tuna. National Park Service and U.S. Forest Service offices usually display photographs of destroyed vehicles to remind you that bears are opportunistic feeders. My favorite photo is of two bears, one in the driver's seat and one in the passenger seat, hanging out of the peeled-back roof. I can hear it now: "Uh, ma'am, we've got good news and bad news. The good news is you now have a convertible. . . ." Store your food correctly, and make sure the bear boxes and your bear canisters are closed.

POINTS OF INTEREST

THE BIG DROP

Many waterfalls can be found on or near the trail, including 100-foot Rainbow Falls and the nearly 600-foot-tall Nevada Falls.

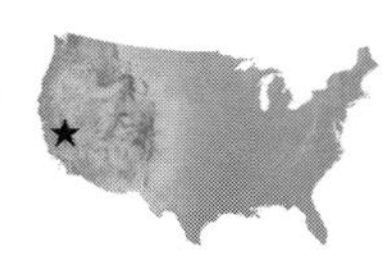

DON'T LEAVE HOME WITHOUT IT

FREE-STANDING SHELTER

Unless you want to carry a mallot to drive in your tent stakes, you'd better bring a free-standing option. When you're not contending with granite floors you'll most likely encounter loose sand and gravel—nothing substantial enough to give your stakes ample bite. A sturdy dome will keep the tent fabric out of your face.

HELL OF A VIEW

The 800-acre Devils Postpile National Monument just south of Yosemite has a unique and fascinating display of joined basalt columns.

BUT HOW BIG ARE THE TERMITES?

Sequoia National Park is home of the biggest tree, in volume, on the planet. The General Sherman tree is 275 feet tall and more than 100 feet in circumference. Many "smaller" trees can be found here, too.

HIGH-ELEVATION ADVENTURES

In addition to Mount Whitney, you'll be hiking amid numerous peaks that exceed 13,000 feet, such as Junction Peak, Diamond Peak, North Palisade, Mount Huxley, and Mount Wynne.

In Their Own Words . . .

Spanning the Sierra crest from Whitney to Half Dome, the John Muir Trail sets the bar for long-distance adventure. Its reputation as one of the most popular trails in the West is certainly well deserved. With its rugged alpine tarns, abundant wildlife, and endless sweeping vistas, we found the JMT truly stunning. Rarely a moment passed that we were not humbled by the massive glacial landscape around us. Towering granite cliffs line much of the trail corridor as it meanders through lush pine forests and climbs over jagged passes. When not enjoying the well graded tread underfoot, we spent afternoons swimming in crisp, clear lakes, and exploring hidden peaks.

However, for all its natural beauty, the John Muir Trail was not a lazy stroll. Churning rivers, vast summer snowfields, taxing climbs, and notorious bear and mosquito populations, not to mention few handy resupply points for more than two hundred miles, presented us with a sizeable challenge. In spite of these obstacles, we were not the only ones to brave the John Muir Trail. The trail was relatively crowded at times and private campsites are becoming a thing of the past. So, don't expect total solitude and apply for permits early. But, despite the popularity, the John Muir Trail has a unique wilderness feel that you will not want to miss.

—Karen Connelly and Ryman McLane, two-time John Muir Trail thru-hikers

lone star hiking trail

130 MILES | TEXAS

TO GO . . .

- winter destination
- crowd factor should be low
- wide assortment of animals
- water available most of the year

OR NOT TO GO?

- not a true wilderness setting in certain sections
- summers are hot and humid
- no detailed guidebook or map set available
- possible difficult fords

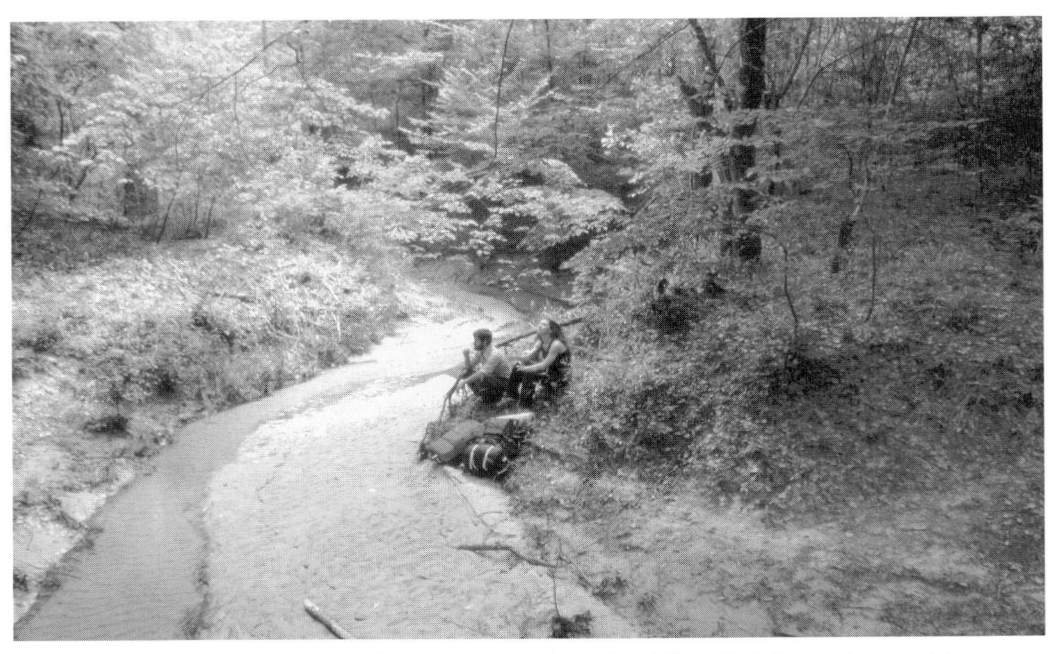

There's a surprising amount of running water on the Lone Star Hiking Trail, if you pick the right season. Avoid the summer months or streams like this one will be bone dry. (USFS)

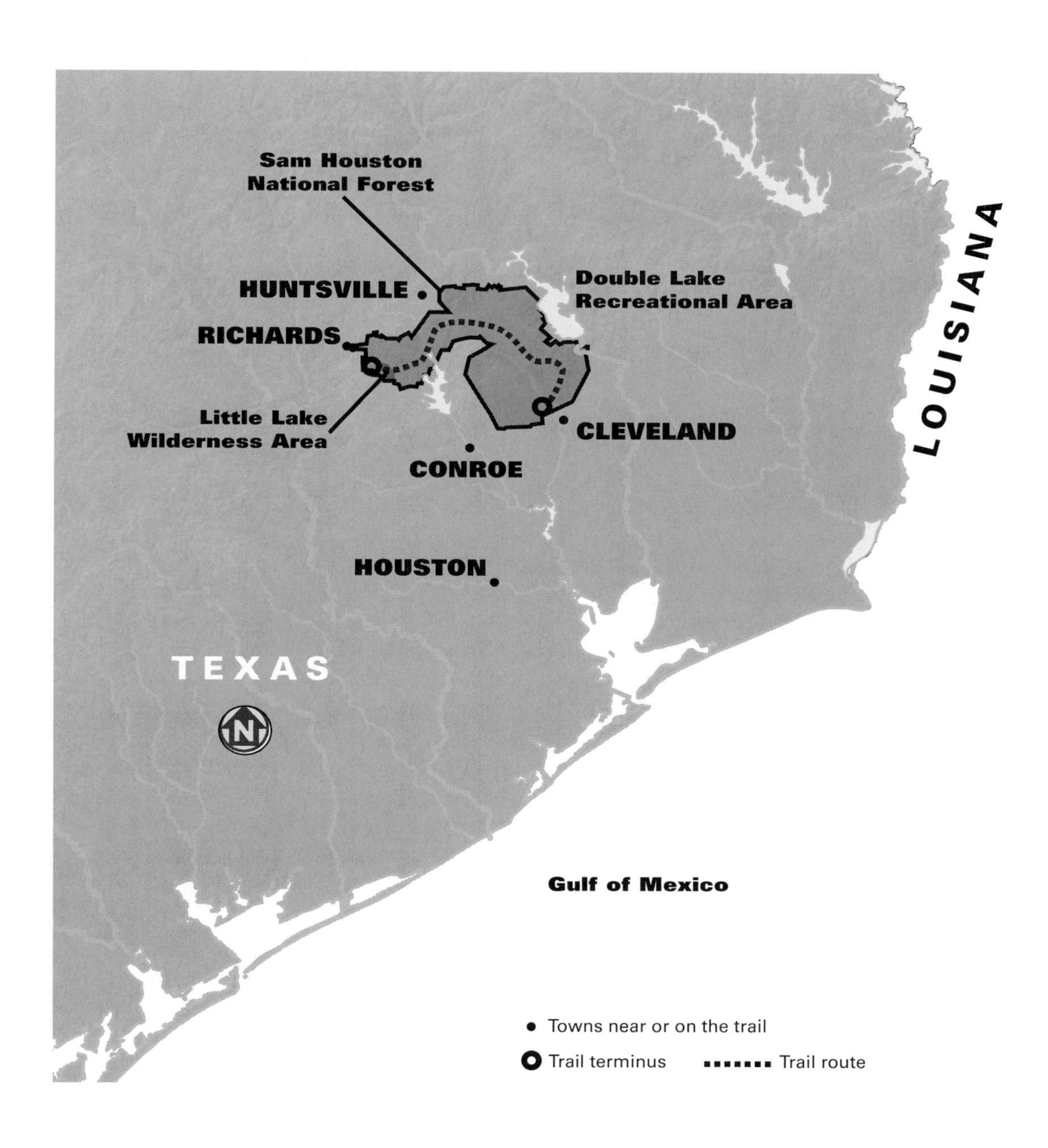
Sam Houston
National Forest
HUNTSVILLE
Double Lake
Recreational Area
RICHARDS
Little Lake
Wilderness Area
CLEVELAND
CONROE
HOUSTON
LOUISIANA
TEXAS
N
Gulf of Mexico
Towns near or on the trail
Trail terminus
Trail route

VITALS

- > Expect to cover 18 miles a day
- > Expect a thru-hike to take 8 days
- > Hiking season: September to May
- > Water availability: Frequent
- > Resupply opportunities: Seldom
- > First year thru-hiked: Unknown
- > Approximate yearly thru-hikers: Fewer than 20
- > Primary contact: Lone Star Hiking Trail Club

Texas comes into this guide showing off its only long-distance hiking trail. The 130-mile Lone Star Hiking Trail (LSHT) primarily travels through the 163,000-acre Sam Houston National Forest, one of four national forests in Texas, located about an hour's drive north of Houston. The LSHT's western terminus is near the town of Richards; the eastern terminus is near the town of Cleveland. Part of the trail is also designated a National Recreational Trail.

When it comes to the highest projected daily mileage, the Lone Star Hiking Trail ties with the Buckeye Trail and the Florida Trail. Due to the smooth terrain of the LSHT, an experienced backpacker with a lightweight pack may be able to average eighteen miles a day. Of the trails in this guide, the LSHT can be hiked end to end in the second-shortest amount of time; it can be hiked fully in just eight days, whereas the Wonderland Trial can be completed in fewer than seven.

The LSHT is a prime location for someone who wants to hike an entire southern trail but doesn't have the time or motivation to hike the Arizona Trail or the Florida Trail, both of which require much more planning and time to complete.

WEATHER

Okay, this is the deal: if you don't like really hot weather, do not try to hike the LSHT in June, July, or August. It gets hot in east Texas. Really hot. Africa hot. It's highly recommended that you do not hike the trail in summer due to heat, humidity, bugs, and lack of water. The terrain is not tough to get through, but the midday heat of Texas is very good at sapping the energy out of any thru-hiker.

TERRAIN

The daily mileage you can cover on the LSHT is high because the terrain is cooperative. If you wanted to, and you are in good shape before starting your intended thru-hike, you could cover more than twenty miles a day, especially because some sections follow old railroad beds. Overall, the LSHT is a pretty flat trail that follows

AVERAGE HIGHS AND LOWS IN DEGREES FAHRENHEIT

	JAN	MAR	MAY	JUL	SEPT	NOV
RICHARDS, TX (320 FT.)	40–60	50–70	65–85	75–95	70–90	50–70
CLEVELAND, TX (160 FT.)	40–60	50–75	65–85	70–95	65–90	50–70

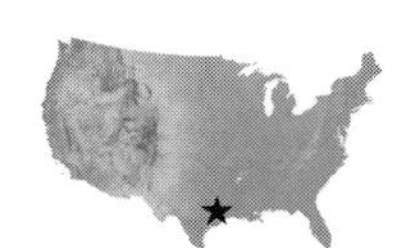

TERRAIN HIGHLIGHTS

- Loblolly and short-leaved pine forests
- Seasonal streams
- Spring blooms
- Deep, shady sections of trail
- Riparian areas
- Logged areas
- Freshwater ponds
- Sand-lined rivers

paved roads, game paths, singletrack hiking trail, forest roads, ranch land, and petroleum pipelines. The hiking surface usually consists of hard-packed sand and pine needles. You'll encounter multiple stream crossings and other wet locales. Because this trail is meant to preserve the wild character of Sam Houston National Forest via a primitive footpath, bridging is rare. In times of heavy rain, some sections may have to be detoured due to flooding.

Vegetation is mostly hardwood forest in wet or low areas, with loblolly and other species of pine on higher ground. In spring the LSHT hosts an incredible array of wildflowers.

WATER

I thought the LSHT would have a big strike against it in this category, but surprisingly this trail has plenty of water to offer a thirsty thru-hiker, including the kind that falls from the sky. Sam Houston National Forest's average annual rainfall exceeds forty inches, which may not be much compared to the rain and snowfall amounts of trails hundreds of miles to the north, but it's usually enough precipitation to provide consistent water sources.

Finding water should not be a major concern if you hike during the right time of year. During the summer months, ponds along the trail can be dry, and many streams are seasonal, so be prepared to cache a lot of water on your route beforehand. There are two potable water sources along the trail, one at Double Lake Recreation Area and one at nearby Huntersville State Park.

WILDNESS

Because national forests are areas of many uses—as opposed to national parks, which are set aside mostly for aesthetic value—the LSHT travels on and near many signs of human-made alterations. You'll come across signs of these national forest activities: "Water-Soil-Minerals" (damming, dirt hauling, drilling), "Vegetative Management" (logging), "Fire Management" (prescribed burning, and attempts at controlling fires), and "ORV Use" (four-wheeling). Try to take these in stride.

It should be mentioned that more illegal activities take place in this national forest than in most other national forests. Methamphetamine labs have been found, and the illegal use of horses and all-terrain vehicles are consistent problems. Many search-and-rescue operations take place, and there are reports of more than 300 written citations a year. Overall, it's not that different from what you would expect to

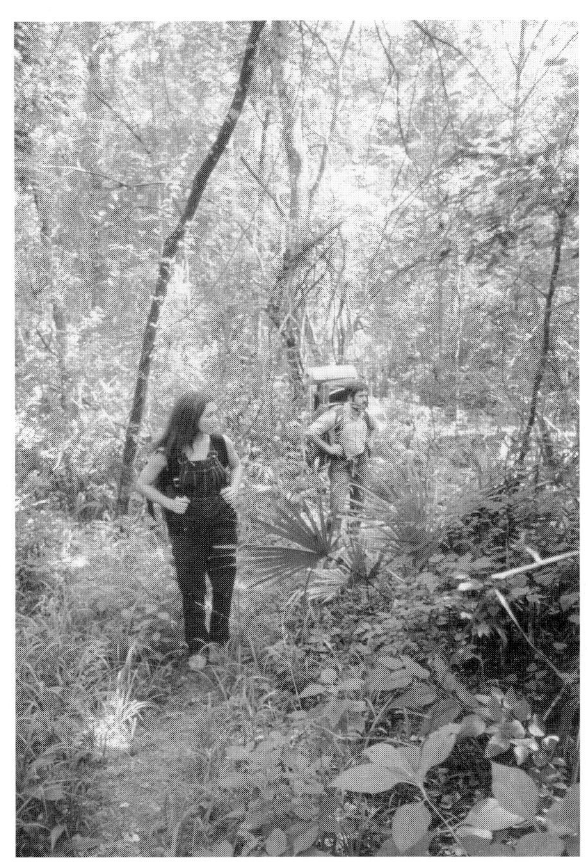

East Texas is also surprisingly lush. This section of the Lone Star Hiking Trail looks more like a jungle than a hardwood forest. (USFS)

see in a typical national forest in the South. That is, except for armed gang members from Houston guarding their meth labs. Actually, I'm just kidding. When I shared an early draft of this manuscript with a high-ranking representative of the LSHT Club, she sternly corrected my casual silliness, asserting that the methamphetamine labs throughout the national forest were "not even on the trail." What a relief!

A hike on the LSHT may include somewhat remote sections interspersed with signs of human impact. Semicivilized camping areas on or near the trail include three campgrounds, two recreation areas, and one state park. Spirited Lone Star Hiking Trail Club volunteers are establishing up to thirteen primitive tent sites, of which four were in place by April 2001.

WILDLIFE

This southeastern Texas trail offers the chance to see large mammals, animals typically found only in the South, and animals whose areas range all the way up to the northeastern United States. Most of the resident critters are harmless, but if you're concerned about mountain lions or snakes, some research before your trip should alleviate most of your worries. In general, if you respect the wildlife and keep on your toes, you won't have any problems.

CRITTERS

- Armadillos
- Bald eagles*
- Beavers
- Black bears
- Common garden lizards
- Feral hogs
- Rattlesnakes, copperheads, water moccasins, coral snakes
- Red-cockaded woodpeckers*
- Turkeys

*Listed as endangered species in Texas

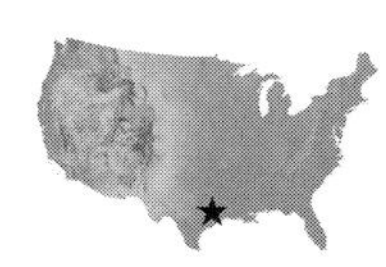

DON'T LEAVE HOME WITHOUT IT

WALKING STICK

The LSHT's flat terrain doesn't warrant a pair of aggressive, new-school hiking poles, but a good-old-fashioned walking stick would provide handy companionship for your 130-mile stroll. Also, there have been some reports of vicious canines near populated areas of the LSHT. Walking softly with a big stick might ensure that you remain top dog.

POINTS OF INTEREST

FORMER RESIDENTS

Sam Houston National Forest has sites that contain signs of human activity from as far back as 10,000 BC. Check with the forest service to see if you can visit one of these archaeological digs. If you find anything interesting and apparently undiscovered, please report it to the forest service.

DOUBLE YOUR PLEASURE

Not only can you buy a soda and take a hot shower at the Double Lake Recreation Center, you can also rent a canoe and tool around on the twenty-four-acre lake stocked with bass, bream, and catfish. Only small electric motors are allowed, so it should be pretty quiet.

UP BIG CREEK

Contained in an area of nearly 2,000 acres with four loop hiking trails, Big Creek Scenic Area (near the Cleveland end of the trail), is home to a diverse range of vegetation. To help preserve the area's natural setting, camping is not allowed.

In Their Own Words . . .

In the three days I've been hiking on the trail I've only encountered five people. One guy was a biker walking the trail to see if it was OK for off-roading. . . . I ran into a couple just before I reached a trailhead at mile eight. He had a rucksack and she had an external frame pack. They turned up a forest road just as I walked by. On the other side of that trailhead I passed a couple day hiking. . . . All five of these folks I saw on Sunday. Saw no one on Monday but I did see a couple of cars and heard a motorcycle go down one of the bike trails near the Lone Star Hiking Trail. I was hoping to encounter some other hikers on my route. Have seen some boot prints but no telling how long ago they were made.

The wind is only gusting a bit along the trail for the past couple of days. I can hear the trees rustling as the gust moves through the forest. I can actually turn my head and track the gust of wind as it moves along in the trees around me. When the gust passes the forest goes quiet. So calm and peaceful.

—Paul "Too Tall" Morgan, 2002 Lone Star Hiking Trail section hiker

long path

345 MILES | NEW JERSEY
NEW YORK

 **TO GO . . .**

- terrain ranging from country roads to steep climbs
- waterfalls and escarpments
- backcountry sections are usually not crowded
- high peaks and Hudson River included

OR NOT TO GO?

- no detailed maps available
- very urban southern terminus
- possible heat, humidity, and bugs
- nearly a third of the route is on roads

At 48,000 acres, Slide Mountain Wilderness Area is the largest wilderness area in southern New York. Its titular peak, 4,190-foot Slide Mountain, towers in the background. This is the highest point within the Catskill Park and on the Long Path. (E. SCHLIMMER)

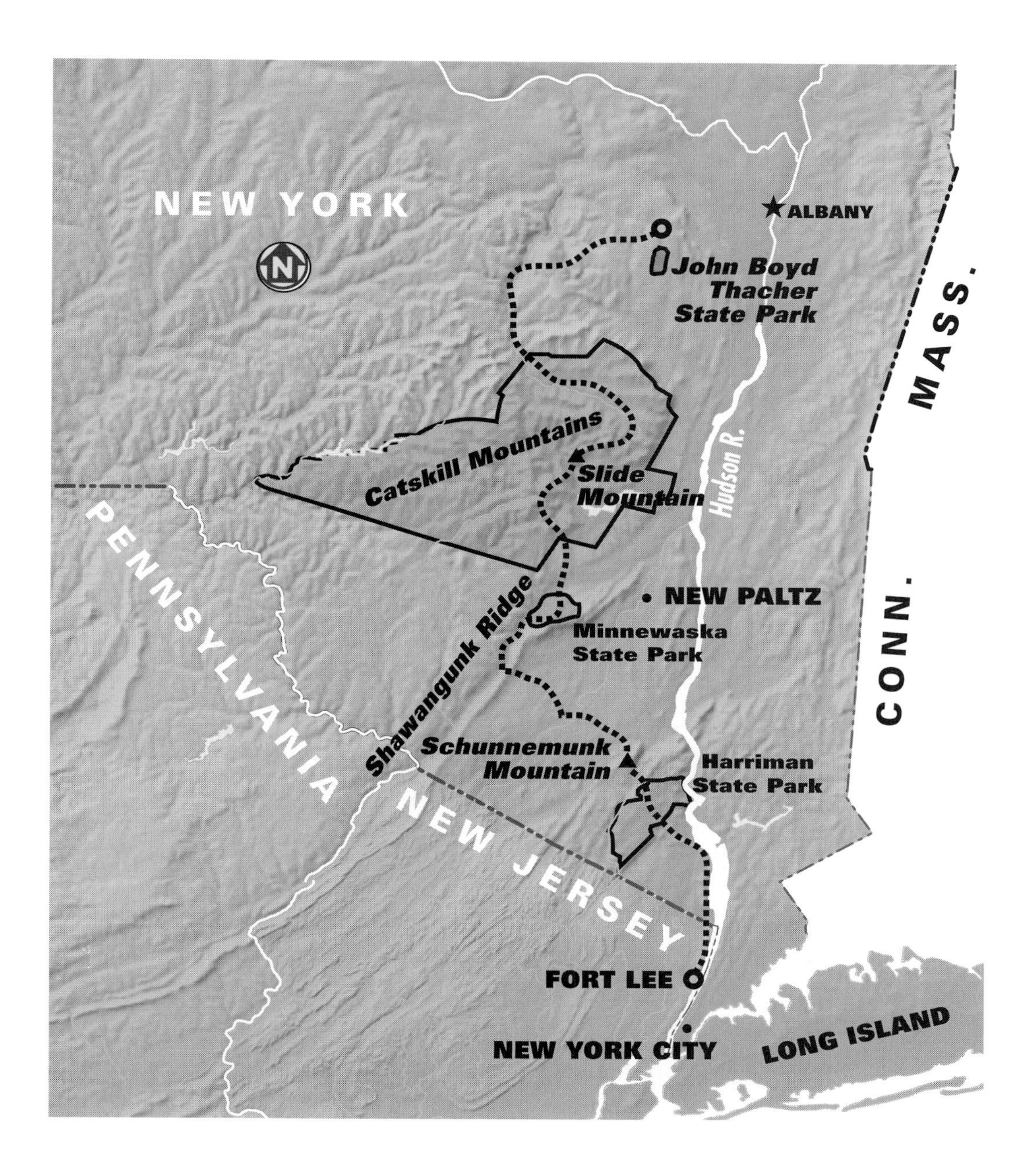
NEW YORK
N
ALBANY
John Boyd Thacher State Park
MASS.
Catskill Mountains
Slide Mountain
Hudson R.
PENNSYLVANIA
NEW PALTZ
Shawangunk Ridge
Minnewaska State Park
CONN.
Schunnemunk Mountain
Harriman State Park
NEW JERSEY
FORT LEE
NEW YORK CITY
LONG ISLAND
Towns near or on the trail
State capital
Trail terminus
Trail route

VITALS

- Expect to cover 15 miles a day
- Expect a thru-hike to take 23 days
- Hiking season: June to November (Hiking is discouraged in April and May due to a fragile surface.)
- Water availability: Sometimes
- Resupply opportunities: Frequent
- First year thru-hiked: 1998
- Approximate yearly thru-hikers: Less than 20
- Primary contact: New York–New Jersey Trail Conference

The Long Path (LP) is one of a handful of long-distance trails in the Empire (Strikes Back) State. Starting on the New Jersey side of the George Washington Bridge (just outside New York City), the LP runs north through New Jersey for twelve miles, then enters New York state. The LP continues north, growing wilder through the nearly 300,000-acre Catskill Park, and currently ends in John Boyd Thacher State Park, near the state capital of Albany.

Although the LP was originally conceived in the 1930s, it is still a relatively young trail and uses many county roads for its route. The civilized sections are being traded in for woods walks to make the LP more pristine. New sections are cut each trail season, over hills and through hollows, with the ambitious idea of having the Long Path hook up with the Northville-Placid Trail in Adirondack Park then continue onward to Canada. Delaying this endeavor are private lands, regulations on building new sections of trail within the Adirondack and Catskill parks, and other obstacles (such as the reasonable idea of having the Northville-Placid Trail retain its original personality).

The Long Path met its first thru-hiker in the late 1990s. While in her mid-sixties, Mary Ann Nissley completed a thru-hike of the then 330-mile Long Path on May 30, 1998. Nissley remains active in the long-distance-hiking world, serving as a Field Editor to the 2003 edition of the *Appalachian Trail Thru Hikers' Companion.*

WEATHER

The weather on the Long Path can be as unpredictable as that on other long-distance trails in New England. Close to the ocean and prone to the typical mixed bag of Northeast weather, the LP can be sunny in the morning, rainy in the afternoon, and cold in the evening (or vice versa). As is said about the Adirondacks to the north: "If ya' don't

AVERAGE HIGHS AND LOWS IN DEGREES FAHRENHEIT

	JAN	MAR	MAY	JUL	SEPT	NOV
FORT LEE, NJ (310 FT.)	25–40	35–50	55–70	70–85	60–75	40–55
ALBANY, NY (240 FT.)	15–30	25–45	50–70	60–80	50–70	30–50

like the weather, just wait ten minutes." The Hudson Valley of New York and even the Catskill Mountains to the west can become unbearably humid, to say the least. Don't expect to make great progress on the Long Path on very humid days.

TERRAIN

The LP's terrain is a mix of ups and downs that will have you "suckin' basketballs," as my friend Pete would say. (That means being out of breath, I think). But there are some extended flats, which give you time to recover while you savor distant views of the Hudson, Schoharie, and Mohawk valleys, which have served as transportation routes for well over 500 years. Hiking tread is mostly broken rocks and slippery leaves, similar to Pennsylvania terrain. The route covers abandoned railroad beds, hiking trails, stream crossings, long ridgelines, escarpments (cliff bands), and rough, rock-strewn climbs and descents.

The Catskill terrain was an uplifted plain a long, long time ago. Later it eroded where drainages developed, so now there are steep-sided peaks with very flat summits. Views can be found, however, because there are boulders, clearings, and escarpments on many of these mountains. The LP is no slouch on its ninety-five-mile trek through the Catskill Park. It climbs no fewer than fifteen peaks exceeding 3,000 feet and comes within a mile of another seven 3,000-foot peaks. An end-to-end hike of the LP ascends more than 30,000 vertical feet.

WATER

You won't be able to find as much water here as on the Northville-Placid Trail to the north, but there should be a good enough amount to ease any worry about finding the next source or rationing what water you have. My good friend who recently finished climbing the 3,000-foot peaks of the Catskills mentioned that during all his adventures in these mountains he never saw a natural lake. And from the moderate research I did on this subject, I found that to be true. The Long Path does pass by lakes and ponds, although nearly all of these are human made. You'll cross a plethora of streams and rivers along your 300+-mile trek, but you'll also encounter dry sections of trail after you start climbing. Basically (and this is a rough guide, because areas on the LP differ so much), when you are about a third of the way up a climb, that's where the water sources end.

TERRAIN HIGHLIGHTS

- The Palisades
- Escarpments
- Waterfalls
- Rocky slopes
- Forested summits
- Steep climbs
- Hemlock-lined streams
- Erratics
- Shallow streams

The New York–New Jersey Trail Conference has put together a great set of maps for the Catskill Mountains, which point out springs along the Long Path, but please note that many of these are seasonal. Before any climbs, fill up at the bottom and you should be fine. Use your own judgment about treating water from popular springs.

WILDNESS

Located near the largest city in the United States, you would think this place would be crawling with people. That's what most other people think, too. What's the end result? A lot of people don't choose the Long Path because they think it's going to be too crowded, thus the crowds aren't bad. Granted, the LP does travel through small towns, and the section that follows the Palisades Parkway at the beginning of the trail is far from wild; it's burdened with high levels of traffic and crowded overlooks.

But as you make your way north, you will probably be satisfied with the amount of wildness, especially during weekdays when most others are at work. The Catskill Park is basically under the same rules and regulations as its larger neighbor to the north, the Adirondack Park, and massive development and logging are not allowed on state land.

Of the series of lean-tos on the Long Path, the most consistent can be found inside the Catskill Park. No camping is allowed above 3,500 feet on all state land. Nearly 30 percent of the current Long Path route is on roads. As such, you will basically never have to leave the trail to resupply. The Long Path travels through the centers of eleven towns on its two-state journey. These villages range greatly in what they can provide a hungry, thirsty, or tired thru-hiker. Some small settlements, such as Bullville (in the central part of the LP) has only a pizza place, post office, and convenience store, whereas Nyack (near the southern terminus) offers everything you will need, including restaurants, supermarkets, and cheap motels. The longest sections without resupply points will be Harriman State Park and the Catskill Park; both require three to six days of townless travel.

The Long Path's route also traverses tons of private land. The landowners have been kind enough to let us hike through their backyards. Don't blow it! Usually camping or fires are not allowed, and some sections are closed during hunting seasons. Leave all public or private lands in better shape than you found them.

WILDLIFE

"A trail near New York City? Cool, I betcha there's lots of rats and stuff." Come on. We are not *in* New York City. We're just near it. Once underway, heading north, you'll be traveling into wilder stuff each day. The Catskill Park is home to more than 500 black bears, among many other mammals.

When hiking through Minnewaska State Park and Harriman State Park, and other areas on the LP, you'll see signs of the destructive porcupine. Nearly anything that has been touched by human hands will be chewed and devoured by the

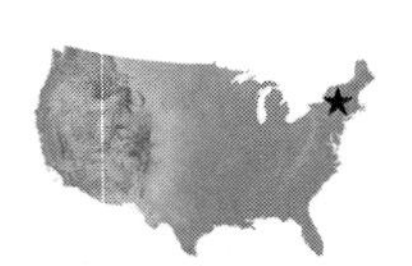

CRITTERS

- Bobcats
- Coyotes
- Field mice
- Porcupines
- Red foxes
- Red-tailed hawks
- Skunks
- Snowshoe hares
- Turkeys

"porkies." Why? Well, they like salt so much that they'll eat just about anything that has a trace of salt on it. Pick up a new trail sign and put it in place? It's fair game as a snack. Many trail signs and even lower portions of outhouses and shelters have fine-wire fencing material on them to protect the wood. So beware; hiking boots and backpacks full of your daily sweat can get chewed up, too.

POINTS OF INTEREST

BUSY BUT BEAUTIFUL

The Palisades on the southern end of the trail are popular with roadside tourists and hikers alike. The first 20 miles of the LP traces the edge of 300-foot tall cliffs that form the western bank of the Hudson River. The view includes the New York City skyline.

AN ISLAND OF WILDERNESS

South of Washingtonville is my favorite part of the Long Path, Schunnemunk Mountain. This area of the trail is being exploited by development, but luckily the sub-

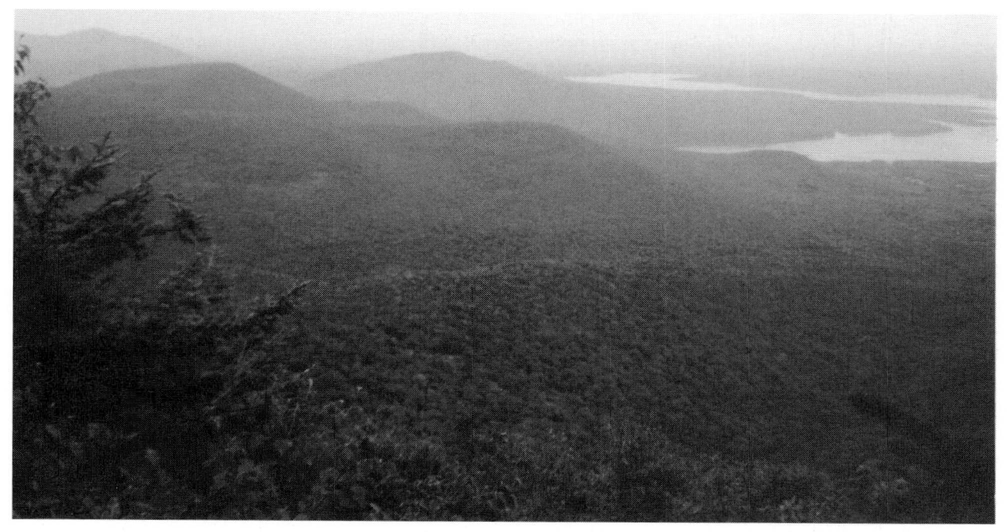

The spectacular view from 3,790-foot Wittenberg Mountain includes the 8,000-acre Ashokan Reservoir, which is owned by the New York City Department of Environmental Protection. (E. SCHLIMMER)

DON'T LEAVE HOME WITHOUT IT

REFLECTIVE VEST

With lots of walking on country roads and with extended sections of the Long Path paralleling the fast and furious Palisades Parkway, a bright-orange vest may help you avoid impact with one of thousands of cell-phone-talking, self-absorbed Downstate drivers. Just don't get pulled over by the fashion police.

urbanites have not yet found a way to build on the gorgeous cliffs that spill from this beautiful five-mile ridge.

THE 'GUNKS

Near Ellenville, just south of the Long Path's midpoint, is Shawangunk Ridge—which can be best described as a really long version of Schunnemunk Mountain (above). Stunted forests of scrub oak and pine, exposed rock hiking, and gorgeous views are included.

THE HIGH AND MIGHTY

The highpoint of the LP is the summit of Slide Mountain (4,190 feet; 31st highest peak in New York). Slide is located in the largest Wilderness Area in southern New York and supports expansive balsam fir and red spruce forests.

FALLING DOWN

From the Palisades in the south to the northern terminus of this 345-mile trail, hikers will see plenty of waterfalls. The big ones include Verkeerder Kill Falls, Vernooy Falls, Buttermilk Falls, and Wildcat Falls. They'll be especially nice on those hot and humid days.

ON THE OTHER SIDE

John Boyd Thacher State Park is just a five-mile hike south of the LP's current northern terminus. Here you will find cliffs, caves, waterfalls, and trails that bring you to all these features easily.

In Their Own Words . . .

First off, if you are looking for a pure-wilderness experience; looking to commune with some of the most gorgeous features the Northeast has to offer, you will want to look outside the confines of the Long Path. Though well maintained and very well marked, the Long Path follows roads for upward of a quarter of its current route. Some of these paved stretches go through busy intersections and parallel highways. On the central and northern sections of the trail you'll be on country roads far from city settings but here you can't drink most of the water since it is polluted by agriculture (well water is polluted on these sections, too).

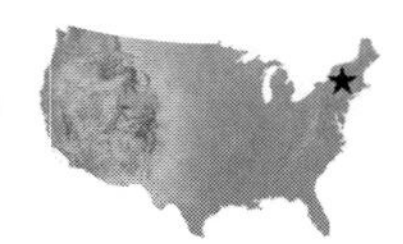

However, those are about all the bad things I can say about this trail. The three major wild areas of the Long Path—Harriman and Highland Lakes State Parks and the Catskill Park—offer wild settings complete with glacial erratics, lakes, expansive hardwood forests, ridgeline hiking, and mountain views. If you start a thru-hike on the George Washington Bridge, you can look forward to wilder and wilder hiking each successive day as you make your way across some of the very attractive terrain of the Empire State. For me, the highlight of hiking 200 miles of the Long Path was the Catskill region, a home of deep hollows, evergreen-clad flat-topped peaks, and plenty of wildlife. On my 200-mile trek I counted more than 30 white-tailed deer.

Like other young trails, the Long Path is a living, growing tread, reaching deeper into the woods, farther from the roads, and farther in overall mileage with each decade. Perhaps it will even meet its sister trail to the north, the Northville-Placid Trail. But until then, this trail retains its Downstate personality. Those who think southern New York state is a land of sprawl and smog are in for a nice surprise if they choose to meet the Long Path.

—Morris Kempshall, Long Path section hiker, climber of all Catskill peaks over 3,000 feet

long trail

270 MILES | VERMONT

TO GO . . .

> gorgeous mountain views
> legendary fall foliage
> Vermont-made cheese, beer, maple syrup, and ice cream
> state highpoint

OR NOT TO GO?

> more than 65,000 vertical feet to ascend
> Appalachian Trail section can be crowded
> bugs are annoying from May to July
> muddy and rough tread in certain sections

The first big view on the Long Trail, if you're hiking south to north, is from the observation tower on Glastenbury Mountain (3,748 feet). The tower rises above the expansive evergreen forests of the aptly named Green Mountain State. (E. SCHLIMMER)

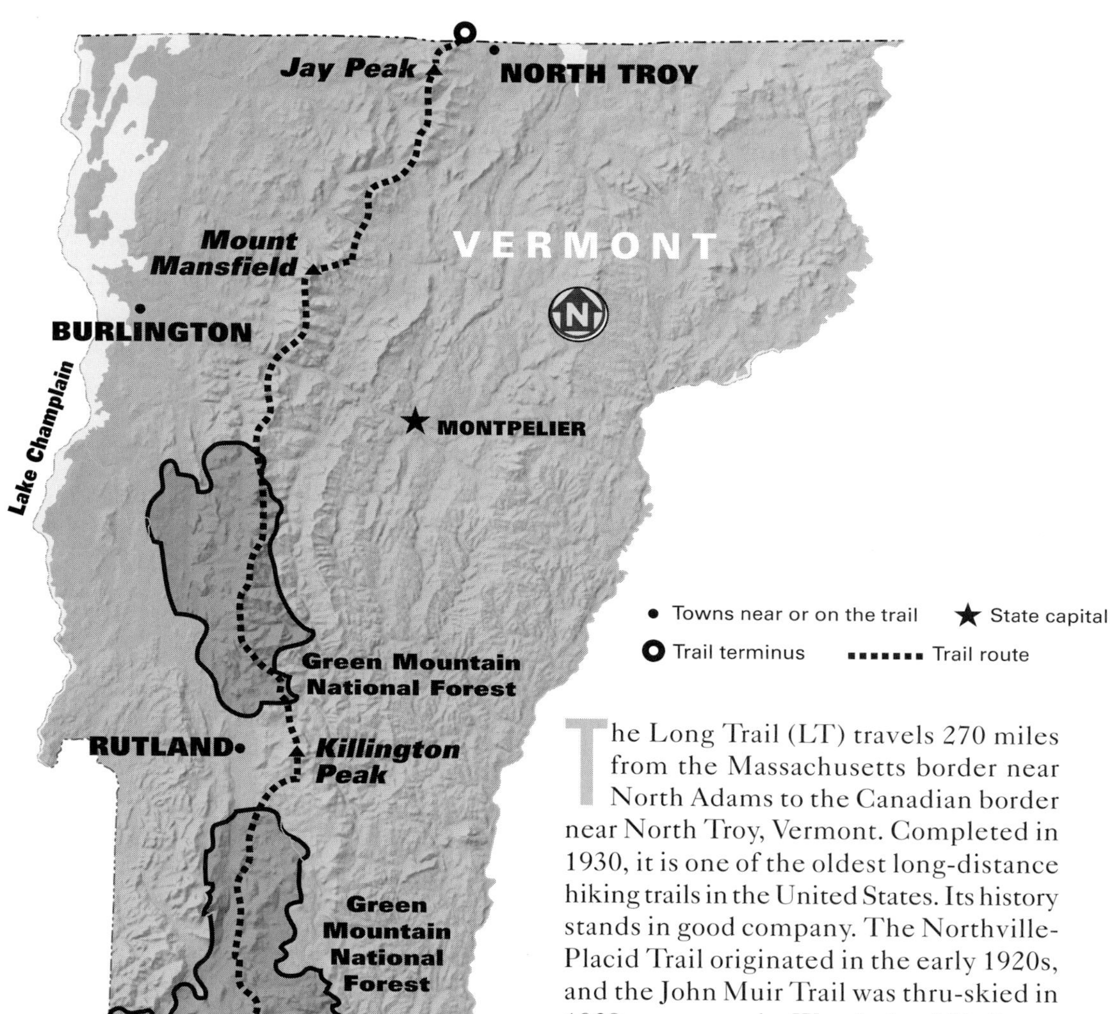

The Long Trail (LT) travels 270 miles from the Massachusetts border near North Adams to the Canadian border near North Troy, Vermont. Completed in 1930, it is one of the oldest long-distance hiking trails in the United States. Its history stands in good company. The Northville-Placid Trail originated in the early 1920s, and the John Muir Trail was thru-skied in 1928; some say the Wonderland Trail predates the Long Trail by fifteen years.

The first hundred miles of the LT are part of the Appalachian National Scenic Trail, which runs 2,170 miles from Georgia to Maine. Located mostly on ridgelines, the LT is a rugged undertaking but is one of the best ways to take in the beauty of New England. Readers of *Backpacker* magazine have voted the Long Trail second best in signage/trail marking, fourth in trail/camp/shelter conditions, and third in difficulty. Overall, the LT was deemed fifth-best long-distance trail in the United States.

The Green Mountain Club did not start recording thru-hikers until 1943, but it reports that the first thru-hikes most likely took place not long after the path was initially

VITALS

- Expect to cover 14 miles a day
- Expect a thru-hike to take about 19 days
- Hiking season: June to late October (Hiking is discouraged in April and May due to a surface that easily erodes. Trails on many Vermont high peaks are actually closed to foot traffic.)
- Water availability: Frequent
- Resupply opportunities: Sometimes
- First year thru-hiked: 1927
- Approximate yearly thru-hikers: 70 to 120
- Primary contact: Green Mountain Club

constructed. The first thru-hike was most likely completed by Arthur T. Safford in the mid-1920s though details of this intrepid hike are not available. The second thru-hiker, a gentleman named Irving Appleby, found lots of press for his hike since it was quite speedy. It was here, at the start of his thru-hike on top of Jay Peak in 1926, that long-distance speed hiking was probably first introduced to the world. He covered the entire Long Trail in only 14 days, 5 hours, averaging eighteen miles per day (in the 1920s the LT's northern terminus was Jay Peak, making the Long Trail 256 miles long). In Laura and Guy Waterman's *Forest and Crag*, Appleby is credited for having the first pompous hiking attitude, immodestly recording in a Long Trail register: "They say [Mount] Mansfield is a tough old climb but watch me hit it! . . . I feel the strength and speed of a panther! . . . If any son-of-a-gun ever does it faster I hope he chokes!" Appleby was back on the Long Trail the next year to attempt a faster traverse and was successful. This time hiking north, he went end-to-end in only 10 days, 19 hours—a very impressive feat.

Not only does speed-hiking find its early roots on the Long Trail, the earliest women's long-distance trail adventures took place here, too. In 1927, a group of three young women—Kathleen Norris, Hilda Kurth, and Katherine Robbins, who dubbed themselves the "Three Musketeers"—completed the Long Trail end to end in 27 days. The story of these self-reliant women was such a shock to the general population that San Francisco's Sunday Examiner announced the women's traverse with the headline: "They Carried No Firearms, and Had No Male Escort." How times have changed.

MOUNT MANSFIELD

The tallest peak in Vermont (and one of five that exceed 4,000 feet), Mount Mansfield (4,393 feet) may well be the largest in overall size, too. The summit of this sprawling behemoth was most likely first reached by Ira Allen and his survey party in 1772. Allen is credited with first ascents of perhaps another six Vermont peaks above 3,000 feet. A legend in Vermont history as one of the rebellious Green Mountain Boys, Ira Allen climbed Mount Mansfield to get a look at the surrounding terrain he had purchased. Upon reaching the summit with its unobstructed view, he saw thousands of acres of swamp, stunted spruce and fir, and cliffs—certainly not the suitable farmland he wanted. He returned to tell prospective purchasers that the land was all straight virgin gumwood of great value. He then sold the rugged land for a sizable profit. This is only one of Allen's shady exploits. At one time both New York and the British had a price on his head, and Allen later spent time in both French and English prisons.

The highest point of the Long Trail will probably not be the aesthetic high point of your trip. This debased mountain has a road, radio towers, television towers, buildings, chairlifts, and a ski center. Summit Stewards are employed for public education. On Mount Mansfield, do not expect to be alone.

Nearly the entire summit ridge breaks above tree line and contains very fragile, rare tundra, so be sure to step only on bare rock or trail. When viewed from the Adirondacks or the White Mountains, the summit looks like a person lying face up, so we have the names "Forehead," "Nose," "Chin," and "Adams Apple" as ridge points. Currently, the University of Vermont owns 400 acres on the summit, which in the opinion of many people are leased to communications interests illegally.

A look to the west from Mount Mansfield's summit provides a stunning view of New York's Adirondack Mountains towering high above Lake Champlain. It is truly one of the most beautiful scenes in the Northeast.

WEATHER

Perhaps Mark Twain said it best of New England weather, noting that the only thing certain is that you can be certain there's going to be plenty of it. The higher mountains of Vermont can see snow fall nearly every month, in addition to receiving strong winds. On average, for every thousand vertical feet gained in New England, the temperature will drop 3.5°, but I have seen as much as a 20° drop from a peak's base to its summit. With that said, LT hikers should be prepared for temperatures ranging from the sticky eighties in gaps to the upper thirties in the high terrain at night.

TERRAIN

The Long Trail guidebook handily divides the trail into twelve sections, and in each section the climbing varies. One section requires little more than 1,000 vertical feet to be climbed, whereas at least one section in the north demands more than 6,000 vertical feet of ascent. I went through every topographic map in my 1992 *Guide Book to the Long Trail* to calculate how many vertical feet the Long Trail ascended end-to-end. The maps are drawn with two-hundred-foot contour intervals, so I knew my figure

AVERAGE HIGHS AND LOWS IN DEGREES FAHRENHEIT

	JAN	MAR	MAY	JUL	SEPT	NOV
NORTH ADAMS, MA (710 FT.)	10–30	20–40	40–65	55–80	45–70	30–45
NORTH TROY, VT (610 FT.)	5–25	20–40	40–65	60–80	45–70	25–45

TERRAIN HIGHLIGHTS

- American beech, yellow birch, paper birch, and sugar maple forests
- Thick hemlock, spruce, and fir forests
- Clear, cold streams
- Hemlock-lined streams
- Rare, above tree-line tundra
- Open rock hiking
- Steep climbs

wouldn't be dead on but it would provide me with a rough estimate. Well, I couldn't believe how much climbing there was on this 270-mile path: 46,200 vertical feet, end to end. Wow. But a year later I found a more accurate source. Most likely this source used United States Geological Survey topographic maps, which were drawn with twenty-foot contours. Here, the figure earned a double-wow. They measured nearly 67,500 vertical feet, 20,000 feet more than my original figure! Mile per mile, the Long Trail is not only the toughest path in this guide, it's the toughest in the United States.

If you're not used to climbing and descending mountains all day, expect to start out at a very conservative pace. Of the 100+ peaks in Vermont that exceed 3,000 feet, the LT climbs thirty of these and comes within a mile of another eighteen 3,000-footers. And it crosses the five peaks in Vermont that exceed 4,000 feet. The Long Trail is no joke.

The tread is mostly rocky-rooty-steep-and-muddy singletrack that winds through hardwood forest below 2,500 feet, ascends into the classic spruce and fir forests of the upper elevations, and breaks through tree line on the summits of Killington Peak (4,235 feet), Mount Abraham (4,006 feet), Camel's Hump (4,083 feet), and Mount Mansfield (4,393 feet).

WATER

The summits of Vermont receive more than a hundred inches of rain and snow each year. In years of heavy snowfall, the taller peaks can hold snowfields until early June, which makes the Green Mountain State a very wet place. In only two days of walk-

THE FIVE TOUGHEST TRAILS IN THIS GUIDE

1. **Long Trail.** At 270 miles with 67,000 vertical feet of total climbing, the LT averages 248 vertical feet per mile.
2. **John Muir Trail.** At 210 miles with 47,000 vertical feet of total climbing (if you're hiking the more popular north-to-south direction), the JMT averages 224 vertical feet per mile.
3. **Wonderland Trail.** At 95 miles with 20,000 vertical feet of total climbing, the WT averages 211 vertical feet per mile.
4. **Metacomet-Monadnock Trail.** At 120 miles with 23,000 vertical feet of total climbing, the MMT averages 192 vertical feet per mile.
5. **Colorado Trail.** At 470 miles with 76,000 vertical feet of total climbing the CT averages 162 vertical feet per mile. ■

ing, you'll pass dozens of mountain- or spring-fed streams in addition to many lakes and ponds, so finding water should not be a problem. Of course you will want to treat all water, especially where a human presence is found. Some of the more remote parts of the Long Trail have springs that are ice cold and taste heavenly.

With all its tall peaks and steep valleys, it's no wonder the Long Trail is the toughest trail in the United States. Looking back to Mount Mansfield from Jay Peak really drives the point home. (ED ROLFE)

WILDNESS

Even though the LT is one of the best-known trails in this guidebook, all you have to do is search around a little and solitude can be found. The first hundred miles, starting from the southern end, have a high chance of being crowded with weekend explorers, summer camp groups, and Appalachian Trail thru-hikers, but once you get onto the Long Trail proper, the numbers drop off. Peaks above 4,000 feet see hikers every day of the week, as do any ponds in the south. As you travel farther and farther north, you may run into fewer people than moose. On my last three days traveling the LT on a south-to-north thru-hike, I encountered only ten other hikers.

As with many of the trails in this guide, you'll be hiking a mix of private, state, and federal land. Resupply points can be reached at least every five days, depending on how far you want to walk to civilization. For a quiet, lonely lunch spot every day, carefully bushwhack a hundred feet or so off the trail and you will not be interrupted or even seen. Shelters, mostly in the form of Adirondack lean-tos, can be found about every four to ten miles, with an outhouse and water at each site. Some lean-tos have mice. Some lean-tos have *commando mice.*

Approximately 10 campsites/shelters are managed by caretakers from June to September. Modest fees apply at these locations.

WILDLIFE

The vast trackless woods of Vermont, especially the northern sections of the Long Trail, are home to large mammals that you would have a hard time finding in more

CRITTERS

- Black bears
- Coyotes
- Foxes
- Moose
- Peregrine falcons
- Porcupines
- Red squirrels
- Ruffed grouse and spruce grouse
- Snowshoe hares

civilized parts of the East. Moose are a highlight. Weighing up to 1,500 pounds, this "horse designed by a committee" is most commonly seen at the 3,000-foot level. Moose may look ungainly and goofy, but they are actually graceful and can run upward of thirty miles per hour.

When hiking the LT, you don't have to worry about being harmed by an animal. The third-hand story that you heard about a moose charging people and a black bear attacking hikers is imaginative and makes for a good tale, but chances of that actually happening are extremely low. Just steer clear of any animals with youngsters, and be wary of moose in rutting season. You'll be fine.

POINTS OF INTEREST

IT'S ALL DOWNHILL FROM HERE

Killington Peak's 4,235-foot summit is Vermont's second highest, it's home to the world-famous Killington Resort, and it's the southernmost above-tree-line terrain east of the Mississippi; take time to enjoy it. Do not step on soil or plants. Step only on trail or bare rock.

SMUGGLERS' NOTCH

If hiking north on the LT, you'll drop 2,600 vertical feet off the highest peak in Vermont into Smugglers Notch, where you'll follow a steep winding road for less than one mile. This rugged defile (which contains boulders as big as your house) obtained its name from illegal smuggling activities dating back to the early 1800s when President Jefferson forbid trade with Canada. Later, during the Prohibition era in the 1920s, the notch was used again; this time to smuggle liquor from our neighbor to the north.

"JAY"

Jay Peak (3,861 feet) provides excellent views of Canada, New York, and New Hampshire. The summit was much more dramatic prior to being blasted with dynamite to make room for a ski lift. Jay Peak is legendary for its annual snowfall, thanks to the "Jay effect."

SCHLIMMER'S SIDE TRAIL

CHAMP

If you head off the trail for a respite in Burlington or any other lakeside town, be sure to keep your eyes peeled for Champ, Lake Champlain's version of the Loch Ness Monster. The first recorded sighting of Champ was in 1609 by explorer Samuel de Champlain, for whom the lake is named. He described a creature that was a "twenty-foot serpent thick as a barrel with a head like a horse." Since then, there have been more than 200 sightings in this lake, which is a 100 miles long and up to 400 feet deep. Each summer, Champ Day is celebrated on the other side of the lake in Port Henry, New York, where you can admire a life-size replica of the reclusive beast. Wow! ■

DON'T LEAVE HOME WITHOUT IT

ASPIRIN!

Mile for mile, Vermont's Long Trail is the most rugged long-distance trail in the United States. This brutal trek will reduce even the hardiest hikers into sniveling wimps. Aspirin will help with the aches and pains, and may reduce the swelling enough that your boots can once again accommodate your turgid feet.

ALL OVER HELL'S HALF ACRE

Located near the northern terminus of the LT, Devil's Gulch winds among boulders and below cliffs. At the bottom, one hiker found an unfortunate moose that apparently fell to its death.

In Their Own Words . . .

The Vermont Long Trail has everything that you'd want to see in New England: Great views, smooth slabs of bedrock, glacial erratics, above tree line terrain, ponds, streams, trees—everything. That's why the Long Trail is legendary.

Down south I got great views from a fire tower on Glastenbury Mountain or the southern Green's random clearings. Then I came across some beautiful lakes in the south-central part of the state. I continued north and started getting into the taller peaks. Killington is the southernmost 4,000-footer in the state, and was just a warm up for things to come. In the southern and central sections, the trail was what I would call crowded, with all the Appalachian Trail thru hikers heading toward Mount Katahdin, but I kept on heading due north while they all headed east into New Hampshire, and there were less people north of the Killington area. The last ninety miles to the border were my favorite. There it's time to relax and enjoy the peace and quiet finally. That was the best part of the trip—just to sit on the side of the trail and not see anyone for a couple of hours. The evergreen forests close in, the weather becomes more unpredictable, and only those seeking a legitimate wilderness experience will head into the woods north of Jay Peak.

But, the Long Trail is definitely not for everyone. It's freakin' hard! That trail's got a mild vendetta against everyone, but it's totally worth it if you're looking for physical challenges, wildness, amazing views, and the opportunity to meet other hikers. You'll be so happy if you stick it out, and then, if heading north, you come around this little turn way up north, and then boom: There it is. The end. Canada. Then you can sit down right on the border swath, one leg in the United States and one in our neighbor to the north and say to yourself, "Man, I just walked the entire length of Vermont."

—Bailey Morgan, 1998 Long Trail thru-hiker, climber of all Vermont peaks over 3,000 feet

mason-dixon trail

190 MILES | DELAWARE MARYLAND PENNSYLVANIA

TO GO . . .

- link with the Appalachian Trail and Horseshoe Trail to form a 250-mile loop hike
- state highpoint as a side trip
- excellent map set available, the best out of all twenty-five trails
- you may become the second person to thru-hike the Mason-Dixon Trail

A lonesome stretch of the Mason-Dixon Trail near Muddy Creek, Pennsylvania. (JAMES E. TRAUTMAN)

OR NOT TO GO?

- 90 miles of road walking
- not a wilderness setting overall
- unfriendly dogs and landowners on some sections
- backcountry campsites a rarity

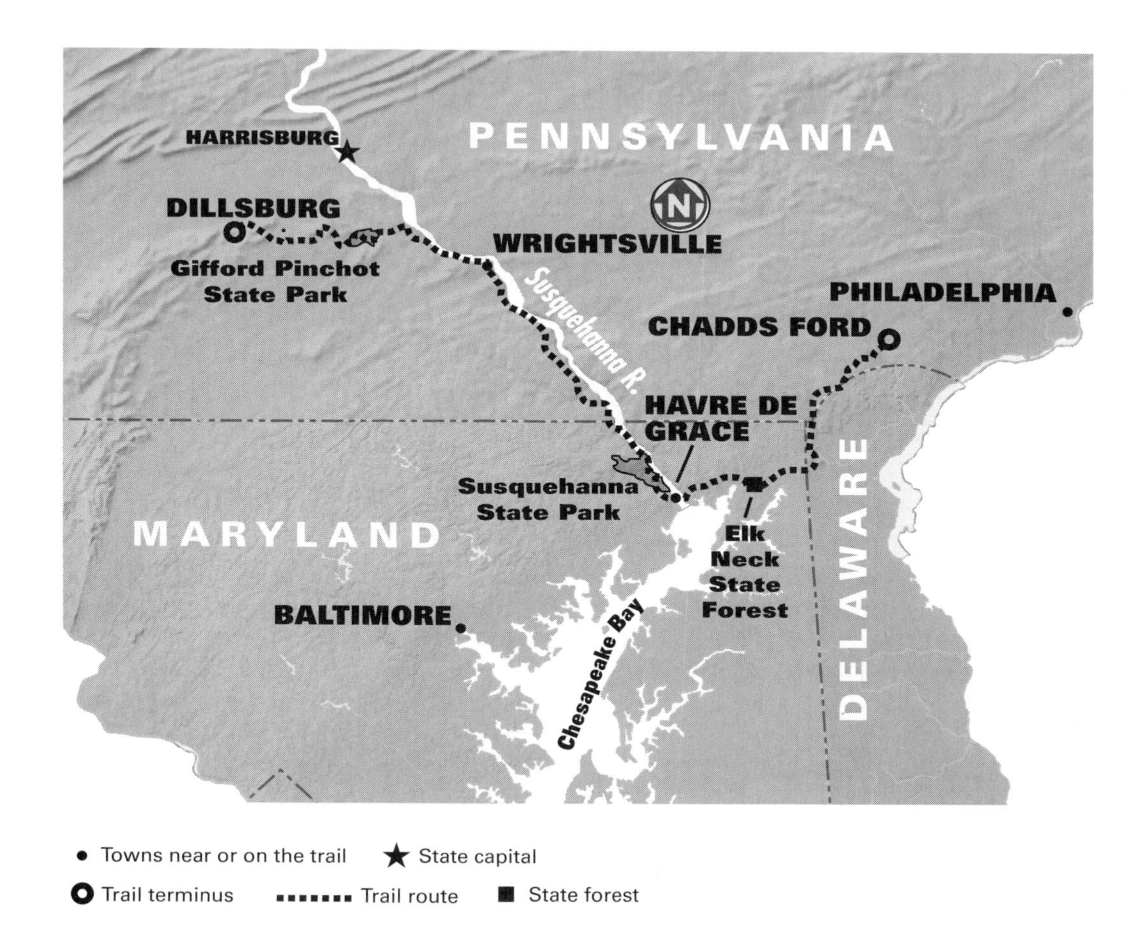

The Mason-Dixon Trail (MDT) was almost not described in this guide; 90 of its 190 miles are currently road walks. But I remembered that variety is the spice of hiking, so here it is, dutifully presented. Departing the Appalachian Trail at Whiskey Springs near Dillsburg, Pennsylvania, the MDT travels southeast through Pennsylvania alongside the Susquehanna River. It then crosses into Maryland, moves up into Delaware, and ends back in Pennsylvania near the town of Chadds Ford. You can make a loop hike totaling more than 250 miles by taking the Horseshoe Trail northwest to the Appalachian Trail. Then follow the Appalachian Trail southwest back to where you started in Whiskey Springs.

The trail is not a backcountry route in most parts, but it is also not completely civilized. Generally, the road walks you encounter are on county roads that don't see much traffic. While in the woods, expect to cover steep terrain among rocky slopes and drainages. You'll find some nice views as well, including those from the northern shore of Chesapeake Bay.

VITALS

- Expect to cover 17 miles a day
- Expect a thru-hike to take 11 days
- Hiking season: April to November
- Water availability: Frequent
- Resupply opportunities: Frequent
- First year thru-hiked: 1993
- Approximate yearly thru-hikers: 1
- Primary contact: Mason-Dixon Trail System, Inc.

A handful of end-to-end completers has tackled the Mason-Dixon Trail in sections but the MDT has only one recorded thru-hiker; Rick Merk, who has thru-hiked it twice.

WEATHER

Planning a trip into Maryland and southeastern Pennsylvania gives you two opposing climates to deal with. You're far enough north to get into significant snow during the winter, and you're far enough south to get an early dose of warm weather in spring and fall. The Mason-Dixon Trail can be hiked in fair weather during the winter, but icy sections of trail can be dangerous. The trail is fairly close to the East Coast proper, so nor'easters can come into town and soak you. Summer days can be very hot even though you're not that far south.

TERRAIN

The MDT is not for hikers who need to be in the woods and away from roads. You'll find yourself in the woods on nearly half of the trail's 190 miles. There are a handful of sections that are in the planning stages of being rerouted into more pristine areas. But with all the private land around, relocating the route to better settings has been a challenge for the trail's advocates, Mason-Dixon Trail System, Inc. (MDTS). Roads consist mostly of paved and dirt country routes, with some short sections that can be busy. Use caution in areas of high traffic, bridges, and tunnels.

The terrain off road is often singletrack hiking trail that slams up and down drainages and follows ridges. The section between Fishing Creek and Otter Creek is considered "difficult with multiple very steep rocky ups and downs," according to MDTS. In fact, this section of the Mason-Dixon Trail reminded Jim Hooper, MDTS president and Appalachian Trail thru-hiker, of the rugged AT

AVERAGE HIGHS AND LOWS IN DEGREES FAHRENHEIT

	JAN	MAR	MAY	JUL	SEPT	NOV
DILLSBURG, PA (600 FT.)	25–40	35–50	50–75	65–85	60–75	35–55
CHADDS FORD, PA (160 FT.)	20–40	30–50	50–75	65–85	55–80	35–55

The tranquil waters of Conewago Lake on the south side of Gifford Pinchot State Park. (JAMES E. TRAUTMAN)

sections of western Maine. Woods paths, dry streambeds, pipelines, and rail beds (rails-to-trails and "real" railroad beds) are used, too. Of the ten maps that describe the trail, the one for the far-western section contains the highpoint of the MDT, which is approximately 1,100 feet. Climbs rarely exceed 300 vertical feet.

WATER

Overall, finding water should not be a problem on the MDT, but as with any other trail, especially outside of New England, there can be periods of drought when finding water will be difficult. However, because nearly half the MDT is near some type of civilization, you should be able to find potable water every day by kindly asking the locals for some. The ten Mason-Dixon Trail, Inc., maps show about fifty-five major drainages, five bodies of water, private residences, and small towns that have water for free or for sale. Spring is the best time for finding water; the end of summer is iffy if you try to use only natural water sources. This is especially true when hiking on ridges or far away from any potable sources. Eighty-five miles of trail are within sight of the massive Susquehanna. Be sure to treat all water found in the woods, including springs. Only tap water is okay as is.

WILDNESS

You should know by now that heading out for a thru-hike of the Mason-Dixon Trail is not the best option for finding a wild setting far from human impacts. This trail is included because it could be an option for someone who wants to do a hike and bike trip. It's a trail that could be used for new hikers who just want to see if they like walking all day, let alone climbing mountains on longer, more remote trails. Someone with a recent injury could use this trail as a recovery trip or a warm-up for a much longer, tougher trail.

Currently, there are four campgrounds on the trail. They can be found in

TERRAIN HIGHLIGHTS

- Oak forests
- Steep, rocky slopes
- Human-made features
- Susquehanna and Delaware rivers
- Chesapeake Bay
- Short ridgelines
- Road walks
- Spring wildflowers

DON'T LEAVE HOME WITHOUT IT

NOSE PLUG OR VICKS VAPORUB

With nearly half of the Mason-Dixon Trail's route on pavement, you can expect to encounter some really ripe road kills, especially in summer. Strap on the plug or dab a little ointment under your nostrils for a more tolerable stroll.

Gifford Pinchot State Park (south of Dillsburg, Pennsylvania), PP&L Otter Creek Campground (in Airville, Pennsylvania [the MDT passes right through the campground]), and Susquehanna State Park and Elk Neck State Forest (both in Maryland). Outside of these, finding places to camp can be a real challenge because of the amount of private land the trail goes through. On road walks there are usually private lands on each side of the trail. This was a problem I encountered on the western portions of the Florida Trail. In cases such as these, I simply wait until dusk and stealthily head off to camp in vegetated areas for the night. I make sure I'm on the road again around dawn, and I leave *absolutely no trace* of my visit. But if hikers took on this practice sloppily, they could jeopardize the relationship between landowners and trail clubs. Remember, you're sometimes seen as "one of them damn hikers," so be sure to represent the rest of us well.

WILDLIFE

Along the MDT you should expect to come across quite a few critters once you're off the roads. On the roads you'll find critters as well, but most likely you'll need a spatula to pick them up. Pennsylvania is where you'll see the most wildlife.

POINTS OF INTEREST

HISTORICAL LANDMARKS

Among the neat things you'll see on your journey are an iron bridge from 1888, Revolutionary War–era roadbeds, houses built as early as 1732, hand-constructed stone arch bridges, and pre–Revolutionary War era smelting furnaces.

THE SUSQUEHANNA

The Mason-Dixon Trail follows eighty-five miles of the Susquehanna River's 400-mile journey from New York to the Maryland coast. The trail rises more than 300 vertical feet above the river in some parts.

CRITTERS

- Bald eagles
- Black bears
- Coyotes
- Rattlesnakes
- Red foxes
- Turkeys

MASON AND DIXON

The Mason-Dixon Line, and thus the Mason-Dixon Trail, is named for two English astronomers and surveyors, Charles Mason and Jeremiah Dixon. Starting in the mid 1760s, these two gentlemen ran a boundary line separating Maryland and Pennsylvania to settle a dispute between Pennsylvanians and Marylanders concerning exactly where their colony demarcation line was supposed to be.

In 1760, an agreement was made between the disputing Penn and Calvert families to hire Mason and Dixon to straighten things out. Prior to 1767, the surveyors completed marking nearly 250 miles of the line, starting from Delaware and working their way west. Mason and Dixon reached the western limit of Maryland in 1773. By 1779, the line was taken all the way to a point that marked the border of Virginia and Pennsylvania (today this point is the Pennsylvania–West Virginia border). This survey line was a general divider between pro- and antislavery states during the Civil War era; today this line divides the North and South culturally. ■

COOL IT NOW

On those hot MDT summer days you may want to cool your toes in Otter Creek, one of eleven streams that cross this trail to empty into the Susquehanna. Otter Creek offers pools deep enough to swim in. Located on the Mason-Dixon Trail System's map number five, this creek is far from the confines of civilization and remains cool even during the hottest weather.

IT'S NOT SO MUDDY

Also located on map number five of the Mason-Dixon Trail is Muddy Creek, which local kayakers like to paddle. There's one cool spot in particular where the water shoots down through rocks lining the creek; you can stand under this natural water spout for an impromptu shower (without soap, of course). This creek is where the first power dam in the area was built, providing electric power to the tiny town of Delta even before Baltimore felt the glow of lights.

SCHLIMMER'S SIDE TRAIL

HIGHPOINTERS TAKE NOTE

Located less than fifteen miles from the eastern terminus of the MDT is the highpoint of Delaware, Ebright Azimuth. At a rowdy 442 feet above sea level, this is an excellent climbing option if you feel you have the stamina to attempt an "E.A." summit bid from your advanced base camp up into the Death Zone. ■

metacomet-monadnock trail

120 MILES | MASSACHUSETTS NEW HAMPSHIRE

TO GO . . .

- beautiful ridgeline hiking
- can extend trip by 51 miles to the north or 40 miles to the south
- dramatic northern terminus on Monadnock Mountain
- thorough guidebook

OR NOT TO GO?

- not a wilderness setting overall
- bug season can be bad
- more than 23,000 vertical feet to ascend end to end
- crossing the Westfield and Connecticut rivers can be difficult

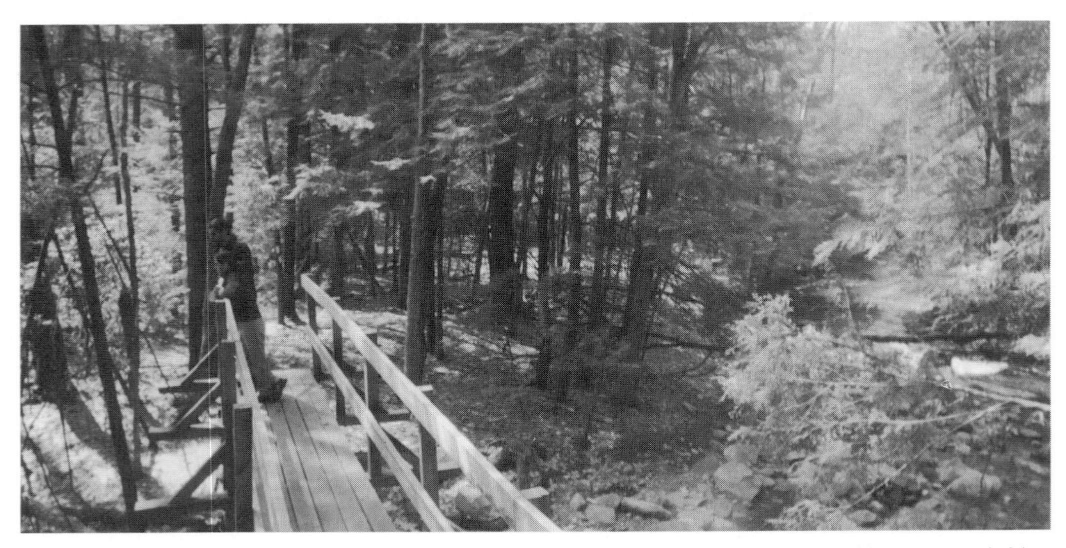

Like all other trails, the Metacomet-Monadnock Trail needs constant maintenance. Here, a new bridge has been installed over Roaring Brook, just east of Leverett, Massachusetts. (E. SCHLIMMER)

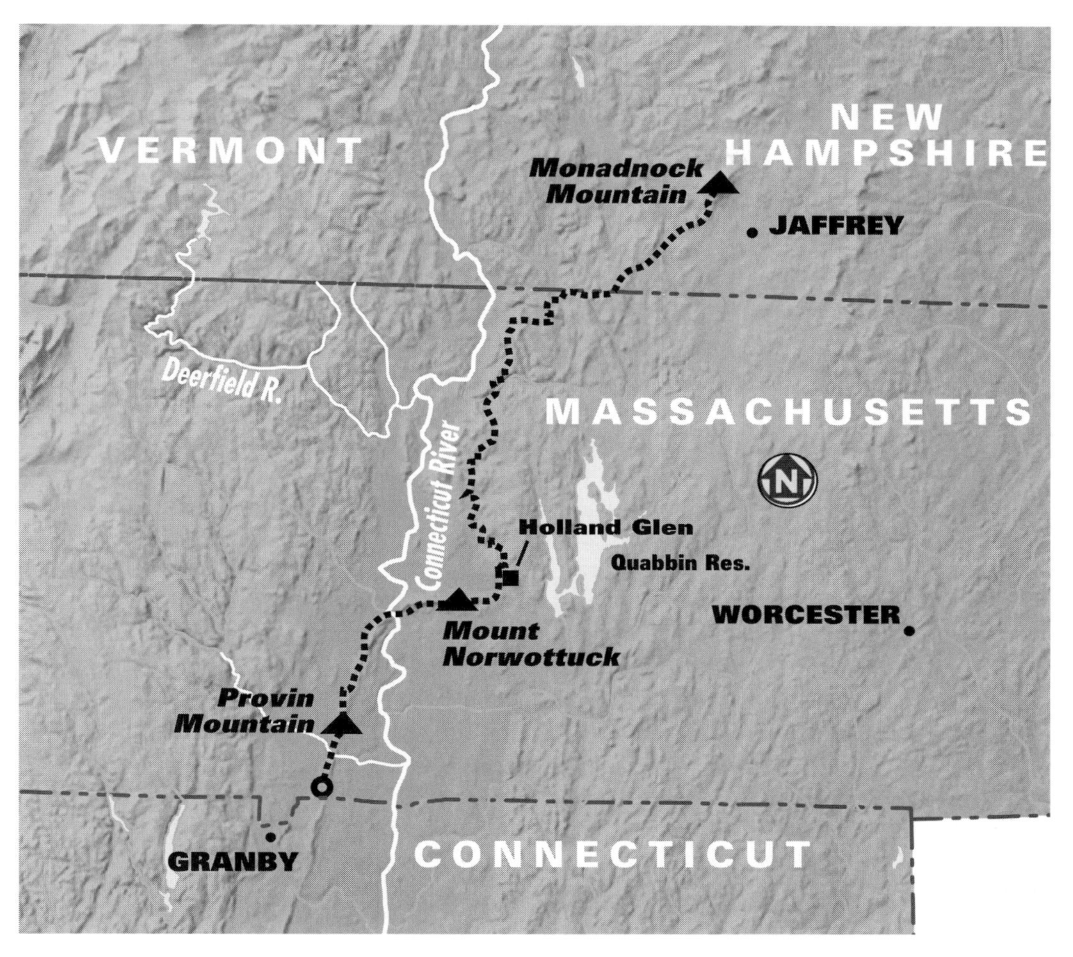

• Towns near or on the trail

○ Trail terminus ▪▪▪▪▪▪▪ Trail route

The Metacomet-Monadnock Trail (MMT) is a frontcountry trail that snakes its way from near the town of Granby, Connecticut, on the Massachusetts border, north through Massachusetts to end on the summit of Monadnock Mountain, in southern New Hampshire. If the 120 miles of walking on the MMT aren't enough, you can also hike the Monadnock-Sunapee Greenway (MSG), which continues north beyond the northern terminus of the MMT. Traveling an additional fifty-one miles, this path ends on Sunapee Mountain (2,726 feet), in central New Hampshire. Below the southern terminus of the Metacomet-Monadnock Trail is a 40-mile trail extension called the Metacomet Trail (MT). Therefore, combining the Metacomet Trail, the Metacomet-Monadnock Trail, and the Monadnock-Sunapee Greenway will enable you to hike a continuous 200+ miles.

VITALS

- Expect to cover 14 miles a day
- Expect a thru-hike to take about 9 days
- Hiking season: May to November
- Water availability: Sometimes
- Resupply opportunities: Sometimes
- First year thru-hiked: Unknown
- Approximate yearly thru-hikers: Fewer than 30
- Primary contact: Appalachian Mountain Club, Berkshire Chapter; Metacomet-Monadnock Trail Conference

Taking this idea a step further, you could hike the MT-MMT-MSG, continue north from MSG's northern terminus, and walk the Appalachian Trail and county roads to the southern terminus of the Cohos Trail. The Cohos Trail travels north for 160 miles to the Canadian border. Thus, any enterprising hiker could accomplish a thru-route of New Hampshire and Massachusetts. The best part of this route may be the name of it: the Metacomet-Metacomet-Monadnock-Monadnock-Sunapee-Appalachian-Cohos route. Now that's a mouthful.

In terms of the fewest days required to hike end to end, the Metacomet-Monadnock Trail ties the Baker Trail and the Northville-Placid Trail for third place. Averaging sixteen miles a day, you can hike the MMT in fewer than ten days. The Appalachian Mountain Club's Berkshire Chapter and the newly formed Metacomet-Monadnock Trail Conference maintain the MMT, as do several state and federal trail and conservation organizations. Sections of the trail have been designated as a National Recreational Trail. The MMT travels close to civilization for its entire route, but you won't find yourself in the breakdown lane of the Mass 'Pike. This mostly ridgeline trail also takes you along remote dirt roads and past beaver ponds and countless tributaries of the Connecticut River.

MONADNOCK MOUNTAIN

This peak's name has been bungled by many, being called Mount Monadnock, Grand Monadnock Mountain, The Great Monadnock, and The Grand Monadnock. But Monadnock Mountain is the name on the most current United States Geological Survey map, so we'll stick with that. Measuring 3,165 feet, this peak is the highpoint of the Metacomet-Monadnock Trail and is its northern terminus. The peak rises dramatically out of the surrounding New Hampshire terrain. In fact, *monadnock*, a Native American word, means "mountain that stands alone" or "isolated mountain."

This label has survived and is used by geologists and cartographers on another peak that rises out of a surrounding plain: Mount Monadnock, located in the Northeast Kingdom of Vermont. This Vermont peak may be the only other mountain named Monadnock in the United States. Currently, Monadnock Mountain of New Hampshire contains forty miles of hiking trails and five major routes to the summit,

AVERAGE HIGHS AND LOWS IN DEGREES FAHRENHEIT	JAN	MAR	MAY	JUL	SEPT	NOV
GRANVILLE, MA (690 FT.)	10–30	20–45	40–70	55–80	45–70	30–50
JAFFREY, NH (1,010 FT.)	10–30	20–40	40–70	55–80	50–70	30–45

each climbing nearly 2,000 vertical feet from the base. The top of Monadnock Mountain has a 360° view into all six New England states.

This wonderful, unobstructed view is one of the key reasons why Monadnock Mountain is the second-most climbed peak on the planet, with more than 100,000 people reaching the top each year. A campground with showers, flush toilets, potable water, and at least twenty tent sites is located at the mountain's base. Monadnock Mountain's first recorded ascent was in 1725 when a party led by Captain Samuel Willard reached the summit while on a mission to find enemy Native Americans.

WEATHER

This southern part of New England has a long hiking season because the elevations aren't usually very high. Expect to get cracking on the MMT earlier than on the Long Trail of Vermont or the Cohos Trail in northern New Hampshire. However, with New England hiking comes New England weather, where a freak snowstorm can roll in as late as April. In the fall, hurricanes can blow in from the south or arctic air can arrive from the north. Nor'easters can also be a threat, because the trail is located fairly close to the temperamental Atlantic Ocean.

Summers are pretty humid and the bugs can be annoying. On a recent March thru-hike, my partner and I were ravaged by mosquitoes on most days, especially in the north. Long pants, bug dope, and a bug net saved my sanity. Thankfully, the stiff breezes we encountered on countless ridgelines helped keep the biting bugs at bay.

TERRAIN

What the Metacomet-Monadnock Trail may lack in extreme remoteness it compensates with its gorgeous, never-ending ridgeline hiking. Dramatic vistas can be found on these ridgelines, along with a break from the mosquitoes and blackflies during the bug season. And come fall foliage time, those vistas glow.

TERRAIN HIGHLIGHTS

- Cliffs and rock outcrops
- Bogs
- Rocky tributaries
- Fall foliage
- Stone walls
- Steep climbs and descents
- Expansive hemlock forests

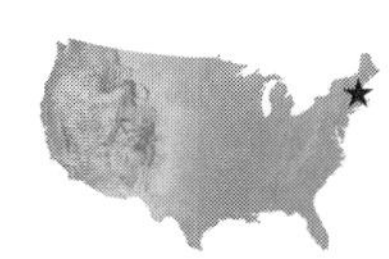

Topographically, the lowest points on the MMT are at the Connecticut and Westfield rivers, both located in the south and each only a hundred feet above sea level. The highpoint of the MMT is the northern terminus at Monadnock Mountain, the only area that reaches 3,000 feet. The climbing required to get from one end of the Metacomet-Monadnock Trail to the other is substantial. I measured 23,300 vertical feet of ascent from the southern terminus to the summit of Monadnock Mountain. This amount of climbing per mile is significant, especially compared to trails that have reputations as being the most rugged in the United States. Of the other trails covered in this guide, the MMT is ranked number three for the most vertical feet climbed per average mile. At 192 vertical feet per mile, this is no walk in the park. (See page 112 for a listing of the five toughest trails.) On this end-to-end trek, you'll climb to an elevation exceeding a thousand feet more than twenty times, and you'll surpass the 1,500-foot point approximately five times. You'll follow game paths, all-terrain-vehicle paths, hiking trails, state park roads, county roads, rail beds, and grown-over, abandoned woods roads from the logging era.

WATER

Along the MMT you'll encounter countless streams, bogs, and swamps, plus the trail has seven major bodies of water near it, including reservoirs and rivers. The most hiker-friendly, reassuring aspect of getting water on the MMT is that you'll pass

METACOMET

Known as King Philip of Pokanoket to the English, and Metacomet to the Native Americans, this Wampanog leader originally befriended Europeans, but as with most other aspects of English-Indian relationships, things turned sour. Due to missionary expeditions, immigrants obtaining land illegally, and the killing of three Wampanog members, King Philip's War started in 1675 and lasted more than two years. Battles took place near sections of today's MMT route. In *Lies My Teacher Told Me*, author James Loewen reminds us of the magnitude of this forgotten part of American history.

> *This was no minor war. "Of some 90 Puritan towns, 52 had been attacked and 12 destroyed. . . . At the end of the war several thousand English and perhaps twice as many Indians lay dead." King Philip's War cost more American lives in combat, Anglo and Native, in absolute terms than the French and Indian War, the Revolution, the War of 1812, the Mexican War, or the Spanish-American War. In proportion to population, casualties were greater than in any other American war.*

Eventually, Metacomet was tracked down and killed by Indians who sided with the English, under the command of Captain Benjamin Church, and Metacomet's head was put on public display in Plymouth, Massachusetts, for the next twenty years. Metacomet's son and wife were captured during this period and were ultimately sent to the West Indies as slaves. ■

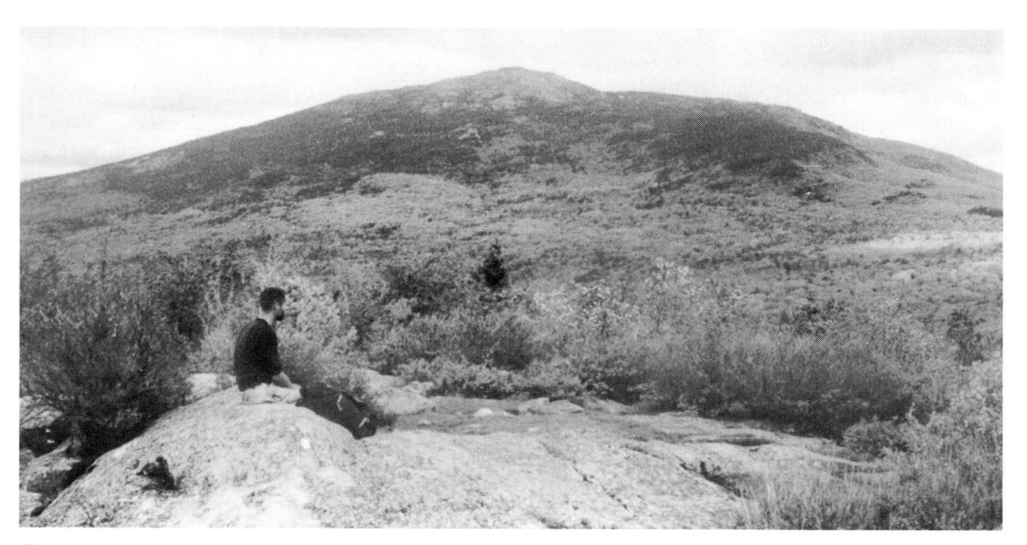

The rocky summit of Gap Mountain provides an inspiring view of Monadnock Mountain. (E. SCHLIMMER)

many homes where the polite hiker can probably get some potable water. Each day you'll pass at least half a dozen houses. Many homeowners surely know that the Metacomet-Monadnock Trail runs near or even through their property. These people may also be willing to provide updates on trail conditions and recommended campsites.

Up on the ridges there is no water at all, so you have to stock up before heading up. Some of the longer ridges extend more than seven miles, so be sure to pay attention to the terrain. The *Metacomet-Monadnock Trail Guide* accurately portrays the terrain and is a good source for taking note of ridgelines. The tactic I used on my MMT thru-hike was this: before getting to a ridgeline, I looked at my map and found the last water source prior to the climb up the ridge. At that water source I drank at least a quart and filled up two one-quart bottles. I drank these two bottles while on the ridge, descended the ridge on the far side, and repeated the process prior to the next ascent. For me, it worked great.

WILDNESS

The Metacomet-Monadnock Trail is not incredibly wild. If you're looking for true wilderness, this trail may not be satisfying enough. Why not? You are guaranteed to cross at least a couple of roads or all-terrain-vehicle (ATV) paths during each day of hiking. In general, the roads you cross are dirt or gravel and not busy, but at times you'll be hiking near or on active ATV paths; the first 30 miles from the southern terminus is an ATV path. In fact, everything south of the Holyoke Range is bikeable. But, after the first 30 miles of the MMT, the ATV paths tended to dissipate and the terrain became much more rugged. Other wilderness spoilers on this hike include

DON'T LEAVE HOME WITHOUT IT

REASONABLE EXPECTATIONS

If you picture yourself sitting in peaceful silence atop the summit of Monadnock Mountain quietly reflecting on the triumphant completion of your 120-mile journey, think again. Monadnock, the second-most climbed peak in the world (and northern terminus of the MMT), offers great scenery, but not solitude. Adjust your expectations accordingly.

power lines, radio and television towers on summits, buried gas lines, homes, and several gravel pits.

To add to the wildness, though, shortly after the start of a northward hike, you have to ford the sometimes-mighty Westfield River, which flows southeast out of the Berkshires. In mid-May 2004, long after the mountain snows had melted even from the north sides of the highest summits of Massachusetts, the Westfield River was still impossible to ford. After finding the crossing spot, my friend Pete and I gave the Westfield River the old college try. We had light packs on, so our concern was not the weight on our backs but the swiftness and depth of the river. We took off our socks, pulled the insoles from our sneakers, and packed them away to keep them dry. Then we put our sneakers back on our bare feet. Next, I gave Pete one of my hiking poles to steady himself. We went in ankle deep, then calf deep, then knee deep, then, finally, thigh deep for Pete and waist deep for me (I'm about seven inches shorter). We were surely at the limit of a safe crossing. We got nearly halfway across, but all we saw in front of us was a deep black hole of a river, probably gut deep for Pete and chest deep for me. We decided to turn back. To get to the other side of the Westfield River, we backtracked on the MMT for a mile, then completed a three-mile road and train-track walk to our destination. Generally, the Westfield River can be successfully forded only from June to September, and only if it hasn't rained recently.

You also have to find yourself a boat to get across the Connecticut River, which comes about midway through the trip. To me, and probably to Pete, too, this was the low point of our Metacomet-Monadnock Trail trek. After arriving at the state boat ramp area, we had to hitchhike across the river. I've hitchhiked many times on roads, but hitching on a river was a new experience for me. Pete and I ended up bumming around the boat ramp for more than two hours looking for a ride. Because I'm a little more outgoing (and I have a degree in public speaking), I was our PR man. I explained to countless boaters our dire predicament, but they showed no sympathy. Excuses ranged from "I have a dog in the boat" to "I don't have time" to "I don't have a life jacket" to "The motor's running funny." Personally, I would rather have heard that they didn't want to give Pete and me a ride because we smelled bad. I hate excuses. Anyway, boat number sixteen finally gave us a ride across the Connecticut River and dropped us off on the sandy beach on the north side of the waterway. It was a two-minute ride.

Lands that the MMT travels over are state reservations, state parks, and private or town-controlled areas. In fact, the majority of the trail passes through private land, so be on your best behavior. Only three lean-tos are located on the MMT, one of them built within the last two years. This new structure is quite palatial and well built. I encountered no established primitive backcountry campsites in 2004, only lean-tos. Mostly, you'll have to resort to pristine camping. Be sure to follow LNT principles.

Nine town centers are located on or within a few miles of the MMT. A key resupply point is conveniently located at mile 65 (if hiking south to north). The Leverett Village Co-op should be able to feed the hungriest of hikers and offers free potable water.

Franklin County, in the north, regarded by many as the most remote part of the Metacomet-Monadnock Trail, has some sections more than ten miles long where you won't cross a paved road; the longest of these roadless sections is nearly twenty miles. Overall, the crowd factor on the MMT is very low. The only places you are guaranteed to see people are the Holyoke Range and Monadnock Mountain. The Holyoke Range, which rises east of the Connecticut River on a southern section of the MMT, is a gorgeous ridgeline composed of countless wooded minor peaks. Mountain bikers and off-road-vehicle enthusiasts use the trails in this area. Also, Mount Holyoke, which rises to almost a thousand feet, has an auto road that wraps around its northern half. This road reaches the Mount Holyoke Summit House (Prospect House), a restored mountaintop facility that is open to the public from May to October. Water and restrooms are downstairs.

To reiterate, there's just about no way in hell you'll find solitude on Monadnock Mountain unless you climb it in winter . . . when it's raining and snowing . . . on a weekday . . . at night. On our recent trip, Pete and I saw twenty hikers on the first 119 miles of trail. We saw seventy-six hikers on the last three miles of trail, on Monadnock Mountain.

WILDLIFE

You have a pretty good chance of spying some critters on this hike, but that's good news and bad news. It's nice to run into the local residents, but chances are you're seeing them because they have nowhere else to go. Urban sprawl, commonly found in Massachusetts, is encroaching on their turf. If you see a beautiful creature, give it the space it deserves; it isn't easy being a suburban critter devoid of all property rights.

CRITTERS

- Black bears
- Bobcats
- Cottontail rabbits and snowshoe hares
- Coyotes
- Foxes
- Moose
- Skunks

SCHLIMMER'S SIDE TRAIL

WORLD'S MOST-CLIMBED MOUNTAIN

In case you're wondering which mountain is the world's most-often climbed, it is Japan's 12,388-foot Mount Fuji. This mountain has been accurately described by William Bueler, author of *Mountains of the World*, as "the most photographed, most painted, most climbed, and most looked at mountain on earth . . ." It's one of the most beautiful mountains, too. The climbing season lasts from July 1 to August 31. Basically, this is the window of best weather; the snow has melted, and the huts, post office, and toll road, among other facilities, are open for operation. During this two-month time frame, as many as 200,000 people climb Mount Fuji, sometimes forming long lines of bodies that stretch from base to summit.

It's estimated that the first ascent of Mount Fuji took place in the eighth or ninth century A.D., because; a book from this period accurately describes Fuji's volcanic crater. Climbing on Mount Fuji, in a recreational sense, began perhaps 700 years later, though climbing this mountain for religious reasons dates back to before 1200 A.D.

In 1963, a toll road was completed up the north side of this peak, reaching an elevation greater than 7,000 feet, making Mount Fuji an even more inviting climb for those who would rather not start from the mountain's base. ■

Moose are becoming more common along the MMT. While hiking northern sections of the MMT near the Massachusetts–New Hampshire border, my friend and I spotted two separate areas that contained moose scat and tracks.

POINTS OF INTEREST

IN THE GOOD OL' DAYS

Along the MMT you'll find old stone walls, cellar holes, abandoned logging roads, and mill dams built by early settlers. These date back to a time when Native Americans still controlled much of the surrounding area.

RIDGE RUNNING

I found Provin Mountain, on the extreme southern section of the MMT, was one of the most enjoyable stretches of the trail. The elevation is modest, only 650 feet, but the smooth, rolling terrain is welcome.

MOUNT NORWOTTUCK

This 1,100-foot peak in the Holyoke Range has excellent views, scree fields, and a series of overhanging ledges and caves known as the Horse Caves. The MMT heads right through a rock crevice that you must shimmy up or down, depending on your direction.

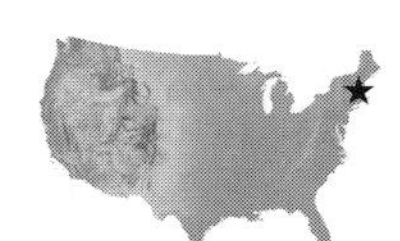

A TASTE OF HOLLAND

Holland Glen, north of State Route 9, is home to a steep and deep ravine, waterfalls, and mature hemlock groves, all protected by the Belchertown Historical Society. This was also one of my favorite parts of the MMT.

MIND THE GAP

If you want a wonderful view of southern New Hampshire but would rather not stand shoulder to shoulder on Monadnock Mountain, nearby Gap Mountain (1,811 feet) is made for you. This rock-topped peak offers a 360° view with Monadnock Mountain as a centerpiece.

In Their Own Words . . .

The Metacomet-Monadnock Trail may be the most difficult trail in Schlimmer's book to pronounce (that, and Tuscarora is a tough one, too, perhaps) and it may well be one of the most demanding, per mile, if you were to hike the whole thing end-to-end. This uncrowded frontcountry path will give you a grand tour of a good portion of the Bay State.

Three specific challenges that come to mind are the Westfield and Connecticut Rivers and the climbing. The Westfield River, as least when I attempted to ford it, looked more like a death trap than the river I expected to cool my toes in. Oh well. Challenges like these should be welcome on the trail. They remind us conceited humans that nature is more powerful than us, whether it be a swift-moving river, hurricane, or heat wave.

The Connecticut River, on the other hand, can be a logistical headache. If it's raining the day you have to hitchhike for a boat ride, probably no one will be on the water to pick you up. I would get comfortable, for you will be sitting there for quite a while looking for a ride. Crossing the Connecticut River north to south is much more difficult than south to north for the south side of the river has a state boat ramp. On the north side of the river you'll just have to hope someone lands at the riverbank to see if you need a ride. Again, get comfy.

The climbing, mile for mile, was surprisingly tough. Somewhat steep slopes covered in busted rock and dust had to be climbed each day. But all the climbing was worth it. Looking west into the rich farm valleys of central Massachusetts from a peak resting five hundred vertical feet above the fields—a view I clearly earned—was my just reward.

The Metacomet-Monadnock Trail seemed to combine the best features of a backcountry and frontcountry experience. Wildness, challenging terrain, and lonely days merged with short road walks, nearby towns, and a trail that can be hiked in only ten days time.

—Seward Chase, 2004 Metacomet-Monadnock Trail thru-hiker

mid state trail

260 MILES | PENNSYLVANIA

TO GO . . .

- extended ridgeline hiking on Pennsylvania's wildest footpath
- excellent guidebook, detailed maps
- crowd factor should be low
- interesting geological features

OR NOT TO GO?

- finding water can be a challenge
- rough, rocky climbs
- human impact
- I still can't figure out the order of maps

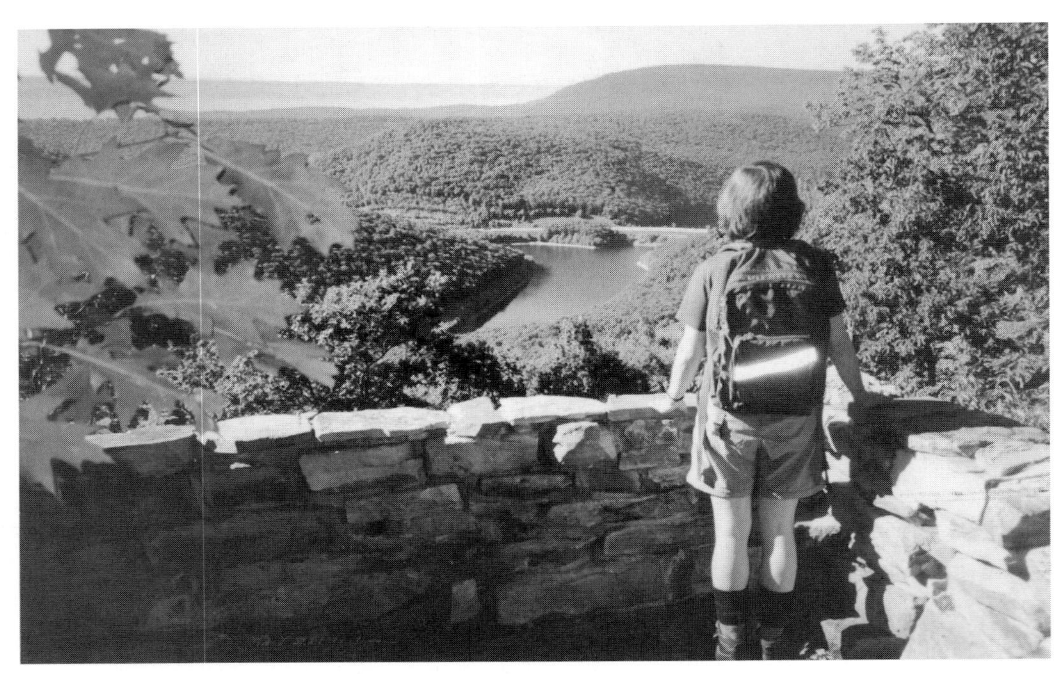

The view from Big Valley Vista is so nice the Mid State Trail Association chose this image for the cover of its Guide to Mid State Trail in the Seven Mountains of Pennsylvania. *This overlook is one of the few places on the Mid State Trail that provides a glimpse of a big body of water; in this case it's the Lewistown Reservoir.* (TOM THWAITES)

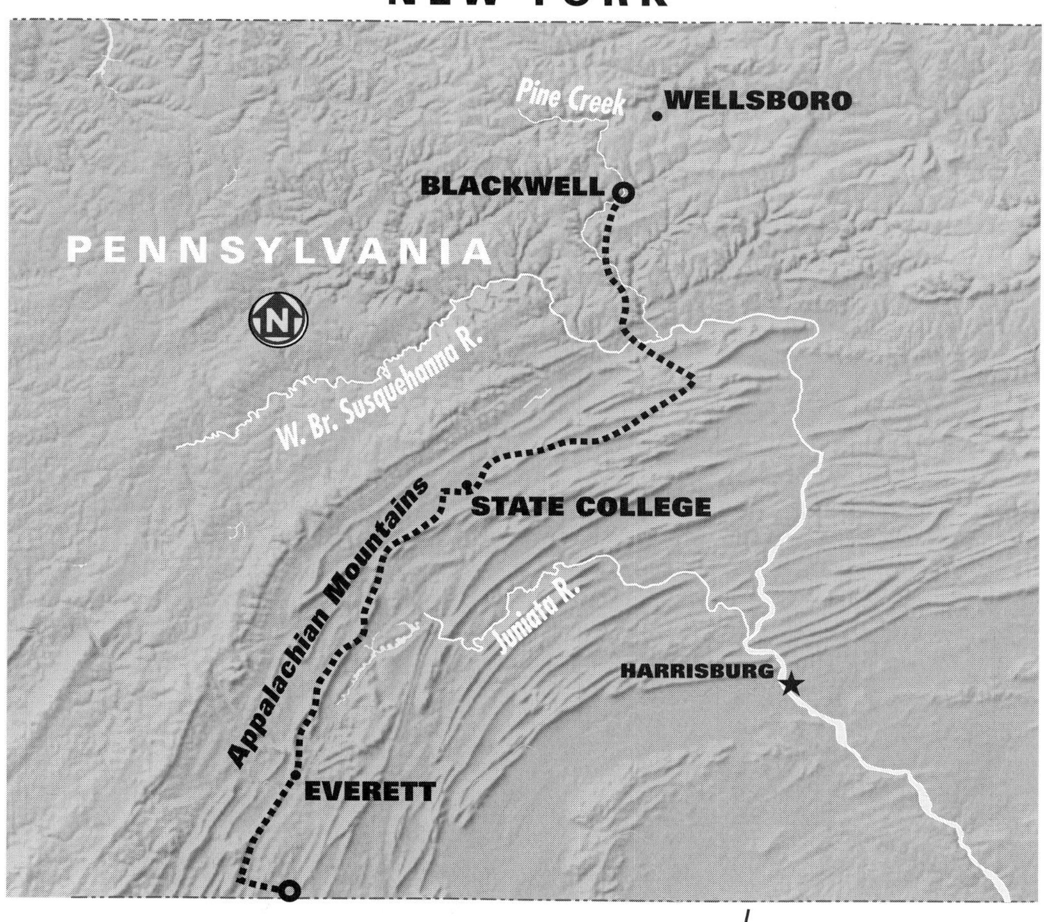
NEW YORK
WELLSBORO
Pine Creek
BLACKWELL
PENNSYLVANIA
N
W. Br. Susquehanna R.
STATE COLLEGE
Appalachian Mountains
Juniata R.
HARRISBURG
EVERETT
MARYLAND

Towns near or on the trail
State capital
Trail terminus
Trail route
PENNSYLVANIA

The Mid State Trail (MST) is one of four trails in this guide that calls Pennsylvania home. It has at least one quality in common with two of the other Pennsylvania trails: like the Baker Trail and the Mason-Dixon Trail, you'll find steep climbs through rough and rocky terrain. But what sets the MST apart from these sister trails is that nearly its entire route is off road, with just four short road walks. Three of these road walks may be reverted to hiking trail soon.

The MST has something else that sets it apart from most other trails in this guide: the metric system. The Mid State Trail Association (MSTA), which formed in 1982 and is the major overseer of the MST, says that "metrication is a patriotic measure designed to help end our cultural isolation and ease our chronic balance of payments problems." This is just the beginning of witty, funny, and simply blunt writings in the excellent *Guide to Mid State Trail in the Seven Mountains of Pennsylvania*. Elsewhere in the guide, we're told that parking at a particular rest stop near the MST is limited to two hours "to discourage drug trafficking and prostitution," and if you're trying to get shuttle service from a busy nearby river-running guide during peak season, the MSTA suggests you "wait for another drought." The guide also says that the springs on the MST are certified to contain "a substantial portion of dihydrogen mono oxide when flowing." (That's H_2O.) Overall, the guide is very well researched, written, and printed. This guide is also available from the Penn State Outing Club. However, I mailed my order to the club with payment enclosed, they received it, and I never heard another word from them. Scoundrels! Then I ordered the guide straight from the Mid State Trail Association. The MSTA proved to be the more reliable supplier.

The Mid State Trail has gone through dozens of reroutes in the past and is currently 260.6 miles (420.2 kilometers) long. Its southern end is near the Maryland border at Everett, Pennsylvania; its northern end is near Blackwell, Pennsylvania. The thirty-four miles of side trails of the MST, according to Tom Thwaites, president of the MSTA for twenty years now, have become "a weakness as they enable horses, mountain bikes, and low-flying saucers to evade negative posting." Is there something in Tom's tap water that he should know about?

The first thru-hiker of this trans-Pennsylvania route may have been Diana Ludwig, of Clarington, Pennsylvania. Ludwig hiked the Mid State Trail in the early 1990s when the southern portion was not yet completed. Her entire route was from

VITALS

- Expect to cover 15 miles a day
- Expect a thru-hike to take 17 days
- Hiking season: April to November
- Water availability: Sometimes
- Resupply opportunities: Sometimes
- First year thru-hiked: Early 1990s
- Approximate yearly thru-hikers: Fewer than 30
- Primary contact: Mid State Trail Association

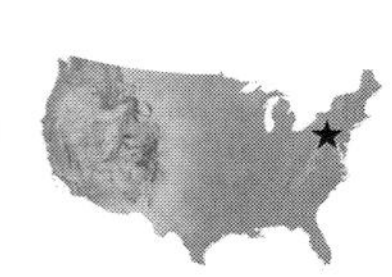

AVERAGE HIGHS AND LOWS IN DEGREES FAHRENHEIT

	JAN	MAR	MAY	JUL	SEPT	NOV
EVERETT, PA (1,020 FT.)	20–35	30–50	45–70	60–80	50–75	30–50
WELLSBORO, PA (1,310 FT.)	15–30	20–45	40–70	55–80	45–70	30–50

U.S. 22 (south of State College) to near Blackwell, which took her about fifteen days. (Diana, an accomplished artist, is no tenderfoot to long-distance adventuring. Besides being the first to thru-hike the MST, she has also soloed the 140-mile Highlands Trail and the 120-mile Loyalsock Trail, in addition to biking a 1,000-mile circumnavigation route of Pennsylvania by herself.)

WEATHER

The central part of Pennsylvania can see the same amounts of snow as the Baker Trail, so unless you're looking for a full-on winter trip, you'll have to wait a little while for the white stuff to melt. Get ready to head out on the MST in late April, which is probably the best time of year to avoid bugs, find plenty of water (once you're off the ridgelines), and walk among springtime blooms.

Summers can be humid and hot, especially while climbing through those very rocky sections of trail. Daytime highs sometimes reach the upper eighties, and humidity rules in the hollows and valleys. The hiking season lasts into early November, but you should be aware that this is the time of year that hunting seasons start. Please remember that many folks with guns are out there, although your chances of encountering a problem are very low.

TERRAIN

I'm not going to lie to you. The terrain on this trail is rough. Many parts of the MST take on characteristics of the most rugged sections of the Appalachian Trail, and the amount of rocky hiking even reaches Ouachita Trail proportions (see page 161). Scree slopes, railroad grades, switchbacks, and steep climbs greet you every day on this 260-mile adventure. Short road walks, easy ridgeline walking, and deep valley exploring will also accompany you from one end to the other through the Seven Mountains Region.

And why is it called Seven Mountains? There have been many definitions over the past hundred years of exactly what this region is, but it's roughly defined

TERRAIN HIGHLIGHTS

- Steep, rocky climbs and scree slopes
- Long ridgelines
- Oak and American beech forests
- Hemlock forests
- River valleys
- Spring-fed streams
- Impacts of civilization

DON'T LEAVE HOME WITHOUT IT

STURDY BOOTS

True, I prefer the lightweight advantage of sneakers, but if there was ever a place to don a pair of heavy stompers, the Mid State Trail is it. The central part of Pennsylvania is legendary for its endless stretches of rocks, and endless opportunities to tweak an ankle.

as a long north-south-running band of ridges and peaks found in central Pennsylvania. The MST traverses all seven major points of this ridge, including Tussey, Fourth, Thickhead, Long, Nittany, White Deer, and Bald Eagle mountains. Of the eighteen maps I received from the MSTA, seventeen have a highpoint exceeding 1,500 feet, fourteen maps bring us over 2,000 feet, and the 2,500-foot mark is sur-

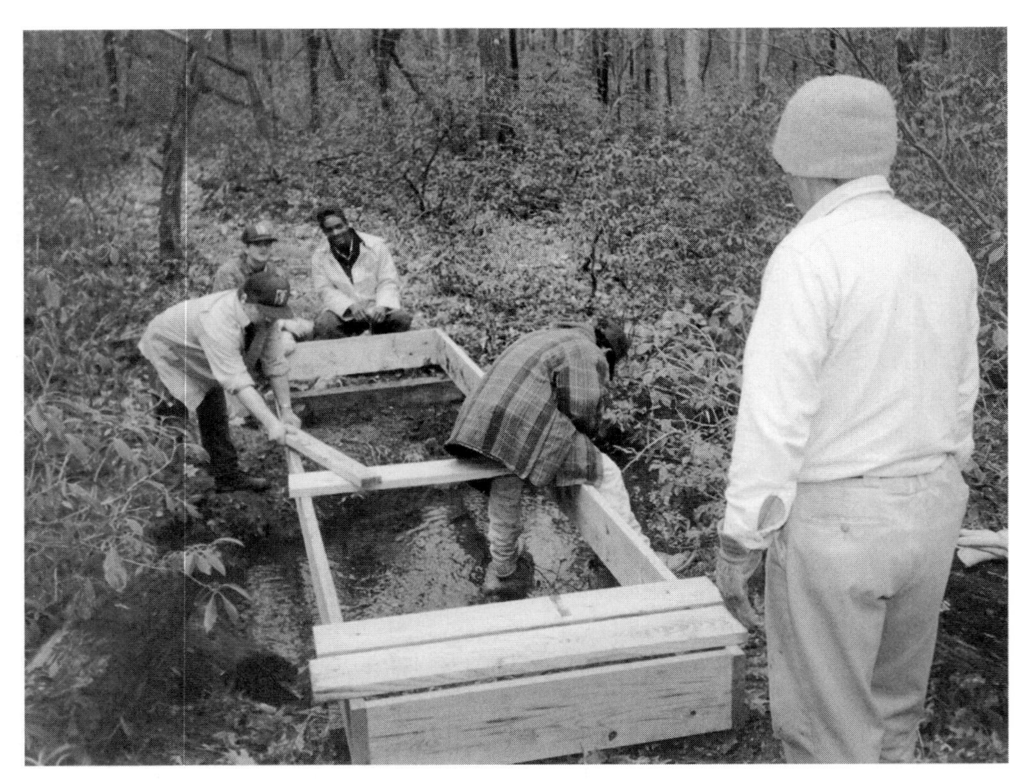

As Tom Thwaites, longtime president of the Mid State Trail Association, reminds us, trails cannot exist without the selfless contributions of trail maintainers. Here a group installs bridging on a section of Pennsylvania's wildest long-distance trail. (TOM THWAITES)

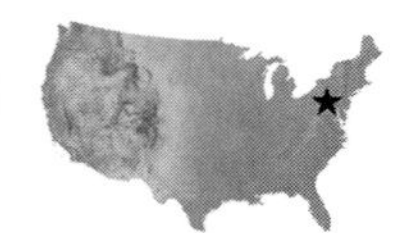

passed on one map. Included on these maps are more than seventy major views marked along the route.

WATER

Filling up your water bottles along the MST is going to be a challenge even in spring. Because the route is mostly on ridgelines, the only place to find water is often well below the Mid State Trail's route, via a blue-blazed side trail. In some cases you may have to climb down steep, nasty sections to grab some water. There are some springs on the ridges, but they total only a handful, and most are seasonal.

Your best bet is to fill up your water bottles in the valleys and pay close attention to any upcoming sources. Potable water can be found in the five towns located on or close to the MST. Post offices, grocery stores, and other services are available at approximately fifteen locations on or near the trail. Eleven campsites on the MST have water available from a hand pump. (Most of these are located off those dry ridgelines we spoke of.)

WILDNESS

Most of the MST is on public land. On your MST thru-hike, you'll head through state forest, state game lands, state forest wild areas, and state parks. Primitive camping is usually allowed in most of these areas except for private land; camping is not allowed on game lands and natural areas. The boundaries of areas are usually not marked on the ground but are indicated on the MSTA's Mid State Trail maps. Fires are generally not allowed at primitive sites from March 1 to May 25 and again from October 1 to December 1.

You won't always be in the woods or on top of pristine ridgelines. Human-made features include quarries, pipelines, and clear-cuts, and on some sections of trail you'll meet equestrians and mountain bikers. Most of the MST is designed for, and designated as, foot traffic only, so you can expect to have some time to yourself among the silence of deep hemlock forests.

WILDLIFE

Like so many other places in the eastern United States, you will surely see our friends the white-tailed deer. Heading through central Pennsylvania is not the wildest experience in the United States, but the MST is legendary for making thru-hikers feel they are in true wilderness and not amidst civilization. A claim of the Mid

CRITTERS

- Black bears
- Coyotes
- Rattlesnakes
- Red foxes
- Skunks
- Turkeys
- Lots of white-tailed deer

State Trail Association, which often holds true, is that you'll see more bears than humans on a thru-hike.

POINTS OF INTEREST

THE BEST VIEW

Featured on the cover of the *Guide to Mid State Trail in the Seven Mountains of Pennsylvania*, Big Valley Vista is one of the few places with a nice view of a big body of water; in this case it's the Lewistown Reservoir.

THE LIGHT AT THE END . . .

You'll hike through the 280-foot Paddy Tunnel, which travels under Paddy Mountain. This tunnel is on a southern section of the MST near State Route 45.

THE FEW REMAINING VIRGINS

In the Detweiler Run Natural Area, east of State College, you'll find virgin white pine and hemlock, which are rare in the Northeast.

AN ANCIENT PATH

The Great Island Indian Path is "the real McCoy." Located near Ravensburg Park (and lacking signage), this old Native American trail is now a side trail off the MST. Its half-mile length has been spared from becoming a road.

SIGNS OF PAST TIMES

Near the halfway point of the Mid State Trail in the West Branch Valley you'll find the remnants of Fort Horn (from 1777), the Pennsylvania Canal, a village of the Delaware Indians, and even the remains of a Prohibition-era still.

In Their Own Words . . .

The Mid State Trail is a wilderness footpath across Pennsylvania from the Mason-Dixon Line to Pine Creek Gorge in Tioga County. It is the longest and wildest footpath in the state. It follows the grain of the ridge and valley region mostly, before crossing the West Branch of the Susquehanna, to reach the Allegheny Plateau. An extension is being built across Tioga County in the north using the lands of Cowanesque and Hammond Lakes, State Game Land 37, Tioga State Forest, and Hills Creek State Park to connect with the Finger Lakes Trail and the North Country National Scenic Trail in New York State. At the Mason-Dixon Line to the south, it connects with the Green Ridge Hiking Trail in Maryland.

Features of the Mid State are its many views and sense of isolation and remoteness. . . . Along the way it crosses five state forests, four state game lands, eight Natural Areas, three Wild Areas, and six state parks. The Mid State Trail visits old-growth timber in Detweiler, Alan Seeger, and Bark Cabin Natural Areas, too.

The Hiking Division of the Penn State Outing Club started construction in 1968 and continued until 1989, and was joined by the Mid State Trail Association in 1982. Bucknell University and Susquehanna University Outing Clubs, CETA Trail Crews, the Standing Stone Garden Club, Girl Scouts, Youth Conservation Corps, Boy Scouts, adjudicated juveniles, PSU Faculty Women's Hiking Interest Group, community service workers, convicts from Huntingdon State Prison, and church youth groups have all worked on the trail. The Mid State Trail is maintained entirely by volunteers from the hiking community.

Camping is permitted along the trail on state forest lands but not on state game lands. The Mid State Trail is a rugged and demanding path. If you hike alone, you may meet more bears than people on your journey. The Mid State Trail was designed, built, and is maintained only for foot traffic.

—Tom Thwaites, Mid State Trail Association president

mountains-to-sea trail

925 MILES | NORTH CAROLINA

TO GO . . .

- crowd factor should be very low
- opportunity to see the entire state
- alternative to the crowded Appalachian Trail
- highpoints of Tennessee and North Carolina

OR NOT TO GO?

- at least 300 miles of road walking
- no accurate maps of the entire route
- limited thru-hiker support system
- watching the film *Deliverance* may change your mind

As the Mountains-to-Sea Trail enters into Linville Gorge, you'll be treated to this impressive view of Shortoff Mountain. (JEFF BREWER)

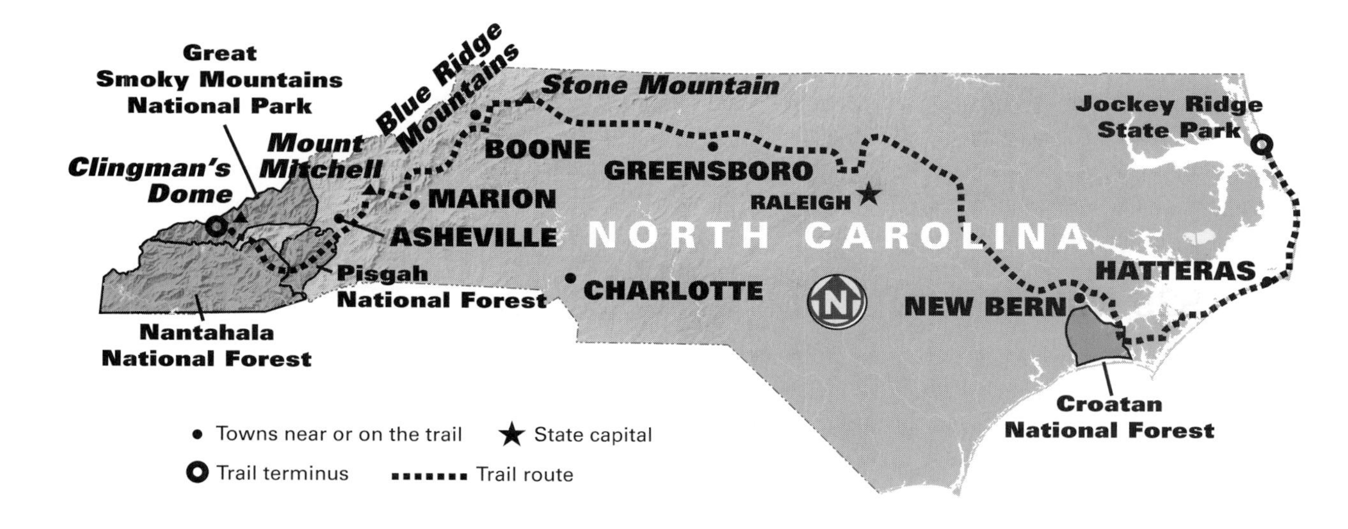

North Carolina, like Wisconsin (Ice Age Trail) and Vermont (Long Trail), boasts a path that takes you from one end of the state to the other. Starting in the far western part of North Carolina on the Tennessee border, on top of the highest peak in Tennessee, and winding its way east to the Atlantic coast, the Mountains-to-Sea Trail (MST) is aptly named. The 925-mile figure may change with the cutting and blazing of newer sections of trail; like many other trails in this guide, the MST is a work in progress.

By spring 2003, 370 miles of the MST were on bike paths and road shoulders, with 450 miles having State Park Trail designation. But with each trail season, the MST moves closer to completion. Currently, the largest obstacle for making this path truly a mountains-to-sea route is the central and eastern portion of the state—the Piedmont Region—where there is little publicly owned land.

Luckily for Southern long-distance hikers, the state of North Carolina fully supports the expansion of this "flagship trail." During a July 2000 session of the General Assembly of North Carolina, the state approved Bill 1311, which authorized "the addition of the Mountains-to-Sea State Park Trail to the state parks system." Major reasons cited by state officials that support the existence of the trail (which must have blushingly flattered the MST) include the following.

. . . to preserve the common heritage of this State, its open lands, and places of beauty; and whereas, the General Assembly enacted the State Parks Act in 1987, declaring that the state of North Carolina offers unique archaeological, geological, biological, scenic, and recreational resources, and that these resources are part of the heritage of the people of the State to be preserved and managed by those people for their use and for the use of their visitors and descendants; and, whereas, a Mountains-to-Sea Trail across North Carolina would offer outstanding recreational opportunities to the state's citizens; would protect riparian buffers and corridors of wildlife habitat along its route; and would possess biological, scenic, and recreational resources of statewide significance. . . .

The private organization assisting state and federal agencies in making this happen, through the spirited work of their volunteers, is Friends of the Mountains-to-Sea Trail (FMST). Headquartered in Louisburg, North Carolina, this group runs volunteer trail projects and petitions individual property owners for the use of their land. As on most other trails in this guide, volunteers, along with state and federal land management agencies, are the backbone of a long trail's existence.

Only four recorded hikers have walked from the mountains of North Carolina to the sea via the MST. The first to thru-hike this path were Allen DeHart and Alan Householder back in 1997. Householder and DeHart currently serve on the Board of the Friends of the Mountains-to Sea-Trail. DeHart is also the author of *Hiking North Carolina's Mountains-to-Sea Trail.* In September and October 2002, Jason Pass hiked and biked the MST averaging 19.6 miles per day. The president of Friends of the Mountains-to-Sea Trail, Jeff Brewer, started a thru-hike during the last week of August 2003 and reached the eastern terminus on the Outer Banks on October 19, fifty-five days later. Jeff unfortunately had to deal with a full-on hurricane during his thru-hike.

Hurricane Isabel did play a huge factor in my trip. I took one day off for it but the next day all the creeks and streams were at flood stage in the Piedmont (Winston-Salem area) of the state. This also made the Croatan Forest very wet with waist-high water at times on the trail. Other than that, the weather was great. As you know, the hurricane tore the Outer Banks up pretty bad as well.

When a hurricane wasn't drenching Jeff, he considered the best section of the MST to be from the town of Marion to Blowing Rock. This 110-mile section is home to Linville Gorge and Shortoff Mountain.

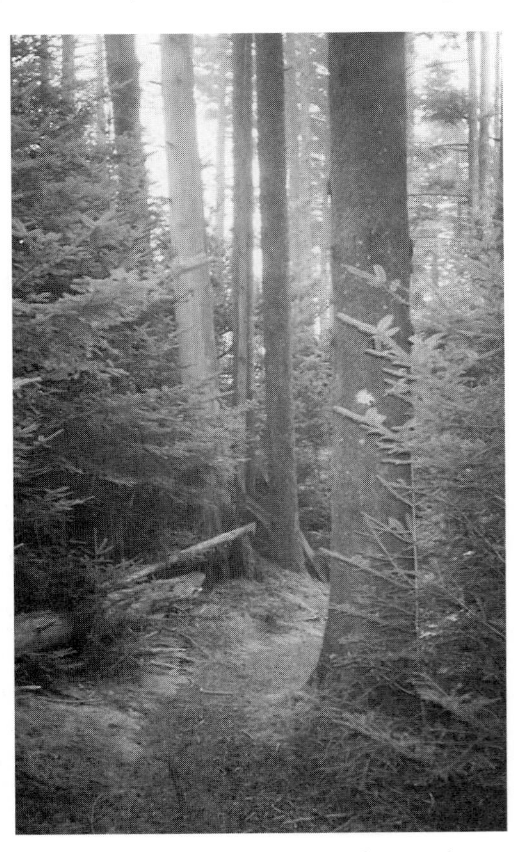

The Mountains-to-Sea trail bed softens as it winds through this inviting fir forest near Bear Pin Gap. (JEFF BREWER)

MOUNT MITCHELL

Of all the mountains to the east of the Mississippi River, Mount Mitchell stands tallest. Located in Yancey County, this 6,684-foot peak boasts

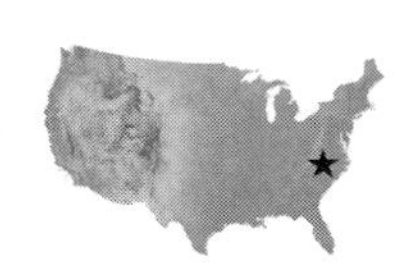

VITALS

- Expect to cover 17 miles a day
- Expect a thru-hike to take 55 days
- Hiking season: April to November
- Water availability: Frequent
- Resupply opportunities: Sometimes
- First year thru-hiked: 1997
- Approximate yearly thru-hikers: 1
- Primary contact: Friends of the Mountains-to-Sea Trail

hiking trails, camping areas, evergreen forests, rhododendron, and wonderful views from its stone observation tower.

Although it's the geographic highpoint of the MST, Mount Mitchell will not be the aesthetic high point of your two-month thru-hike. Currently the peak hosts a nearby auto road, a restaurant, employee quarters, maintenance buildings, a concession stand, and a gift shop, to be enjoyed by throngs of camera-toting tourists.

Some nasty weather may keep these pedestrians confined to their cars, however. The record low for the state of North Carolina occurred on this summit in 1985 when the mercury dipped to a heartless –34°. The highest temperature ever recorded on the summit was just 81°. A peak wind gust of 178 miles per hour was recorded on top . . . right before the anemometer blew off the mountain.

REV. ELISHA MITCHELL, D.D.

On the summit of Mount Mitchell is the grave of Reverend Elisha Mitchell, D.D. (1793–1857). Dr. Mitchell, a Yale graduate and professor of chemistry, math, and geology at the University of North Carolina, conducted the first statewide survey in the United States, tackling western North Carolina's high peaks from 1824 to 1828. Mitchell may have been the first person to summit Mount Mitchell in 1835 after viewing it from nearby Big Butt (5,940 feet). The good doctor had his doubters, though, and in 1855, an intense controversy ensued between Dr. Mitchell and Senator Thomas Clingman (who has two southern high peaks named for him) over whether Mitchell did in fact summit the highest peak east of the Mississippi.

In June 1857, Mitchell—still in the heat of dispute while on a third expedition to the summit—fell to his death at a forty-foot waterfall, now called Mitchell Falls (no pun intended). After finding his body, the searchers spent several grueling hours carrying the corpse to the summit, where they planned to bury it, only to have to carry it back down the mountain. Margaret Mitchell, the doctor's daughter, requested that the body be buried in Asheville, North Carolina. On June 15, 1858, after a statewide demand to move the body back to the mountain, Elisha Mitchell made one last ascent of the peak; he was finally laid to rest just below the summit observation tower, where he remains today. ■

Mount Mitchell is the centerpiece of 1,855-acre Mount Mitchell State Park—which in 1915 became North Carolina's first state park. This high land was preserved primarily due to concerns over excessive logging, water-quality degradation, and extreme fire danger.

WEATHER

With nearly a thousand miles of trail, at elevations ranging from nearly 7,000 feet to sea level, the Mountains-to-Sea Trail weather within a single thru-hiking season can range from 90° for road and beach walks to snowstorms in late summer and early fall. On

THE SOUTHERN DIALECT

Horace Kephart, in his classic work *Our Southern Highlanders*, explains the Appalachian dialect he encountered during the first decade of the twentieth century while living in what is today's Great Smoky Mountains National Park. Not much has changed concerning speech in the hundred years that followed Kephart's arrival in the hills. The English language is so modified in the southern Appalachians that it has been called by many a legitimate dialect. After spending four months as a trail boss in the high peaks of western North Carolina, I agree. Below are some of the linguistic labyrinths a thru-hiker may have to sort out when on the Mountains-to-Sea Trail or the Tuscarora Trail.

Non-verbs serving as verbs. Horace Kephart recorded a Southerner estimating, "That bear'll meat me for a month." I heard, "I reckon I ain't had no time to get breakfasted" and "We're gonna trail it today" (going to work on the trail today).

Redundancies. I heard a man referring to diesel as "diesel gas"; another man told me his dog "done did" get tangled in a rhododendron thicket. Kephart's neighbors described "rifle guns," "ham meat," and a "preacher man." Sometimes Kephart found the double descriptions to be contradictory, "male cow" and "automatic revolver" being two classics.

Altered tense. A man told me, "I reckon I done seen where somethin' got eat" (he saw where an animal may have been eaten) and "I reckon I ain't done seen it." Kephart overheard, "I done done it."

Multiple negatives. Kephart recorded the double, triple, quadruple, and, yes, even quintuple negatives: "I ain't never seen no men-folks of no kind do no washin' (quintuple)." I heard, "I reckon we didn't go to no party" (double) and "If I'm missin' work then I ain't got no money to pay no bills" (triple).

Ya'll come back. In certain southern locales, there is rarely one person referred to in conversation— only groups. It's unknown how many people were present during the conversation Kephart overheard. "Let we-uns all go over to youerunses house." He recorded "we-all" and "you-all" often, too. Kephart labeled these pieces "double-barrel pronouns." I had a conversation with one southern gentleman who gave me this salutation: "Well, y'all come back and see us. We'll be here." I replied, "Oh, I'll be back." Then he responded, "All right, you-all take care. We'll see y'all later." ■

AVERAGE HIGHS AND LOWS IN DEGREES FAHRENHEIT	JAN	MAR	MAY	JUL	SEPT	NOV
ASHEVILLE, NC (2,130 FT.)	30–45	35–60	50–75	65–85	55–80	40–60
CHAPEL HILL, NC (510 FT.)	30–50	40–60	55–80	65–90	60–80	40–60
HATTERAS, NC (5 FT.)	40–55	45–60	60–75	75–85	70–80	50–65

June 21, 2003, the first day of summer, the morning temperature on Mount Mitchell's summit was a bone-chilling 36°. This reading was repeated on June 22. Brrr!

Once you're out of the mountains on the western sections of trail, the weather is dramatically more predictable; the elevations are below 3,000 feet in the central and eastern portions of the state. The coast has pleasant temperatures most of the year, but hurricane season can level the Outer Banks (and any unsuspecting thru-hikers). Be prepared for possible layovers if a strong storm is on its way toward the coast.

TERRAIN

The Mountains-to-Sea Trail throws just about everything imaginable at thru-hikers, some features challenging, some of them remote, some of them boring. But most of the features are in a pretty setting as the MST travels through thirty-seven of North Carolina's one hundred counties.

On the west end of the MST, you'll hike up and down the highest peaks in the eastern United States. Peaks that exceed 6,000 feet include Chestnut Bald, Mount Mitchell, Clingmans Dome, Waterrock Knob, Black Balsam Knob, Craggy Dome, Richland Balsam, and Blackstock Knob. Upon leaving the Appalachian Mountains, you will start to encounter the deep hardwood forests of the South and, continuing on, finally reach the Atlantic coast, where the Mountains-to-Sea Trail ends in Jockey's Ridge State Park. This park is home to the tallest sand dune on the East Coast, rising a full 140 feet above the beach.

WATER

The only sections of trail where a lack of water may be a concern include the high peaks of the Appalachian region near the MST's western terminus. The Smoky

TERRAIN HIGHLIGHTS

- Sand dunes
- Small Southern communities
- Bike paths
- Evergreen-clad summits on two state highpoints
- Road walks
- Waterfalls
- Ferry rides on Atlantic coast
- Blazing fall foliage

The Mountains-to-Sea Trail joins the Neusiok Trail for a 22-mile journey through the enchanting pine savanna in Croatan Forest. (JEFF BREWER)

Mountains may receive up to ninety inches of precipitation each year, but this rainfall reaches the base of these tall peaks fast. During the summer months, wise thru-hikers will pay attention to upcoming mountainous terrain and carry plenty of water when in the high hills. In the Piedmont and eastern sections of the MST, summers can get brutally hot, so carry plenty of water on these flat sections, too.

You'll pass by six scenic waterfall areas, five major lakes, four major bays, and ten rivers on your two-month trek, crossing the Neuse River multiple times. You can get across the massive Oregon Inlet via a 2.5-mile bridge walk, and you'll pass two giant swamps—one in Croatan National Forest and the other in Cedar Island National Wildlife Refuge. Of course, because the MST heads through many small communities, a savvy thru-hiker will want to keep an eye out for potable water sources, too.

WILDNESS

Like other trails in progress, the MST has very wild sections interspersed with not so wild sections. Currently the longest continuous marked and maintained section is more than 130 miles long, but again, about 400 total miles of trail are on roads and bike paths. This, I would assume, is the primary reason why thru-hiker Jason Pass decided to bike 200 miles of the MST and walk the remaining 725 miles. The Tennessee Eastman Hiking and Canoeing Club reports that one of the two first MST thru-hikers, Alan Householder, concurs that "hiking and biking would be a great combination or alternative to just an entire hiking experience." In central and

DON'T LEAVE HOME WITHOUT IT

TRUST

While hiking in the southern Appalachians I was treated to a whole host of friendly favors by Southerners. One guy drove up to the trailhead, gave me an ice cold soda and drove away. On another occasion, a man came out of the woods, invited me back to his tent and cooked me breakfast. While in the hills, people approached me and struck up conversations like we were long-lost friends. And when hitchhiking, it never took long to get picked up. Southern hospitality certainly lives on.

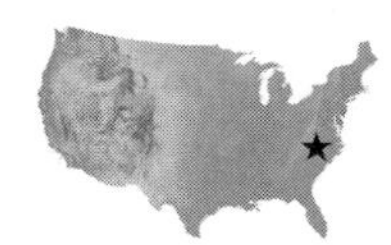

CRITTERS

- Beavers
- Bobcats
- Coyotes
- Eastern cougar*
- Feral hogs
- Rattlesnakes and copperheads
- Sperm whales*

*Listed as endangered species in North Carolina

eastern sections of the MST there is no trail—only a rough idea of where it will eventually go.

End to end on this trail, you'll cross through three national forests, three national parks, and six state parks. Nearly fifty towns are near or on the trail, including the cities of Asheville, Goldsboro, Greensboro, and the state capital, Raleigh, making resupplies a snap.

Although the trail is not defined for its entire route, it's still wild in certain sections. You must ford the often-thigh-deep North Fork of the Catawba River as well as Linville Gorge. Many streams in the Smokies are not bridged, and only a few shelters can be found on this 900+-mile route. You may want to save a thru-hike of the Mountains-to-Sea Trail until further work has been done so that more sections are off road.

WILDLIFE

A problem that critters of North Carolina have in common with wildlife in other parts of the country is ecosystem spoilage. The reason why you may see so many deer and bears on the Mountains-to-Sea Trail may be the result of urban sprawl and destruction of their fragile habitat. The North Carolina Wildlife Resources Commission explains this well, noting the current situation with human-bear interaction in the Tar Heel State. This is from their "Nuisance Wildlife: Coexisting with Wildlife" brochure.

Black bears once roamed the entire state of North Carolina. Due to increasing human populations and associated development, bears no longer occupy the Piedmont and are found only in the eastern and western parts of the state. Further, many new homes are built in occupied bear range each year. Despite all this, bear numbers have increased over the last [10 to 15] years. As a result, bears and people are coming into contact with each other more frequently than before.

Beside the negative impacts of sprawl, there remains the serious issue of black bear poaching in the South. Many illegally obtained black bear gall bladders are harvested in the South and end up in Asia, where they are believed to be a potent aphrodisiac. This problem is especially intense in the Great Smoky Mountains National Park and adjacent land.

In addition to the 700 bears in North Carolina, other animals are stressed from the encroachment of their turf. Please give them the room they deserve.

POINTS OF INTEREST

IN THE WEST

The Appalachian Mountains of the South are home to nearly 200 peaks exceeding 5,000 feet, which should keep your legs and lungs occupied for quite a while. These gorgeous evergreen- and rhododendron-clad summits have cooler temperatures than those in the valleys below, and significant snow in winter. However, ground-level ozone, a nasty beetle infestation, and acid rain are destroying this ecosystem and making far-reaching views a thing of the past.

IN THE EAST

In summer, cooler temperatures are found on the far-eastern end of the Mountains-to-Sea Trail, among sand dunes, shorebirds, and whales.

HIGHPOINTERS TAKE NOTE

You'll climb the highest peak in Tennessee (Clingmans Dome, 6,643 feet) and the highest peak in North Carolina (Mount Mitchell, 6,684 feet).

BIG, BIG ROCK

Stone Mountain, located in Stone Mountain State Park, rises 600 vertical feet above its enormous base and offers excellent views of northwest North Carolina and southern Virginia. Nearby scenic Stone Mountain Falls drop more than 150 vertical feet.

SOUTH HARPER CREEK FALLS

The South Harper Creek Falls area, in Pisgah National Forest, is home to wonderful waterfalls in an amphitheater-like setting of bare rock. You'll pass five other scenic waterfall areas on the MST, too.

In Their Own Words . . .

The Mountains-to-Sea Trail is a cross between two very different long trails: the Cohos Trail of New Hampshire and the Florida Trail of the South. On the western end of the Mountains-to-Sea Trail you have the highest peaks in the Eastern United States, made up of the Great Smoky, Plott Balsam, Great Balsam, and Black Mountain Ranges. Here you'll find evergreen-clad 6,000-foot peaks, rhododendron- and mountain laurel-covered 5,000-foot summits, and hardwood hills of 4,000 feet. To find a hardy and high boreal environment outside the South, you would have to drive fifteen hours to New England. But here, you can reach this unique terrain with only two hours of steady climbing.

Below 3,500 feet on the western sections of the Mountains-to-Sea Trail, you'll feel like you are trekking through a South American jungle rather than the woods of the East. Mosses, briars, vines, shrubs, and expansive hardwood and softwood forests greet Mountains-to-Sea Trail hikers as they slowly but surely work their way toward the Outer Banks of the Carolinas, if heading east.

The Mountains-to-Sea Trail follows the Cape Hatteras Beach trail from Hatteras to Nags Head. Here you'll cover miles and miles of sandy beach. (JEFF BREWER)

Upon reaching the flats on the eastern parts of the Mountains-to-Sea Trail, your ecological trip is not over. Sand dunes, whales, swamps, and shore birds will greet you. A thru-hike of the Mountains-to-Sea Trail, by starting on the highest peak in Tennessee and ending on the Atlantic Ocean, is the ecological equivalent of walking from Quebec to North Carolina, a distance of more than 2,000 miles.

. . . You can get in on the ground floor and become one of the first to tackle this cross-state route. That is, if you like to climb thousands of vertical feet, hunker in April snowstorms, and ford rushing rivers.

—T. R. Buell, Mountains-to-Sea Trail wanderer,
Mount Mitchell State Park trails director

northville-placid trail

135 MILES | NEW YORK

TO GO . . .

- wilderness setting
- crowd factor can be low
- fishing opportunities in remote areas
- possible thru-ski route

OR NOT TO GO?

- bugs can be of Biblical proportions
- no extensive views
- route is often muddy
- middle of nowhere southern terminus

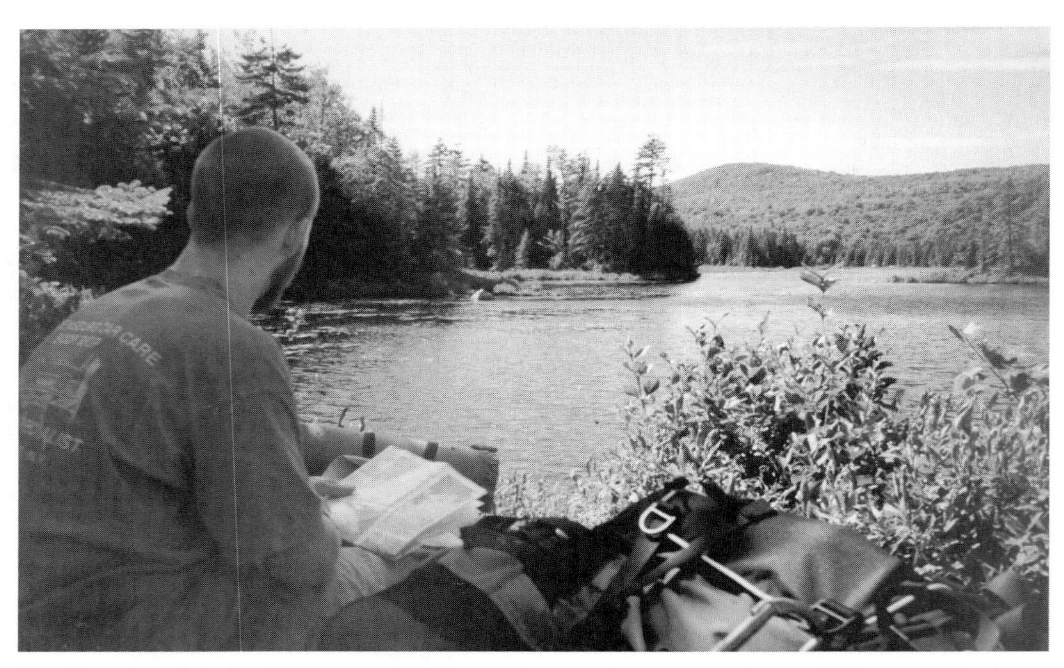

The West Canada Lakes Wilderness Area boasts dozens of remote ponds—and billions of biting bugs. (E. SCHLIMMER)

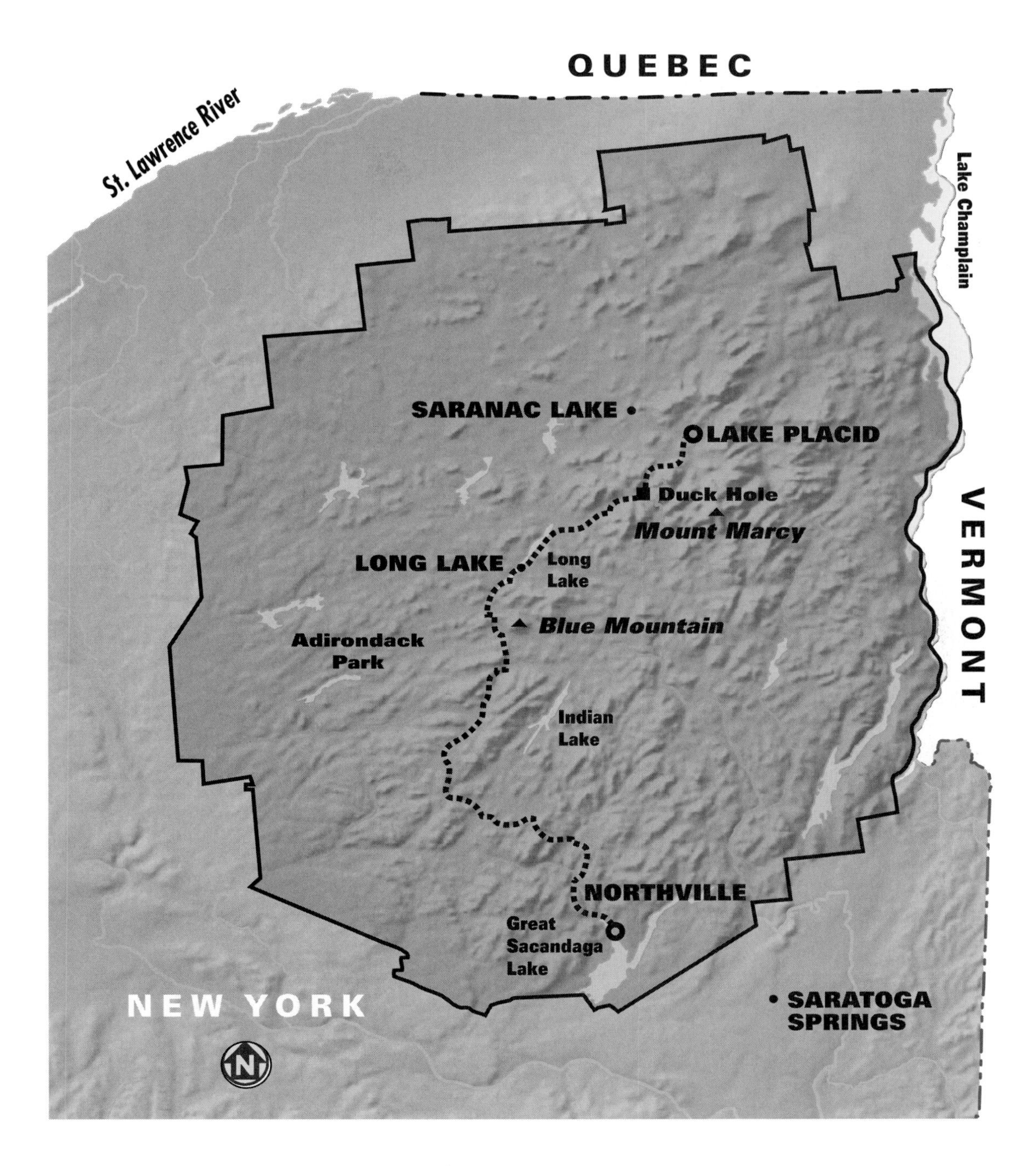
QUEBEC
St. Lawrence River
Lake Champlain
SARANAC LAKE
LAKE PLACID
Duck Hole
Mount Marcy
LONG LAKE
Long Lake
Blue Mountain
Adirondack Park
VERMONT
Indian Lake
NORTHVILLE
Great Sacandaga Lake
NEW YORK
SARATOGA SPRINGS
N

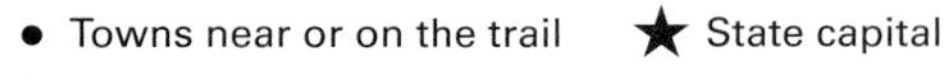
Towns near or on the trail
State capital
Trail terminus
Trail route

This secluded beach on Tirrell Pond is an excellent spot to kick off your shoes and cool your aching dogs. (JEFFERY CASE)

This trail, located in New York's Adirondack Mountains, is a treasure for anyone wanting to immerse him- or herself in a park that's bigger than Yosemite, Yellowstone, Glacier, and Great Smoky Mountains national parks combined. The Adirondack Park is unusual in that there are private lands within its boundaries, and its geology is different from that of the nearby Appalachians. The Northville-Placid Trail (NPT) has been a well-kept secret for years. And the Adirondack Park itself is not well known either. To preserve the area's wild character, it's necessary to practice strict Leave No Trace principles.

The NPT's southern end is at Northville, northwest of Saratoga Springs, and its northern end is near Lake Placid. The trail is geared more toward the walker than the mountaineer, with the route following old tote roads, lazy streams, deep moun-

VITALS

- Expect to cover 15 miles a day
- Expect a thru-hike to take 9 days
- Hiking season: June to October (Hiking is discouraged in April and May due to a surface that easily erodes.)
- Water availability: Frequent
- Resupply opportunities: Seldom
- First year thru-hiked: Unknown
- Approximate yearly thru-hikers: 50 to 80
- Primary contact: Adirondack Mountain Club

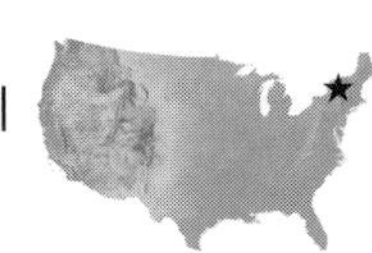

AVERAGE HIGHS AND LOWS IN DEGREES FAHRENHEIT

	JAN	MAR	MAY	JUL	SEPT	NOV
NORTHVILLE, NY (800 FT.)	10–30	20–40	45–70	60–80	50–70	30–45
LAKE PLACID, NY (1,880 FT.)	5–30	15–40	40–65	55–80	45–70	25–45

tain valleys, and lakeshore after lakeshore after lakeshore. Because both ends of the trail are on roads, only 122 miles of the 135 miles need to be walked for a true thru-hike. In terms of fastest traverse times, the Northville-Placid Trail ties for third place with the Baker Trail and the Metacomet-Monadnock Trail. Averaging fifteen miles a day, you can hike the NPT in fewer than ten days.

WEATHER

Expect the range of temperatures to be moderate and not as varied as the nearby Long Trail. It can become fairly humid, because a lot of hiking is in valleys, but the trail passes so many bodies of water you can usually find a stiff breeze to provide comfort. Prepare to get rained on at least once during your trip, and if you decide to head out beyond early October, flurries are a distinct possibility. September is crisp and clear, though I've seen snow fall in the Adirondacks in this month, too. During a typical winter, the central portion of the trail has a significant snowpack from November to May. The hiking season's temperatures are usually pleasant.

TERRAIN

The NPT climbs no significant peaks during its 135-mile journey through the Adirondack Park. The elevations stay around 1,700 feet, with the highpoint reaching a hair over 3,000 feet in the beautiful Fishing Brook Range near the town of Long Lake. Following a valley route, the NPT visits more than twenty bodies of water and a handful of major tributaries. To the east and west of the trail rises a series of mountains. Six 4,000-foot peaks and another five 3,000-foot peaks are within a long, hard day's climb. All of these peaks, except two, lack trails and require full-on bushwhacking.

Forests are composed mostly of hardwoods, including beech and maple, with

TERRAIN HIGHLIGHTS

- Beech and maple forests
- Remote lakes
- Meadows
- Deep valleys
- Clear streams
- Swamps
- Signs of early logging
- Glacial erratics
- Nearby peaks exceeding 4,000 feet

DON'T LEAVE HOME WITHOUT IT

BUG DOPE AND HEAD NET

Perhaps the buggiest trail in the guide, the NPT is teeming with airborne bloodsuckers. I suggest you bring as much DEET as you can carry and ensconce yourself in sheets of mosquito netting. You are warned.

---

only swamps and the height of land having any significant areas of spruce and fir. Small sections of old growth forest can be found in the Adirondack Park, but they are rare—though this park, along with Great Smoky Mountains National Park in Tennessee and North Carolina, is said to have the largest remaining stands in the East. Ninety-seven percent of the Adirondacks has been logged in the past 150 years, so in actuality you have a small chance of finding big trees. Lakeshores are usually lined with cedar, white pine, and hemlock. Blowdown (downed trees) may be encountered on remote sections, especially because chainsaws have limited legal use in designated wilderness areas, and Adirondack trail crews are backlogged severely.

WATER

If you can't readily find water on the Northville-Placid Trail, you must not be on it anymore. You're lost. With multiple ponds, streams, rivers, and lakes, finding water on the NPT is not a problem. Some springs can be found along the way, and the prudent hiker may treat these deep sources as well (no pun intended). With all this water, though, come muddy sections of trail. Be sure to stay on the trail and do not cut around mud holes. This saves trail crews, rangers, and volunteers valuable time and money by not having to brush in side paths. In warmer weather the water also breeds clouds of mosquitoes and blackflies.

WILDNESS

A trail that travels through the heart of the Adirondacks is an explorer's dream come true. Although the number of hikers on the NPT has been increasing steadily, it is still a rather unpopular place compared to the Eastern High Peaks Region to the northeast. The typical NPT hiker is the older hiker who doesn't want to go up and down peaks all day, or it will be the hiker who enjoys lazy days, covering as many or

SCHLIMMER'S SIDE TRAIL

BLUE MOUNTAIN

From the NPT, a five-mile side trail will take you to the top of this 3,750-foot peak. Ranked seventieth highest of the Adirondacks, Blue Mountain lies near the exact center of the Adirondack Park. The summit features exposed rock and a restored fire tower, both of which provide excellent views. ■

Crosssing Ouluska Pass Brook in the High Peaks Wilderness Area. (JEFFERY CASE)

as few miles as he or she wants, far from swarms of other hikers. During the summer months, areas within a day's hike of trailheads have to be shared, but the more remote sections seem empty. All you have to do to be by yourself is search around a bit for those off-the-beaten-path locales, or go in the off season (but not the mud season, April and May). "Bug season" really keeps the crowds away. Years ago, while serving as a Forest Ranger in the Adirondacks, I'd patrol the most northern sections of the NPT. When the bugs were at their worst, I'd see just a few people a day on this lonely trail. The rest of the hiking public had the good sense to stay home, away from the clouds of biting bugs.

The NPT has many classic Adirondack lean-tos with nearby tent sites. Each campsite usually has an outhouse and water. Some heavily used sites are in poor condition. The most pristine sites are the ones farthest from roads. The Northville-Placid Trail passes through four wilderness areas: Silver Lake, West Canada Lakes, Blue Ridge and High Peaks Wilderness Area—which has many rules and regulations.

The only resupply areas near the trail are the tiny towns of Piseco (in the south), Blue Mountain Lake, and Long Lake (both near the halfway point of the NPT). These three towns have so few businesses that most thru-hikers mail themselves food packages to the respective post offices. It's a good idea to check the hours of operation before you send packages general delivery.

WILDLIFE

With its six million acres (that's about the size of Vermont), the Adirondack Park has plenty of room for wildlife to roam around, and plenty for the hiker to see. The exciting news is that the moose has made a return to New York, and the best place in the state to come across one is on the central portions of the NPT.

CRITTERS

- Beavers
- Black bears
- Coyotes
- Fishers
- Great blue herons
- Moose
- Pine martens
- Red foxes
- Red squirrels
- Turkeys

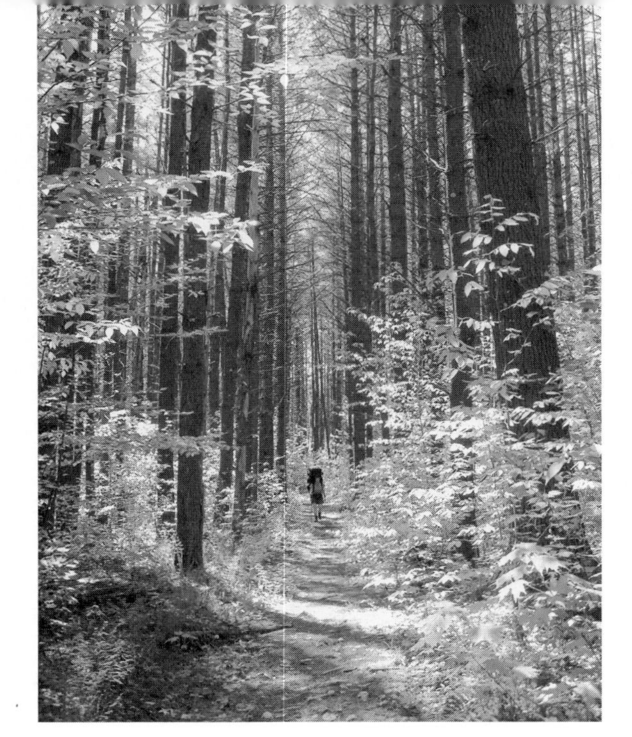

A lone hiker is dwarfed by the towering pines in the High Peaks Wilderness Area north of Long Lake. (JEFFERY CASE)

POINTS OF INTEREST

THE ADIRONDACK MUSEUM

Located just a few miles west of Blue Mountain, the museum can actually be reached via a side trail off the NPT. This outstanding property offers a tour of Adirondack history, culture, and ecology. Weekends at the museum are usually crowded.

LAKE PLACID

Known as the Olympic Village for hosting the 1932 and 1980 Olympic Winter Games, Lake Placid has also hosted the Great Outdoor Games and Ironman Triathlon. Needless to say, this town is very hiker-friendly. Its gorgeous lakeside location is nestled among peaks more than 4,000 feet tall.

DUCK HOLE

This pond, set in the Western High Peaks, is deep enough to swim in, hosts two lean-tos, and provides expansive views of the Sawtooth Range and MacNaughton Mountain. Please hang your food well because bears visit this area often.

In Their Own Words . . .

The Northville-Placid Trail is not that long but, you know, it's long enough. When I thru hiked it in the last two weeks of August in 1995 I really didn't see many other people; maybe ten or fifteen hikers over the 135 miles. It would definitely have to be one of my favorite long trails. The only thing is, if you don't like bugs, mud, and being out in the middle of nowhere, with no views, then you probably shouldn't go. Other than those detractions, I would recommend it. It all depends on what you're looking for. If you're looking for wilderness, the Adirondacks provide.

Read through the guidebook, review the maps, talk to the locals, and then see what you think. This trail is not perfect, but what trail is? And some sections are better than others, like most long-distance trails. The Northville-Placid Trail can be a satisfying path for woods-savvy hikers in search of natural beauty and solitude, who also don't mind sections of trail flooded by beavers and choked with blowdown, or summer months dominated by antagonistic bugs.

Use of the Northville-Placid Trail, including the presence of thru-hikers, has increased

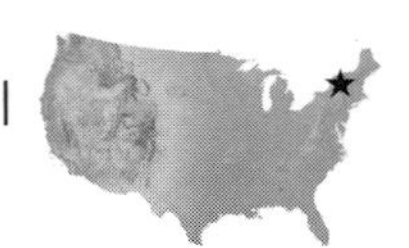

since I first hiked it end-to-end, but it is not crowded. And let's say that you do come to a campsite on the Northville-Placid Trail that's already taken. That doesn't have to be looked upon in a negative light. You can get to know those people. Where are they from? Are they thru-hiking? Have they seen any bears? Why does their dinner look so much more delicious than yours? If you're not that social, just keep on trucking. Pristine camping is allowed, but it would be best to stay at already-impacted sites.

The Northville-Placid Trail may grow wilder each year. A key bridge to a side trail has been removed at Duck Hole and some lean-tos have either been relocated away from water sources, or are slated for removal. The tread is still a jumble of leaves, rocks, mud, and more mud, though.

—Seymour Hamilton, 1995 Northville-Placid Trail thru-hiker,
former Northville-Placid Trail forest ranger

ouachita trail

225 MILES | ARKANSAS OKLAHOMA

TO GO . . .

- long hiking season
- crowd factor is low
- cool rock slides
- excellent guidebook

OR NOT TO GO?

- rugged and rocky tread
- very hot summers
- wicked little climbs
- dry sections

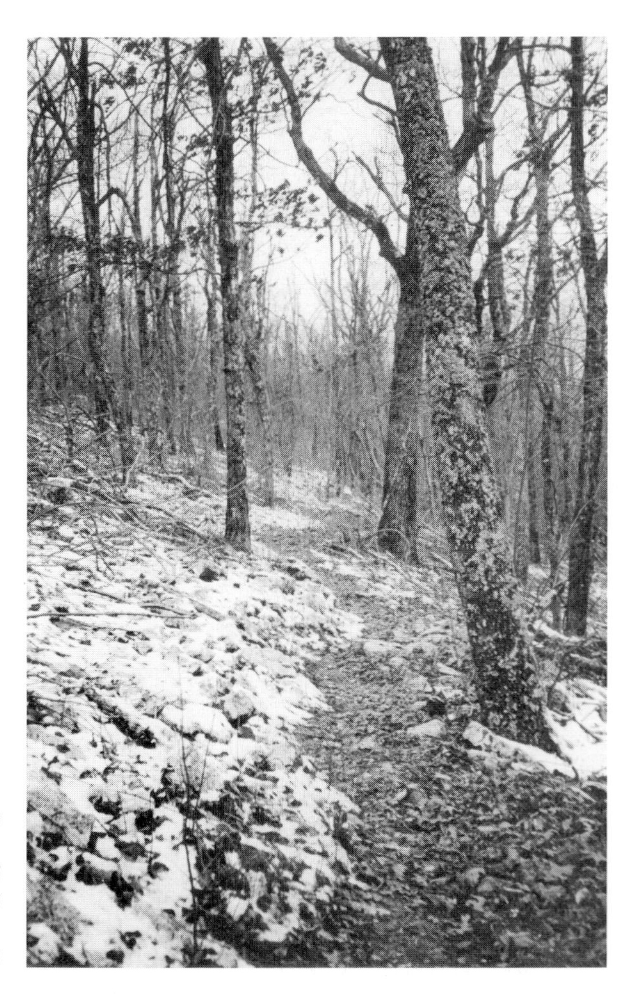

Even in the middle of February, the 225-mile Ouachita Trail receives only an occasional dusting of snow. *(E. SCHLIMMER)*

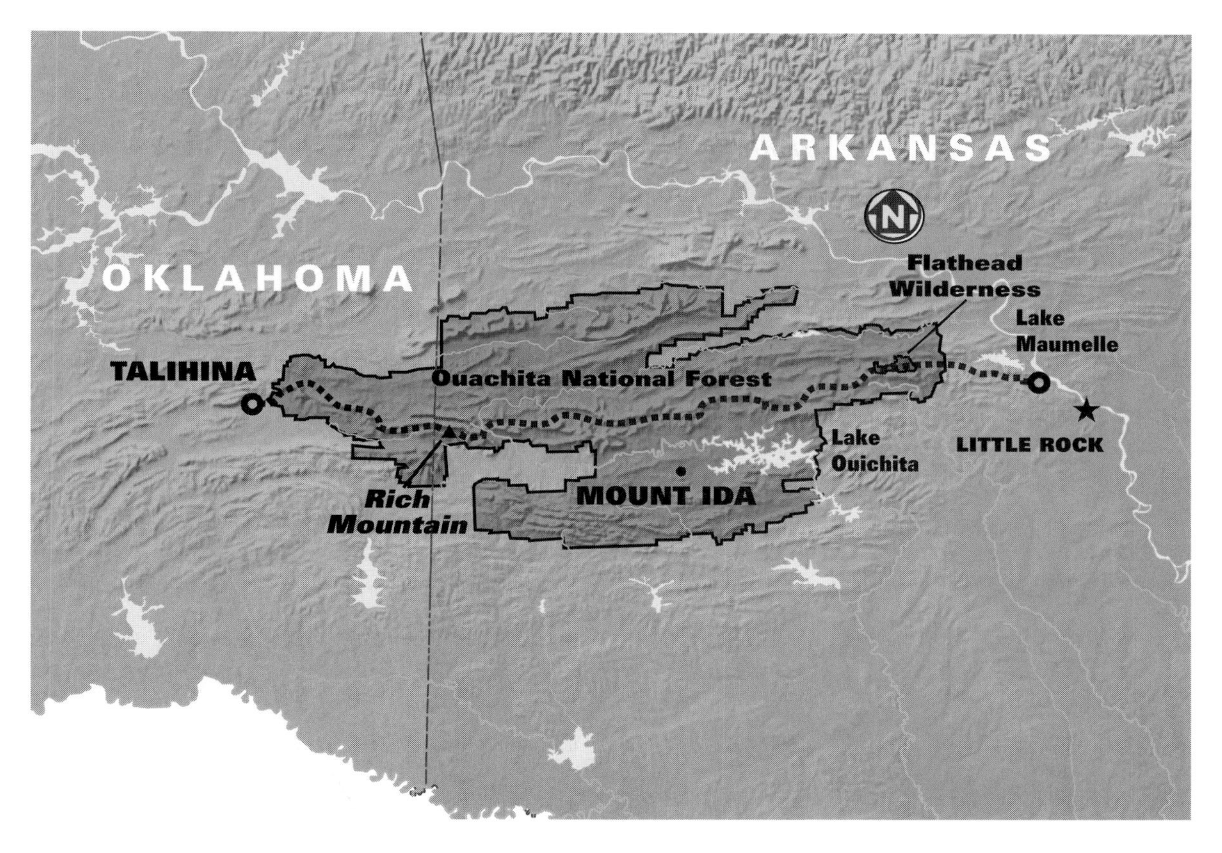

The Ouachita National Recreation Trail (OT), located mostly within the 1.6 million-acre Ouachita (pronounced *wha-shi-tah*) National Forest, is the longest trail in the Oklahoma–Arkansas area, at a stout 225 miles. The OT stretches from Talimena State Park, near Talihina, Oklahoma, to Pinnacle Mountain State Park, near Little Rock, Arkansas. The OT owes its success to the efforts of many, but one man immediately comes to mind: writer and hiker Tim Ernst. Tim describes himself as

a genuine trail nut. Have been for a long time. Not your ordinary peanut variety of nut, but rather more like a cashew or macadamia. Pretty much everything that I do relates in one way or another to trails, to the outdoors or to something similar.

And I believe him. Who else has completed more than 19,000 hours of volunteer trail work? Tim has thru-hiked the OT pushing a measuring wheel and carrying a tape

VITALS

- Expect to cover 14 miles a day
- Expect a thru-hike to take 16 days
- Hiking season: October to May
- Water availability: Seldom
- Resupply opportunities: Seldom
- First year thru-hiked: Circa 1983
- Approximate yearly thru-hikers: Fewer than 30
- Primary contact: Tim Ernst of Cloudland.net

recorder, so a good reason to hike the OT is just to read the ultra-thorough guidebook he produced. Tim has written nine other books about Arkansas hiking, and four of those are books of photography. See, he told you he was a trail nut!

The first person to thru-hike the Ouachita Trail was Jim Rawlins around 1983. Rawlins, a famed outdoors person from North Little Rock, Arkansas, is known as the "Ouachita Trail guru." He also wrote the foreword to the third edition of Tim Ernst's *Ouachita Trail Guide* and is the author of the original guidebook to the OT.

To be honest, when I imagined Arkansas and Oklahoma, I thought of souped-up pickup trucks and four-wheelers, but there is wild land out there to be explored—at least 225 miles of it. In the past, *Backpacker* magazine readers have voted the OT fourth best in signage/trail marking and third best in solitude.

WEATHER

Weather on the Ouachita Trail creates a hiking season that has more in common with that of the Arizona Trail than closer trails of the upper Midwest. But it should be mentioned that winter in the Oklahoma and Arkansas region can be quite cold and flurries may fly when it gets cold enough (but major snowstorms are rare). If you don't like to hike around in near freezing temperatures, it would be best to wait until after February to tackle the OT. However, it is apparent that the absolute worst time of year to be on the OT is summer. Water becomes an issue (see below), the heat alone can be brutal, and there are thunderstorms.

TERRAIN

The OT really comes alive in spring, when you'll find yourself hiking through a kaleidoscope of colorful wildflowers. But the most common features on the two-state OT are short, very steep climbs that crest 2,000 feet in elevation eleven times—

AVERAGE HIGHS AND LOWS IN DEGREES FAHRENHEIT

	JAN	MAR	MAY	JUL	SEPT	NOV
TALIHINA, OK (740 FT.)	30–50	40–65	60–80	70–95	60–85	40–65
LITTLE ROCK, AR (350 FT.)	30–50	45–65	60–80	70–95	65–85	40–60

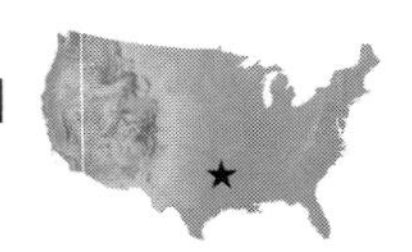

TERRAIN HIGHLIGHTS

- Exposed outcrops
- Many kinds of lichens
- Rock slides
- Oak forests
- Yucca and cacti
- Cypress trees
- Occasional streams
- Summit and ridgeline views

you are in the Ouachita Mountains after all. Thankfully the trail also has many switchbacks. And rocks. Lots of rocks. Rock slides, dubbed "rock glaciers," are giant scree slopes that appear to have recently moved. Many slopes contain rocks that appear to be stationary, covered with colorful lichens.

The western end of the trail is definitely the roughest; at times you are literally waist deep in rocks. To bring the point home, I flipped open Tim's *Ouachita Trail Guide* and picked four different pages at random. I found these descriptions:

- "The trail crosses a dry drain as it runs around the right side of the rocky hill, then begins to drop. It gets a little steep and rocky."
- "The trail crosses several dry drains as it heads on downhill some. There are some big pines here and there, and another rock outcrop."
- "And the sheer rocky hillside is pretty nice, too."
- "In fact, as the trail goes through many rock gardens there really is no trail tread at all—just rocks."

WATER

Finding water is the main concern when it comes to planning a thru-hike. On the OT, *you should be more concerned with getting your hands on water than anything else.* The dry season usually starts in June and lasts until September. It is highly advised that you do not hike the Ouachita Trail during this time. Water can be unavailable for stretches exceeding ten miles, and the temperatures combined with the humidity get very nasty. If you want to hike during this time of the year, pay close attention to any water sources listed in Tim's guide and keep your eyes peeled. You may want to cache water as well.

If you do find water, and think you might not encounter any more for a while, fill up all water containers (including your stomach). If arriving late in the day, it might be best to make that spot your camp for the night so you have cooking water and all the water you can drink. In the morning, leave with a pack full of water. When you start your hike, pay attention to what you see. It may sound obvious but if you come across a stream only every seven miles, there isn't much water out there. If you find streams every mile, you should be all set. The wet season on the OT is generally from late February to May; the months in between the dry and wet season can go either way.

Rocks, rocks, and more rocks greet every hiker's feet on the Ouachita Trail.
(E. SCHLIMMER)

WILDNESS

A problem the OT had in the past was clear-cutting. But with the efforts of local Ouachita Trail hikers, bikers, and even forest service folks, the OT now has a 200-foot corridor on each side of the tread that prohibits the practice. However, just because clear-cuts don't cross the trail anymore does not mean you should not expect to see signs of logging.

There are only two easily accessible resupply points off the trail. Right now the trail has approximately nine Adirondack lean-tos, with more shelters slated for construction. For section hikers there may be a shuttle service available from local outfitters. Mountain bikes are allowed on some portions of the trail, but pack stock is not. You should be by yourself for most of your hike.

WILDLIFE

As far as two-legged animals go, you'll see only those who carry backpacks. You won't see them on motorized vehicles or pack stock; the Ouachita Trail is closed to those users. You won't see many on mountain bikes, either; biking is only allowed on certain sections of the OT.

Four-legged creatures, such as bears, do inhabit the area, as do smaller critters. And you may encounter some non-legged, slithering creatures. This 225-mile trek hosts a wide variety of wildlife, because the terrain and climate can take on characteristics of both desert and temperate environments.

POINTS OF INTEREST

LOW FLYING PLANES

The peak of Rich Mountain has a nice view, probably less appreciated by those aboard any of the fifty planes that have crashed into this mountain or the immedi-

CRITTERS

- Bald eagles
- Black bears
- Lizards
- Rattlesnakes, copperheads, water moccasins
- Slit mouth snail*
- Turkeys

*Listed as an endangered species in Arkansas

DON'T LEAVE HOME WITHOUT IT

AGAIN, WATER AND MORE WATER

As with the Arizona Trail, you'll need to carry plenty of water on the Ouachita Trail, and you'll need to know where the next source is. Additionally, lightweight hikers might want to bite the bullet and carry a water filter. Sure, iodine tablets are plenty sufficient to purify OT waters, but a water filter's intake hose can fit into much tighter spaces than, say, your widemouth drinking bottle. If you stumble upon a trickling rill, a filter can mean the difference between a source of water and a source of frustration.

---

ate area. Located on the Arkansas–Oklahoma line, this 2,600-footer is the highest peak in the Ouachita Mountains and the highest point on the Ouachita Trail.

HALFWAY THERE

Located near the OT's midpoint is Big Brushy Campground, an overnight area that's rarely used (it's near a road). There are a half dozen hiking trails that originate from this spot and some tie into the OT to make loop hikes. On this section of the OT there's enough water in some streams to take a dip.

NOT SO FLAT

Despite its name, the Flatside Wilderness Area has many steep climbs up pinnacles and beautiful ridgelines. This area, on the trail's eastern section, provides nice views.

THIS IS NOT A MIRAGE

Near Pinnacle Mountain State Park, on the extreme east end of the OT, lies Lake Maumelle. The OT travels above the lake's north shore. There are many water sources on this section and short ups and downs, though overall the section is fairly easy to traverse.

In Their Own Words . . .

This 223-mile trail from Talimena State Park in Oklahoma to Pinnacle Mountain State Park near Little Rock, Arkansas, has as many challenges and downright hard places as it has beautiful streams and vistas.

Unlike the Ozark Highlands Trail, which goes up and down all day long, the Ouachita Trail will climb to a hogback ridge, and stay there for hours. So knowing where the water is (or is supposed to be), and when the springs and creeks are dry, can make a hike one to remember, or one you would like to forget!

There is much to see and enjoy on the Ouachita Trail, but there are also real life dangers, and a few "tricky situations," especially for the novice backpacker. For example, there are some months only a fool would get out on the trail.

—Jim Rawlins, "Grandfather of the Ouachita Trail,"
from the *Ouachita Trail Guide* foreword

ozark highlands trail

165 MILES | ARKANSAS

TO GO . . .

- excellent guidebook written by a local
- nice rock formations
- rugged wilderness setting in sections
- abundant waterfalls

OR NOT TO GO?

- steep, rocky climbs
- difficult fords
- summer is blazing hot
- dry sections in summer

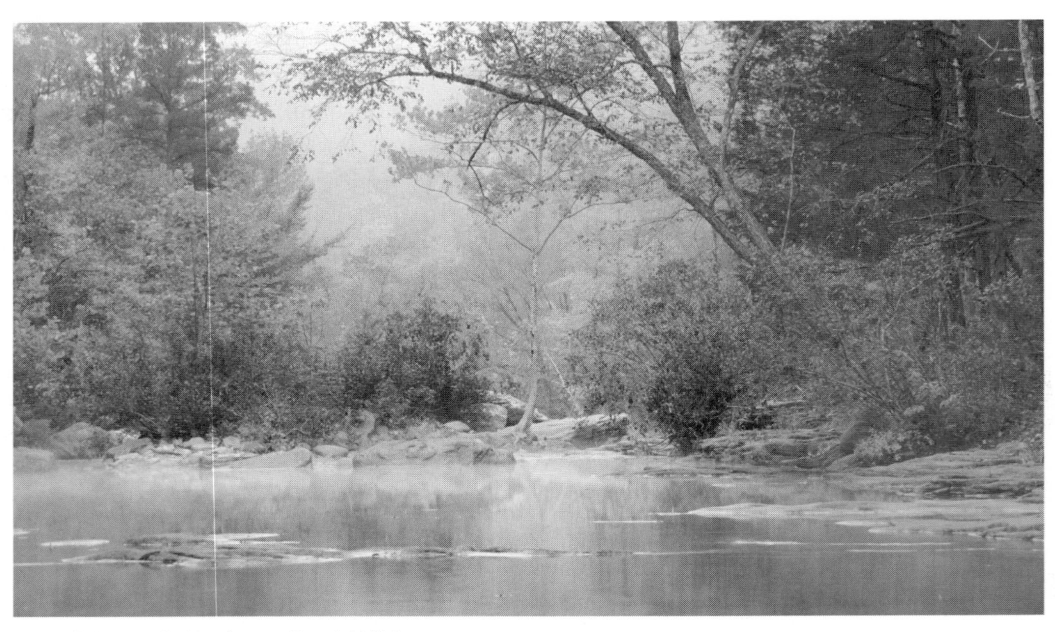

Near Arkansas's Hurricane Creek Wilderness. (RANDY WILSON)

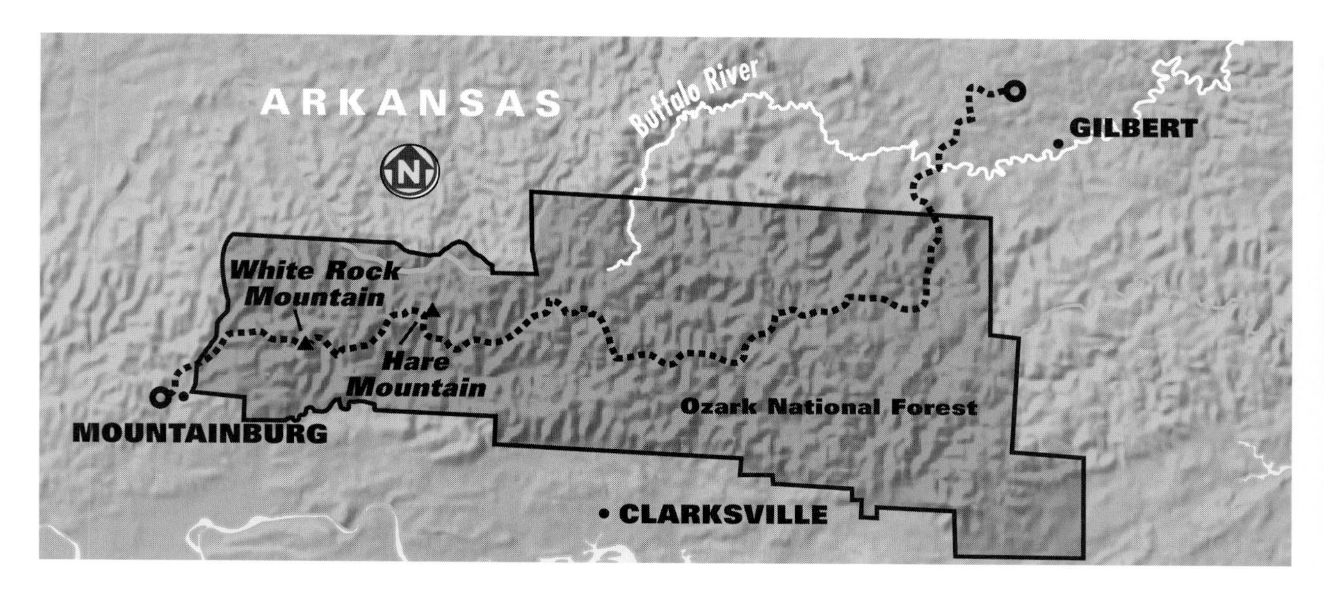

• Towns near or on the trail

O Trail terminus ▪▪▪▪▪▪▪ Trail route

The Ozark Highlands Trail (OHT) has a bit in common with its sister trail to the south, the Ouachita Trail. Both offer rocky hiking among the hills and views of Arkansas. Both will keep a southern hiker occupied for weeks on end. And both trails have a good friend in Tim Ernst. Tim is back at it again! He's hiked, measured, and written about the entire length of this trail, too. Tim has traversed the OHT twice with a measuring wheel and at least once with a tape recorder to give us descriptions from nearly every step of the way. The guide is also a journey through the culture of Arkansas and an introduction to the characters of the Ozark Highlands Trail. As you travel through Frog Bayou Creek, the Ben Hur Trailhead, Greasy Creek, and over Potato Knob, you'll get to know Carl "The Wildman" Ownbey, James Boomer, and Dave Gasche, among others, in stories involving death, bear attacks, deer hunts, and jugs of whiskey.

If you liked the Ouachita Trail but thought it was a bit too long, maybe the Ozark Highlands Trail is a better option. From its western terminus near the town of Mountainburg to its eastern point on the Buffalo River near Gilbert, this National Recreational Trail currently stretches 165 miles. But, the trail isn't done yet. It's actually slated to travel down the Buffalo River for a good stretch then connect with the Ozark Trail. Eventually you'll be able to hike all the way to St. Louis, making a thousand-mile route when complete. In a past issue of *Backpacker* magazine, readers rated the OHT the number one trail in the United States.

And who would you guess was the first person to thru-hike the Ozark Highlands Trail? That's right, Tim Ernst.

VITALS

- > Expect to cover 12 miles a day
- > Expect a thru-hike to take 14 days
- > Hiking season: October to May
- > Water availability: Frequent
- > Resupply opportunities: Frequent
- > First year thru-hiked: 1984
- > Approximate yearly thru-hikers: Fewer than 40
- > Primary contact: Ozark Highlands Trail Association

You can give me the nod for [thru-hiking] the Ozark Highlands Trail in 1984. That is when we finished the very last part of the existing trail. I'd done many previous thru-hikes of all that had been completed before that, even doing the entire route in 1975 from end to end before a foot of trail was built.

WEATHER

The weather on the Ozark Highlands Trail is similar to that on the Ouachita Trail; they're only about seventy miles apart. You can hike the OHT year-round because there is no significant snow on the trail except in an odd snowstorm. Temperatures in the middle of winter can drop to 10° at night, but if you can tolerate the cold, the OHT is an excellent option. Plus, you probably won't see any other hikers. Spring is the most inviting time to go, when there is lots of water, and spring blooms are coming out to greet the sun. The worst time is July, August, and September. Temperatures reach the nineties, and there is plenty of humidity to match. The OHT has a lot of streams crossing it, but many of them run seasonally. If hiking in summer, don't expect to make great progress, and be ready to carry about a gallon of water to make sure you can make it to the next water source.

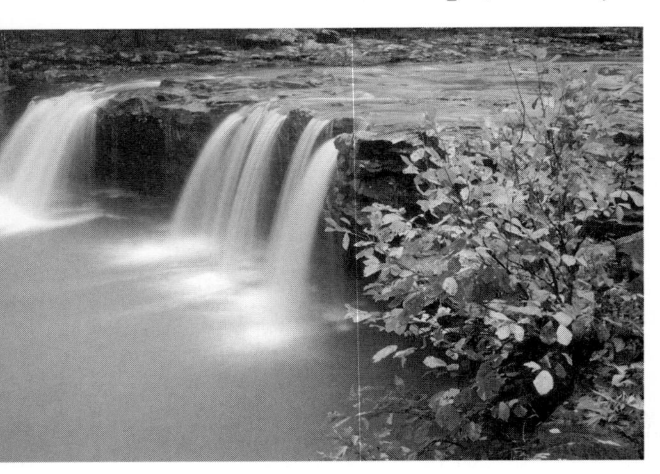

Unlike the Ouachita Trail to the south, the more northern Ozark Highlands Trail has an abundant supply of water; as evidenced by Falling Water Creek in the Richland Creek area. (RANDY WILSON)

TERRAIN

Don't worry, the Ozark Highlands Trail isn't quite as rough as the Ouachita Trail, and it's even more beautiful. Now, I didn't say it wasn't rough. It is rough. The OHT is characterized by rocky, short, steep climbs, but there are lots of switchbacks to help you along. The elevation reaches beyond 2,000 feet seven times, and there are many climbs exceeding 800 vertical feet, with a few exceeding 1,000 feet. The biggest climb is 1,500 vertical feet. The majority of tread consists of singletrack hiking trail, and

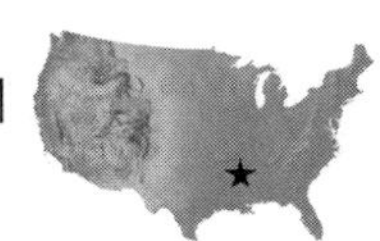

AVERAGE HIGHS AND LOWS IN DEGREES FAHRENHEIT	JAN	MAR	MAY	JUL	SEPT	NOV
MOUNTAINBURG, AR (740 FT.)	25–50	40–70	55–80	65–95	60–90	40–65
GILBERT, AR (600 FT.)	25–50	35–65	55–80	65–85	55–85	35–65

there are also forest service roads, all-terrain-vehicle paths, and railroad beds to pass over. Nearly the entire route is on U.S. Forest Service land, and the OHT has a protective 400-foot corridor (200 feet on each side of the tread), just like the Ouachita Trail, to ensure that logging will not cross the path. This doesn't mean that you won't see some signs of human meddling, however.

The biggest attraction of the OHT is its many waterfalls. You'll see a dozen falls in just a few days of hiking—another reason why spring is so nice here. The falls are spectacular, but you'll reach them at a price. Currently there are few footbridges on the Ozark Highlands Trail, so you'll have many fords to deal with. At least one person has died while hiking the OHT; he drowned in a stream he was attempting to ford. Use caution during stream fords. If you cannot cross safely, head upstream to check things out. In rare circumstances, you may have to wait it out. I flipped open a few random pages in Tim's *Ozark Highlands Trail Guide*, this time looking for mentions of streams and waterfalls.

- "[The trail] remains on the road, crossing a small creek with a class A waterfall [less than five feet tall]."
- "Unless you want to spend a lot of time looking around for a better crossing, you will normally have to cross here wet."
- "At this writing, there is a large tree across the creek that will get you to the other side just fine."
- "Off to the right is a nice falls and pool, which then spills over a ledge for a class D falls [more than fifteen feet tall]."

WATER

Despite all the waterfalls, in late summer you can expect to encounter waterless sections up to fifteen miles in length. That's a long way when you're climbing and descending rocky slopes all day. You could cache water ahead of time, but you can probably get away with just paying attention to your map and stocking up at all water

TERRAIN HIGHLIGHTS

- > Waterfalls
- > Oak forests
- > House-size boulders
- > Rocky climbs
- > Seasonal streams
- > Flat-topped peaks
- > Rock bluffs

DON'T LEAVE HOME WITHOUT IT

MODESTY

If you encounter a guy that looks like a "trail nut," it might be Tim Ernst—the hardest working volunteer on the Ozark Highlands Trail (and often the hardest working volunteer in the entire United States). You ain't got squat on Tim, so don't talk smack.

points. You'll pass a few ponds and swamps, but for the most part you'll be getting your daily water out of streams. At least two of the campgrounds you walk through have had their wells shut down because the water in them has become unpotable.

WILDNESS

The OHT is a popular trail. There is more interest in the Ozark Highlands Trail than the Ouachita Trail, but you won't be crowded on either hike. An aspect that improves this trail's wildness is that you can camp nearly anywhere on forest service land if you're at least 200 feet from water and trails. This gives you a chance to camp in beautiful pristine spots each night—if you are an LNT-savvy camper. If you're not experienced, it would be best to stay at any of the established backcountry sites or in one of the eight campgrounds you'll pass. The OHT does not have consistent bridging as of this writing (and I hope none in the future). This makes the trip all the wilder. But, you will encounter human-made features such as forest service roads, homestead sites, gas wells, and pipelines.

You need to resupply only once on this thru-hike, which means you can spend more time hiking and less time shopping. The best place to resupply is in the town of Ozone, located about half way along the OHT. Ozone's general store burned down recently, so you'll have to rely on the town post office. Another resupply opportunity is in the nearby town of Pelsor (at mile 125 if you're hiking from west to east). Pelsor, about a mile south of the trail, has a post office and a store.

WILDLIFE

Critters and a couple of other hikers will be your only partners on the Ozark Highlands Trail. Some critters you may not look forward to sharing your time with, though, are the mosquitoes, chiggers, and other biting bugs that come out in force around May. Heading into the woods of Arkansas beyond July would not be bad bugwise, but then you run into the heat of summer. Just another reason to hike in the cooler months.

CRITTERS

- Bald eagles
- Beavers
- Black bears
- Copperheads, rattlesnakes, and water moccasins
- Coyotes
- Elk
- Lizards
- Turkeys

POINTS OF INTEREST

VAN'S

On the western end of the trail is Van's Crevasse, home to caves, gigantic boulders, and four waterfalls that exceed fifteen feet in height.

FROM THE HORSE'S MOUTH

Tim Ernst has called White Rock Mountain "one of the prettiest areas in the state." Near the OHT's western terminus, this mountain features the two-mile White Rock Rim Loop that follows the high bluffs that circle its peak.

LAND OF SPIRITS

At Spirits Creek, near White Rock Mountain, you'll find large rock slabs, boulders, bluffs, waterfalls, and pools. A note on the bluffs: some are actually closed from dusk to dawn because people have fallen off the edge and died. Please be careful.

OHT HIGHPOINT

At 2,380 feet, Hare Mountain is the highest point on the OHT and it offers a view of the highest point in Arkansas (Magazine Mountain, 2,753 feet). On Hare Mountain's flat top you'll find signs of summit farming, including an 800-foot-long rock wall built during the pioneer era. Within a mile of the summit is a campsite and well. Use the bear pole to hang your food, please. Hare Mountain is located 40 miles east of the western terminus.

KODAK MOMENT

At Marinoni Scenic Area (55 miles east of the western terminus) you'll find a natural rock bridge where wild azaleas, magnolia trees, bluffs, and waterfalls will amaze you.

In Their Own Words . . .

Arkansas is blessed with extraordinary natural resources: beautiful mountains and forests, clean water, and abundant wildlife. But one of the most splendid assets in our state is the one-million-acre Ozark National Forest, created by President Theodore Roosevelt in 1908.

It is no exaggeration to say that the Ozark Highlands Trail, which runs 165 miles through the heart of the Forest, is one of the great scenic hiking trails in America. The vistas from White Rock Mountain, the waterfalls, and the many creeks and campgrounds make hiking the Ozarks one of the greatest experiences going.

In addition to appreciating the scenery, you will also notice that the trails you'll travel are unusually well maintained. We in Arkansas take great pride in our natural resources, and are committed to maintaining them as God surely intended.

—Dale Bumpers, former Arkansas governor and United States senator,
from the *Ozark Highlands Trail Guide* foreword

river-to-river trail

170 MILES | ILLINOIS

TO GO . . .

- arguably the best Midwest hiking
- opportunities for rock climbing and caving
- hiker traffic is low

OR NOT TO GO?

- shared horse route
- not as expansive or wild as many other long trails

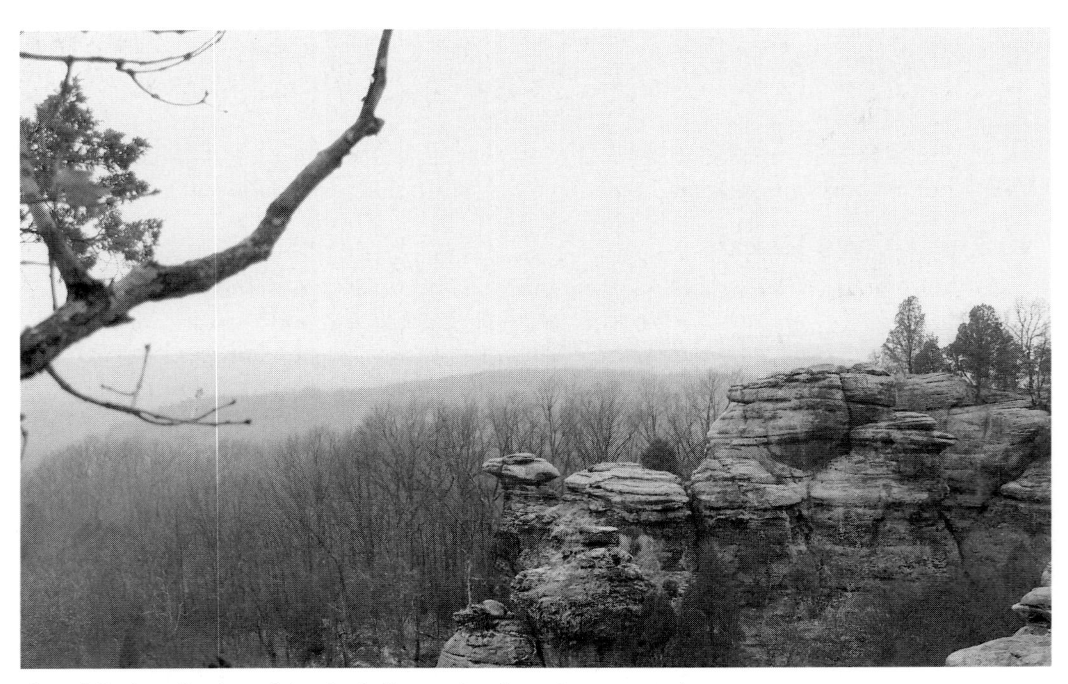

Camel Rock at Garden of the Gods Recreation Area. (ERIC JOHNSON)

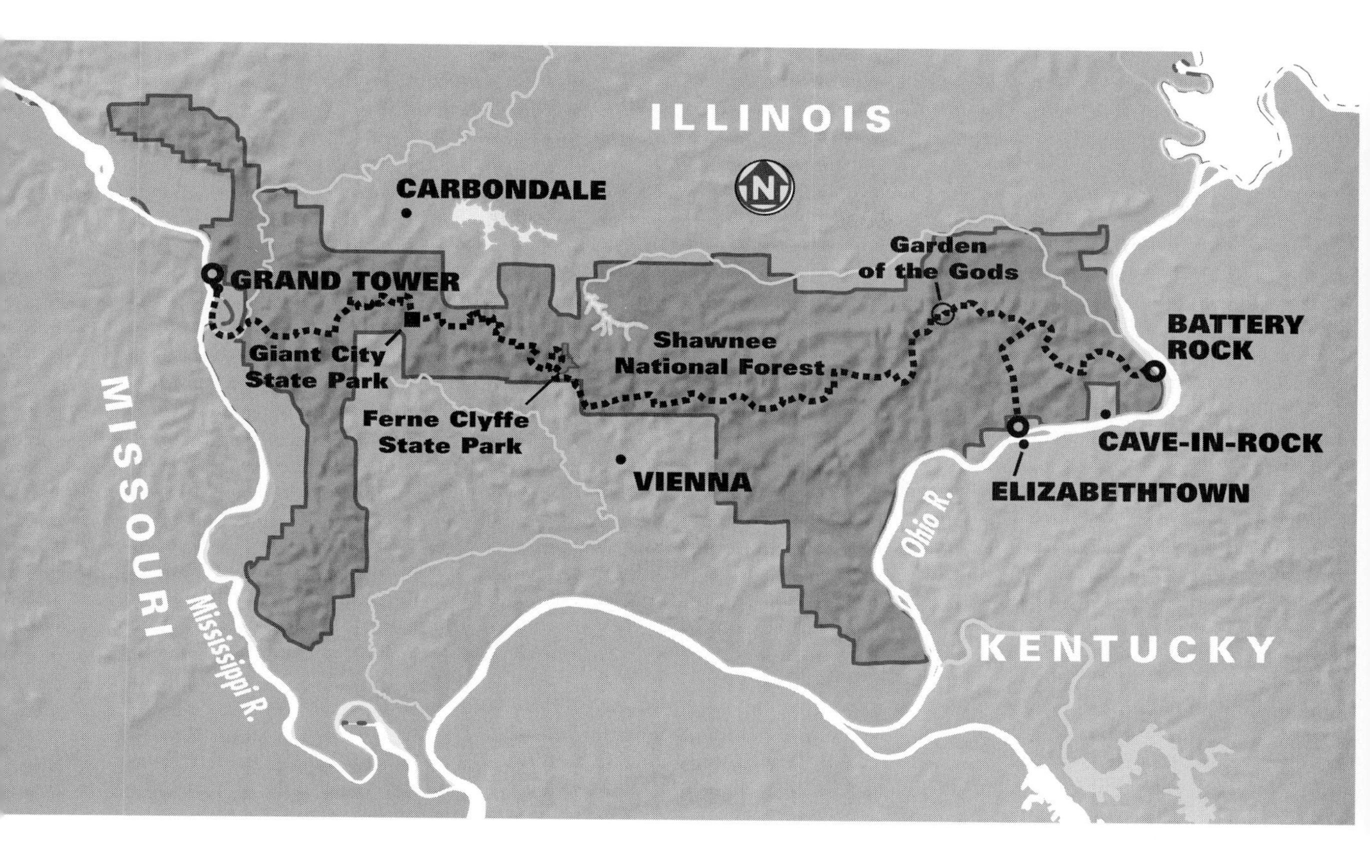

● Towns near or on the trail ■ State park
○ Trail terminus ▪▪▪▪▪▪▪ Trail route

As a section of the much longer American Discovery Trail, the River-to-River Trail (RRT) travels through the Shawnee Forest of Illinois, from the Ohio River in the east to the Mississippi River in the west. "Illinois hiking—isn't that one of those oxymorons?" Bite your tongue. There's a lot for the backpacker to see in this state. The path meanders through a diverse landscape complete with large mammals, interesting geological formations, and different types of vegetation. It can be hiked almost year-round—if you like to hike when it's pretty hot or fairly cold. The trail is nearly all contained within the 280,000-acre Shawnee National Forest, so there should be no concern about finding trails away from urbanized terrain. The 170-mile figure is kind of rough (I came across figures of 146 miles and 160 miles, too), because River-to-River Trail improvements are taking place often.

WEATHER

The weather you'll encounter mostly depends on when you decide to quit your job and thru-hike the River-to-River Trail. The RRT can be hiked nearly year-round, because this part of Illinois has somewhat mild winters. Fall is certainly the best time to hike here, with the colors coming out, the bugs dying off, and crisp, cool nights to put you to sleep. Snow can fall in winter, but it's generally not enough to warrant snowshoes or skis. Daytime highs in winter may reach the upper forties, with subfreezing temperatures arriving after sunset. During the summer, the most uncomfortable month is August, when temperatures can reach 90°, with some humidity thrown in just to make it feel a little hotter. Springtime can be fairly wet if there was a recent good dump of snow or heavy rain.

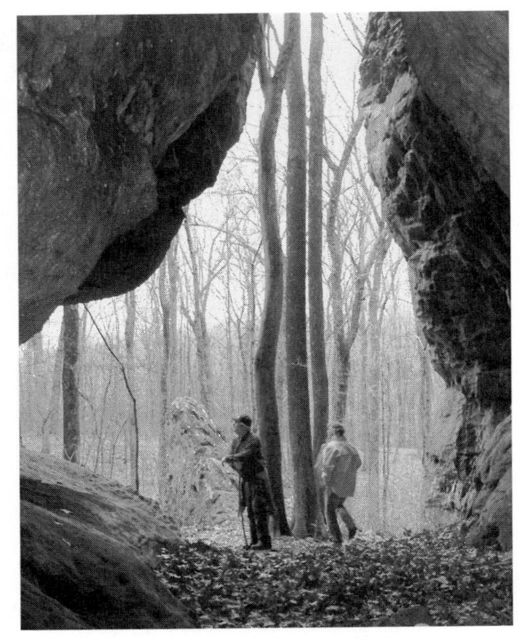

The River-to-River Trail is known for its many caves, shelter bluffs, and rock clefts. *(ERIC JOHNSON)*

TERRAIN

Just reading about the terrain of the River-to-River Trail will make you seriously consider this path for your long-distance hike. Elevations are not characterized by long, grinding climbs, although the RRT does have several short, steep climbs to throw at a hiker. Overall, the terrain can be regarded as rugged, with muddy spots and a plethora of rocks that can slow your pace to one mile per hour. However, this pace is fine for viewing the hardwoods blazing with color in fall and for gazing at the geological formations, which include tall cliffs and deep caves. Land this wild is a rare commodity in this part of the country. As such, southern Illinois sells itself as a unique Midwest destination.

WATER

If you hike the RRT during the colder months of the year, water will be more difficult to find than between March and June. Nearly all campsites and campgrounds on the RRT have a water source that is seasonal, and there are a good

AVERAGE HIGHS AND LOWS IN DEGREES FAHRENHEIT

	JAN	MAR	MAY	JUL	SEPT	NOV
CAVE IN ROCK, IL (400 FT.)	20–40	35–60	50–75	65–90	55–80	35–60
GRAND TOWER, IL (360 FT.)	25–40	40–60	55–80	70–90	60–85	40–60

TERRAIN HIGHLIGHTS

- Freshwater streams
- Cave systems
- Oak and beech forests
- Rocky outcrops
- Meadows
- Escarpments
- Waterfalls
- Hollows

number of streams, ponds, and lakes (and some swamps if you're in a pinch), within the national forest. On each end are the huge aforementioned rivers, too. Expect to find water a couple of times through each day of hiking, but in mid- to late summer it would be wise to fill up at each source, no matter how small.

WILDNESS

If your intent is to hang out with large mammals in expansive and dramatic areas, then, of the twenty-five trails in this guide, I would not recommend the River-to-River Trail above others. This book is designed to be used regionally, so backpackers from nearby St. Louis, Evansville, and Kansas City will want to pack up their things and head for the RRT. Conversely, prospective long-distance hikers from Montpelier, Vermont, Bozeman, Montana, or Millinocket, Maine, will probably not spend the time and money to travel to an area that could be considered marginal to their own backyards. This means there are not many hikers on the RRT.

Other good news is that the River-to-River Trail is a young, somewhat overlooked route, with no recorded thru-hikes prior to the early 1990s. The crowd factor on this long path is usually low, and the best way to avoid any potential crowds would be to inquire about scheduled group hiking and horse packing trips. Organized hiking clubs in the area can be of help digging up this usage information. The trail is shared with horses, but mountain bikes are not allowed on most parts of the trail. All-terrain vehicles are not allowed anywhere inside the national forest except with a special-use permit. Dogs are allowed on national forest lands but should be kept on a leash, especially in camping areas. Over your 170-mile journey, you'll come across thirty established places to camp, and most have a seasonal water source. Resupplying on the RRT will not be as challenging as hiking its rough terrain. Starting from Battery Rock (the eastern terminus near the town of Cave in Rock) you will

VITALS

- Expect to cover 15 miles a day
- Expect a thru-hike to take 11 days
- Hiking season: March to November
- Water availability: Frequent
- Resupply opportunities: Frequent
- First year thru-hiked: Early 1990s
- Approximate yearly thru-hikers: Fewer than 30
- Primary contact: River-to-River Trail Society

CRITTERS

- Bluebirds, pileated woodpeckers, northern flicker, northern parvla, yellow-throated and Cerulean warblers, Acadian flycatchers
- Bobcats
- Copperheads and rattlesnakes
- Coyotes
- Eastern cottontails, swamp rabbits
- Grouse
- Wild hogs

pass near or directly through the towns of Herod, Eddyville, Ozark, Goreville, Makanda, Alto Pass, and Grand Tower (on the western terminus). It should be mentioned that these towns are very small though. Out of the eight towns listed above, six of them were not even listed in my road atlas's population section. The two towns that were listed—Goreville and Grand Tower—have only 940 and 620 people, respectively. However, every one of the above towns has a post office.

WILDLIFE

Upon learning that Illinois is ranked nearly last out of the fifty states when it comes to undeveloped lands remaining, you may think this place would be home only to the alley cat, junkyard dog, or sewer rat. But Shawnee National Forest has its share of wild residents. If you had the choice of traveling anywhere in the United States on your next backpacking trip, and viewing wildlife was high on your wish list, yes, you would find places with bigger and "better" animals. But for the Midwest hiker, the RRT has an ample selection of wildlife.

POINTS OF INTEREST

HEAVENLY HIKING

Garden of the Gods Wilderness Area is on the trail's eastern portion and offers your best bet for solitude, in addition to unique rock formations with names such as Camel Rock, Noah's Arc, and Mushroom Rock. This was ranked the best backpacking spot in Illinois according to the April 2004 issue of *Backpacker* magazine.

ROCK CLIMBING

With all the rocky outcrops on the RRT, you're bound to see people hanging off them. Join them in places such as Fernclyffe State Park, midway along the trail.

GORGEOUS

The 1,000-acre Panther Den Wilderness Area may be the smallest of the seven Wilderness Areas the RRT passes through, but here you'll find sandstone cliffs, creeks, rolling hills, white-tailed deer and maybe even a bobcat or black bear. Despite its name, you won't be seeing any panthers. The so-called Panther Den is actually a 70-foot-deep canyon near the center of the wilderness area.

DON'T LEAVE HOME WITHOUT IT

AN OPEN MIND

No one, and I mean no one, imagines taking their annual hiking trip through Illinois. However, you'd love the River-to-River Trail's features if you could shake your preconceptions. Illinois, particularly southern Illinois, has much more to offer than what you've seen from its highways. It's not all corn and soybeans down there.

In Their Own Words . . .

A feature of interest is that this area is a transition zone for many species of plants and animals. The division between north and south and even east to west overlaps to a considerable degree, so it is possible to see an eastern and western bluebird, a northern and southern garter snake, blue herons, cypress swamps, and mosses and lichens that have adapted from the ice age. Because trail walking is quieter than walking on leaves, it is possible to walk up on wildlife before either knows of the others' presence. Remember to bring a camera! There are poisonous snakes, both copperheads and rattlesnakes. I have never seen a poisonous snake on the trail, nor have there been any reports of hikers seeing them or being bothered. There are reports of bobcats and other unsubstantiated reports of cougars, but undoubtedly you will never be bothered by these.

To honor the spirit of those who first immigrated to Illinois, the guide follows an east to west description. It is interesting to consider the hopes and dreams of those people as they viewed the new land and began the search for their place in this wilderness. We can still see some of the beautiful vistas and gorgeous valleys of those early days, and in some small way compare our efforts with theirs. Perhaps as we notice that all of the most beautiful places have wagon roads to them, we will realize that they too shared a spiritual need for the power of such beauty.

—John O'Dell, River-to-River Trail Society president, author of *The River-to-River Trail Guide*

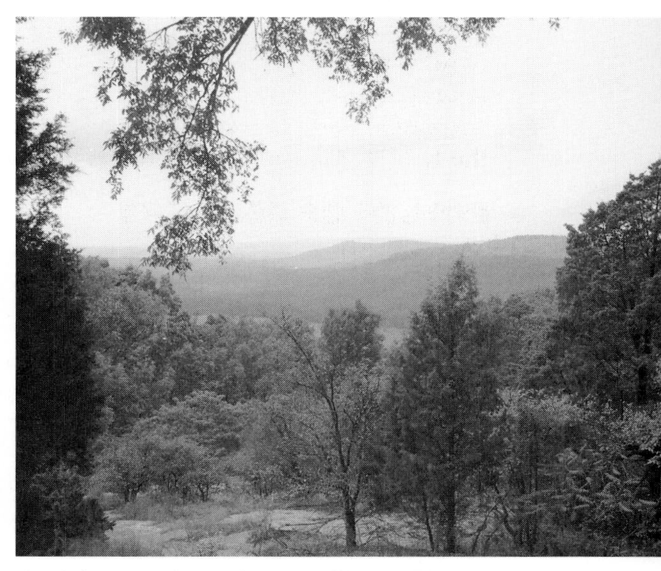

A brief 100-yard spur from the River-to-River Trail will take you to this view from atop High Knob. (ERIC JOHNSON)

shore-to-shore trail

220 MILES | MICHIGAN

TO GO . . .

- assortment of mammals
- unique shore-to-shore route from one Great Lake to another
- possible thru-ski route
- 130 miles of SST side trails to be explored

OR NOT TO GO?

- times of heavy horse traffic
- not a singletrack path overall
- hiker-oriented guidebook unavailable
- not a true wilderness setting in certain sections

Many riders and hikers regard this eastern stretch along the gorgeous high banks of the Au Sable River to be the most beautiful part of the Shore-to-Shore Trail. (KATIE FRITZLER)

MACKINAW CITY
Lake Huron
Lake Michigan
MICHIGAN
N
EMPIRE
SCHECKS
GRAYLING
Huron National
Forest
LUZERNE
OSCODA
Au Sable River
CADILLAC
Towns near or on the trail
Trail terminus
Trail route
Side trails

VITALS

- Expect to cover 17 miles a day
- Expect a thru-hike to take 13 days
- Hiking season: April to October
- Water availability: Frequent
- Resupply opportunities: Frequent
- First year thru-ridden: 1964
- First year thru-hiked: Unknown
- Approximate yearly thru-hikers: Fewer than 20
- Primary contact: Michigan Trail Riders Association

The Shore-to-Shore Trail (SST) in Michigan exists thanks to our friends the equestrians. The Michigan Trail Riders Association is the main group that was dedicated to the birth of, and now the maintenance of, this 220-mile path that winds its way across "the mitten" of Michigan. The western terminus is the shore of Lake Michigan at the town of Empire; the eastern end is on the shore of Lake Huron, near Oscoda. The Shore-to-Shore Trail basically makes a beeline across the state, but near the trail's midpoint there's a side trail that heads north for eighty-five miles, and there is another arm nearby that heads south for forty-five miles. Part of the SST is overrun by the 4,200-mile North Country National Scenic Trail for a short distance north of the town of Kalkaska. Overall, the SST is not geared toward hikers as strongly as most other trails in this guide, but it's still a nice path with a helpful organization that oversees the trail.

Help from the Michigan Department of Natural Resources and the U.S. Forest Service contributed greatly to this trail's completion in 1964. A group of horse riders celebrated the completion of this trail by executing the first end-to-end ride, held that same year.

WEATHER

When it comes to cold weather, the Shore-to-Shore Trail (SST) is not mild mannered even when compared to the higher Superior Hiking Trail to the north or the trails of the Northeast. However, as opposed to the SST, many trails in the Northeast are inaccessible in winter even if you own a good pair of snowshoes. Winter certainly does arrive here in Michigan, and to help you fight cabin fever the SST is one of the few trails in this guide that is an option for long-distance skiers during fair snow years. A clue to the reliability of snowfall each season is that six downhill ski areas are located in the 150-mile-wide, 30-mile-deep band of land between the towns of Empire and Oscoda. It is certainly not impossible to cross-country ski the Shore-to-

AVERAGE HIGHS AND LOWS IN DEGREES FAHRENHEIT

	JAN	MAR	MAY	JUL	SEPT	NOV
EMPIRE, MI (620 FT.)	15–30	20–40	40–70	60–80	50–70	30–45
OSCODA, MI (540 FT.)	15–30	25–40	45–65	60–80	50–70	30–45

TERRAIN HIGHLIGHTS

- > Fall foliage
- > Rural settlements
- > River valleys
- > Great Lakes shorelines
- > Freshwater ponds
- > Swamps
- > Moderate hill climbing

Shore Trail, because the tread is wide and the climbing is usually modest. A thru-ski of this path is not a walk in the park, however.

Located close to many of the Great Lakes, the SST is subject to lake effect snow, wind, and fluctuating temperatures miles from the shores of Lake Michigan and Lake Huron. At its midpoint, the SST is only approximately seventy-five miles from either lake. Don't expect to start an SST thru-hike until April. You should plan on completing your hike prior to the first day in November.

TERRAIN

The daily mileage that can be averaged across this 220-mile adventure may seem high, but the tread is very clean and there are no major climbs. The tread consists mostly of county roads, woods trails in river valleys, and wide jeep trails, with a durable surface of sand, compacted soil, hardpan, or mud. You'll travel through beautiful hardwood and conifer forests. The most challenging parts of the SST are the river crossings. Most major drainages do have bridges, but some do not. After heavy rains you may have to detour around once mild-mannered streams that have become dangerous torrents. Use your own judgment when facing obstacles, and remember that it's always best to err on the safe side when attempting a ford.

WATER

You may expect a great amount of water on a peninsula that juts out between two Great Lakes, and, well, you'd be correct. The SST crosses all types of water sources, including major river systems, small streams, ponds, and a couple of swamps (I'm especially apprehensive to be in Mayhem Swamp during bug season). The trail does head through some low, wet areas, but the Michigan Trail Riders Association has done a good job hardening and elevating the tread or completing trail relocations to help keep your feet dry and help protect fragile areas. Keep in mind that after heavy rains some unbridged large drainages may have to be detoured. Overall, you'll be

DON'T LEAVE HOME WITHOUT IT

SUGAR CUBES (NOT BJORK'S BAND)

Regarded equally as a hiking trail and horse-riding trail, you may want to get on the good side of all those equestrians. Bring some yummy snacks for the horses. Constantly say "dagnabit," "howdy," "what in tarnation?" and "shucks" to help fit in, too.

Light fog hangs over Au Sable River at this crossing near South Branch Trail Camp. (AL AND KATIE FRITZLER)

able to find ample water daily. Just keep an eye out for it, and be sure to purify all water, because this trail is so popular with horse riders. Most campsites have a reliable water source in addition to a latrine.

WILDNESS

The Shore-to-Shore Trail may satisfy all but hikers in search of the wildest terrain. Overall, the trail is more of a frontcountry setting than a deep wilderness setting, but the most civilization you'll find end to end is small towns, suburban residential areas, and twelve established campgrounds. This proximity to populated areas makes resupply runs easy if you need them.

It's important to note the horse packing trips. It is highly recommended that you do not thru-hike during the horse riding times listed below. The Michigan Trail Riders Association (MTRA) holds group rides during these periods. Contact the MTRA for specific dates. The numbers of equestrians expected to attend each ride are given as well.

Blossom Ride in May: 90 to 100 riders
First June ride: 100 to 150 riders
Second June ride: 200 to 240 riders
September ride: 200 to 240 riders
October ride: 100 riders

Needless to say, you probably won't find much solitude on these dates, and some of

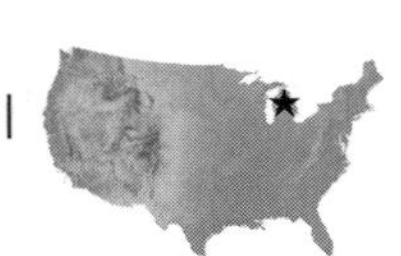

the rides run from shore to shore. The MTRA is helpful to hikers as well as horse riders. Drop them a note to get the full scoop.

On the Shore-to-Shore Trail, it's important to have a multiple-use-friendly mind-set. Mountain bikers do ride sections of the SST, though they are not allowed on most parts. Day hikers tackle the most scenic sections, including the Au Sable River valley and remote sections in the Huron National Forest. Riders can be found just about anywhere, especially during the event rides. When encountering a horse, use basic hiker-horse safety measures. First, make sure the horse rider sees you. Next, step to the lower side of the trail and give the horse and rider a gentle, friendly hello. Try to stay relatively still until the rider and horse pass, then be on your way again. Remember that hikers yield to horses; mountain bikers yield to hikers and horses.

If you see a trail user misbehaving, I encourage you to report this to a representative of the piece of land you are on, be it private, state, or federal. In my travels, I've been plowed over or nearly plowed over by skiers, hikers, horse riders, mountain bikers, and power boaters. When someone doesn't recreate responsibly and puts your safety in jeopardy, be sure to give them "a good dressing-down"—tell them to cut it out! In many cases, offenders are simply ignorant of their unsafe habits. If they knowingly behave unsafely, I give you permission to forcibly whack these people in the shins with a stout stick. (Of course, my permission might not hold much sway with local juries.)

WILDLIFE

I went to Michigan once to visit my very normal, good-natured sister, whom I love. I hated that visit. It was disturbing. It was the carbon-copy suburbs. It was . . . Detroit. I vowed to never go back. But after decompressing from my visit and researching the northern part of Michigan and the Shore-to-Shore Trail, I would consider heading back there for a long-distance hike (not Detroit, but Michigan in general). My initial visit to Michigan was like heading to Little Rock and vowing never to hike the Ozark Highlands Trail, or relaxing in the slums of Boston and refusing to hear of the Metacomet-Monadnock Trail. I kept an open mind about each trail I found during my initial search for long-distance paths, and it paid off in the end. The Shore-to-Shore Trail is a pretty nice path.

In addition to pleasant temperatures, gentle terrain, and a feeling of moderate wildness, the SST is home to abundant wildlife. The only critter that can hurt

CRITTERS

- Black bears
- Coyotes
- Elk
- Horses and riders
- Kirkland warbler (rare)
- Massasauga rattlesnake
- Snowshoe hares
- Wild turkeys

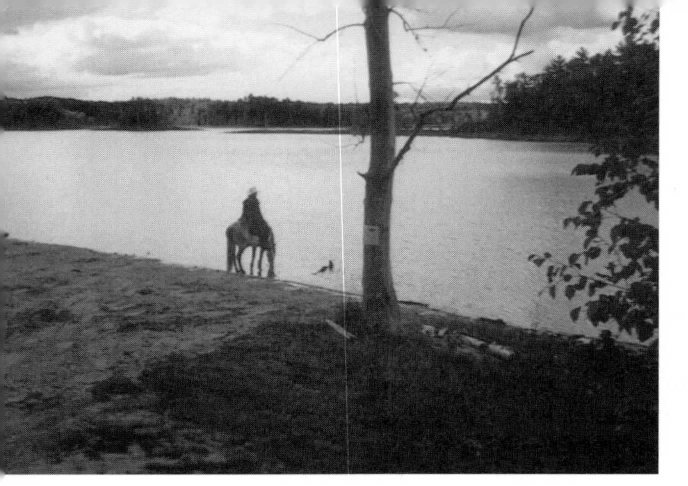

The Shore-to-Shore Trail exists thanks to the steadfast efforts of the Michigan Trail Riders Association. With Lake Huron and Lake Michigan marking its endpoints, and smaller bodies in between, the 220-mile Shore-to-Shore Trail may challenge the assumption that you can lead a horse to water, but you can't make him drink. (AL AND KATIE FRITZLER)

you is the Massasauga rattlesnake, but what are the chances of having a bad run-in? Very slim.

POINTS OF INTEREST

LAKE HURON

Out of the five Great Lakes of Canada and the United States, Huron is ranked second largest concerning surface area. In this size category it is ranked fifth largest freshwater lake in the world. The lake contains the two largest bays of the Great Lakes—Saginaw Bay (just south of the SST's eastern terminus) and Georgian Bay (nearly enclosed by the shores of Ontario). These bays are so enormous that if Georgian Bay was counted as a lake it would make the list of twenty largest lakes on Earth. Lake Huron has the most shoreline of any Great Lake since it has more than 25,000 islands. One such island—Manitoulin Island—is the largest freshwater island on the planet. As with other great lakes, Lake Huron has brought down many ships; five lake-bottom preserves and an Ontario national park safeguard some of the most important sites. The lake's maximum depth reaches approximately 750 feet while the surface elevation holds at nearly 580 feet above sea level. Because Lake Huron and Lake Michigan meet each other in the Straits of Mackinac they are, hydrologically speaking, one large lake.

ON THE BOARDWALK

Positioned over a large swamp, the Luzerne Boardwalk is a wooden walkway a thousand feet long and six feet wide, which includes a sixty-foot bridge span. Located only a mile from downtown Luzerne, it's a nice area for birding and relaxing.

RIVER WALKING

The Au Sable River valley in the Huron National Forest is particularly beautiful. Indeed, it is a designated National Scenic River. At times, the SST travels on sand and stone banks high above the water below.

LAKE MICHIGAN

Lake Superior and Lake Huron are bigger than Lake Michigan, but Lake Michigan is still a monster in its own right, ranking as the sixth largest freshwater lake in

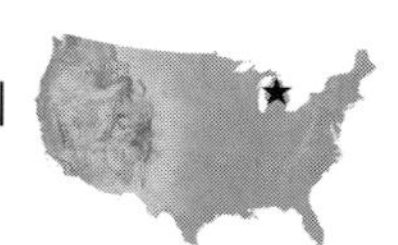

the world in terms of surface area. Millions of people visit the lake yearly, particularly the shorelines near the western terminus of the SST. Here you will find the largest freshwater sand dunes in the world. Lake Michigan's deepest point is 925 feet. This lake rests 580 feet above sea level. Samuel de Champlain, the French explorer for whom Lake Champlain is named, called Lake Michigan *Grand Lac*—just one of its many names. The French had also dubbed Lake Michigan the Lake of the Stinking Water (quite the opposite of Lake Huron's "freshwater sea" moniker), Lake of the Puants, and possibly Lake of the Pauns. (The Winnebago Indians that lived in this area were called the Pauns by French explorers.)

In Their Own Words . . .

There are a lot of different obstacles along the trail. Some of the trail goes through residential areas. There are some busy road crossings. Parts are along dirt roads, with little or no traffic. There are some steep hills to climb. Most of the trail has gorgeous scenery. I like early June and September rides. There is always wildlife to see: deer, fawns, turkey, elk, and I have even seen bears while riding. There are rivers to cross, most have bridges, while others do not. . . . The residential areas can be tiresome even for horse riders, but the rest of the trail more than makes up for it. My opinion is that the best and most beautiful part of the trail is between South Branch and McKinley Camps, and the trail follows the Au Sable River. Come and experience it for yourself. I am sure you would enjoy it.

—Anonymous Michigan Trail Riders Association member
and Shore-to-Shore Trail rider

superior hiking trail

235 MILES | MINNESOTA

TO GO . . .

- high-quality trail maintenance
- gorgeous, varied terrain
- 90 miles of hiking beyond the north end with more options in the future
- state highpoint as a long side trip

OR NOT TO GO?

- bugs can be bad
- may not be a solitary trip
- chances for ornery weather
- Pressie

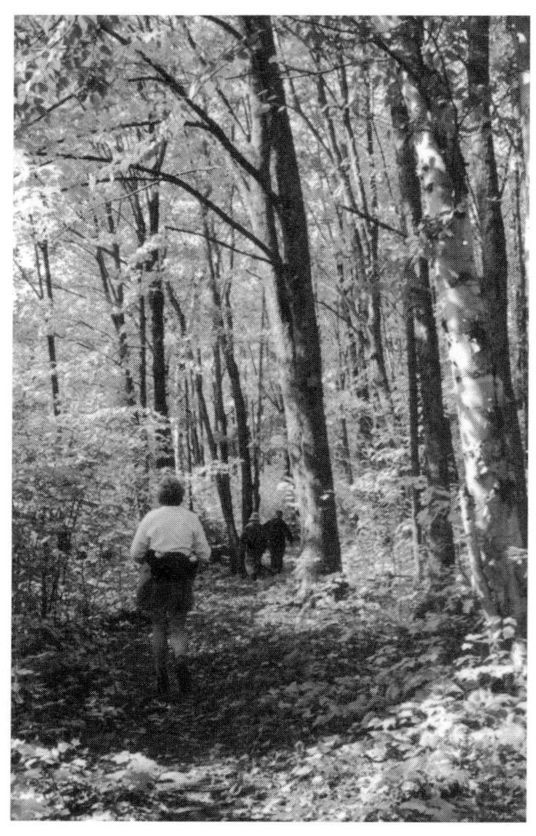

Thick stands of paper birches and red maples flank the trail near the Caribou River on the Superior Hiking Trail. (RUTH HILAND/SUPERIOR HIKING TRAIL ASSOCIATION)

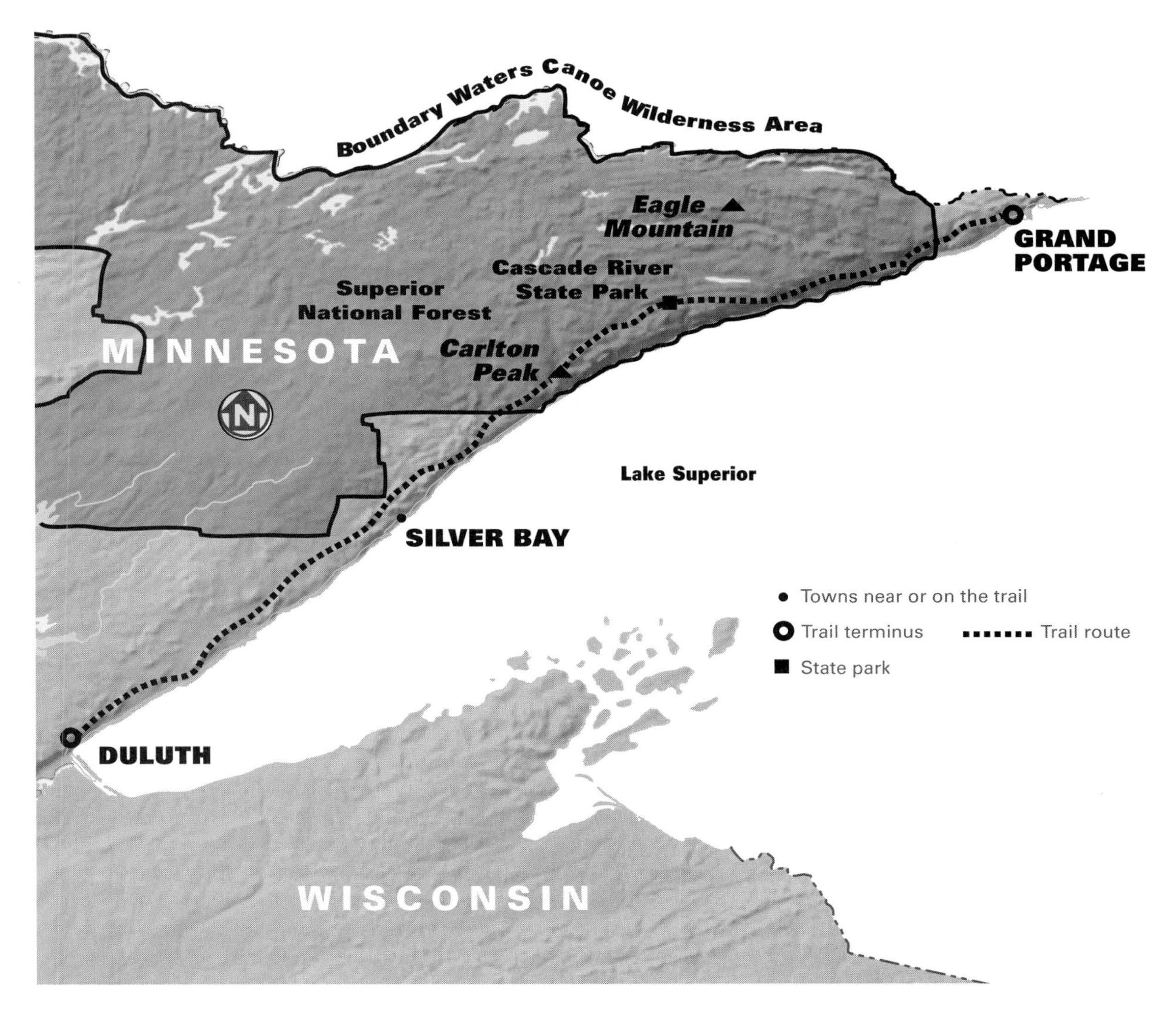

To be honest, I was so turned on to the Superior Hiking Trail (SHT) that I contemplated keeping it just for myself and anyone else already fortunate enough to know about this gem. But here it is. I wouldn't be able to sleep at night knowing I kept such a nice trail from my readers. The Superior Hiking Trail starts northeast of Duluth and ends far to the northeast on the Canadian border, west of Grand Portage and north of Hovland. The north end of the SHT connects to the Border Route Trail, which continues nearly due west approximately ninety miles to end in Ely, Minnesota. The SHT is slated to extend from its current southern terminus to the Wisconsin border, for a total of more than 300 trail miles. After this is done, the SHT will become a link trail on the 4,200-mile North Country National Scenic Trail.

The excellent trail maintenance and information presented by the Superior Hiking

VITALS

- > Expect to cover 15 miles a day
- > Expect a thru-hike to take 16 days
- > Hiking season: May to October
- > Water availability: Frequent
- > Resupply opportunities: Sometimes
- > First year thru-hiked: 1990s
- > Approximate yearly thru-hikers: Fewer than 70
- > Primary contact: Superior Hiking Trail Association

Trail Association and Minnesota-based federal and state agencies, helped the readers of *Backpacker* magazine flatter the SHT like no other trail in existence. In past years, the Superior Hiking Trail placed fifth in best scenery, fourth in best wildlife, first in best signage/trail marking, and first in trail/camp/shelter conditions, and overall was voted the second-best long-distance hiking trail in the United States, second only to the Wonderland Trail. Way to go Superior Hiking Trail and Superior Hiking Trail Association! The SHT is one of the few long-distance trails with a shuttle to help section backpackers and day hikers get around to different parts of the trail. Along the way, this foot-traffic-only trail heads through gorges, over summits, and

LAKE SUPERIOR

It was a real headache researching Lake Superior to find out what claims, if any, this lake held. Some sources said that Lake Superior is the largest lake in the world, but is that in surface area, volume, depth, or amount of freshwater? After scrolling through website after website and thumbing through encyclopedias, I gave up trying to find the same figures twice, for no one seemed to agree. In the end, this is what I came up with.

Surface Area. All sources I examined agreed that Lake Superior is the largest lake in the United States. These sources also agreed that Lake Superior is the second-largest lake in the world. The largest lake in the world, in surface area, is actually the Caspian Sea (of Asia), which is approximately 152,000 square miles in size. However, the Caspian Sea is not a *freshwater* lake. (The Caspian Sea is still considered a lake because it's landlocked, but its water is salty.) Therefore, Lake Superior is the largest freshwater lake in the world in terms of surface area. Lake Superior's surface area is less than 32,000 square miles. To give you an idea of how big that is, the state of Maine is a little more than 33,000 square miles in size.

Volume. Lake Superior is the fourth-largest lake in the world in terms of volume. One source stated that Lake Superior was the second-largest lake in the world, but I found more sources that disagreed with that claim than agreed with it. The Caspian Sea is the largest lake in the world in terms of volume, with 78,200 cubic kilometers of water. Second-place Lake Baikal of Russia has 23,600 cubic kilometers of water, and Africa's Tanganyika has 19,000 cubic kilometers. Superior is ranked fourth, with 12,100 cubic kilometers of water.

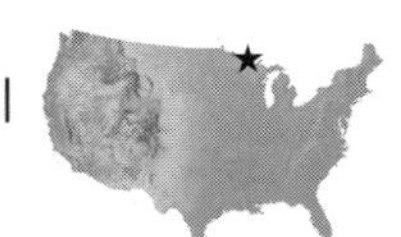

DON'T LEAVE HOME WITHOUT IT

BINOCULARS
Albeit a clunky item for a dedicated lightweight backpacker, a pair of binoculars can bring you closer to the abundant wildlife you'll encounter along this remote trail. The SHT provides an excellent habitat for moose and wolves, so keep your eyes peeled and your binoculars ready. And train your eyes on the lake whenever you can. You might just spot Pressie.

---

next to waterfalls, through a mix of private, county, state, and national forest land. At times, the SHT's general terrain reaches elevations of 1,600 feet; its highpoint is 1,800 feet.

WEATHER

The weather on the SHT is highly influenced by one factor that keeps things cool or hot during your SHT thru-hike: the direction of the wind. When the wind is coming from the interior of the North Shore, you can rely on short-term warm weather.

Depth. All sources agreed that Lake Superior is not the deepest lake in the world or the deepest lake in the United States. Its maximum depth is slightly more than 1,300 feet. The deepest lake in the world is Lake Baikal, which is approximately 5,500 feet deep. The deepest lake in the United States is Crater Lake, in southwest Oregon, at about 1,940 feet deep.

Lake Superior, at an elevation of approximately 600 feet, receives thirty inches of precipitation annually. This massive body of water can get downright rowdy. The average water temperature is less than 50°, waves in excess of thirty feet have been recorded, heavy fog can be persistent, and these conditions have doomed at least three hundred ships. And if that isn't enough, you may have to deal with Pressie!

Pressie is Lake Superior's version of the Loch Ness Monster and seems to be a lot more ornery than Lake Champlain's mysterious Champ. Pressie is claimed to be more than seventy feet in length, and since its first sighting in the late 1800s it has killed at least one deer and almost killed a fisherman by strangling him, or so the tale goes.

But Pressie isn't the only killer in Lake Superior. Pollution is a problem. Lake Superior is the cleanest Great Lake. Thanks to its enormous size, Lake Superior isn't as susceptible to the effects of acid rain as much as other U.S. bodies of water, but Polychlorinated biphenyls (PCBs), mercury, cadmium, arsenic, lead, and agricultural runoff are still an issue. The water quality has been degraded enough that state agencies recommend only limited ingestion of certain fish. To get the full scoop on current threats to the health of Lake Superior, contact the Minnesota Pollution Control Agency and/or the Sierra Club North Star Chapter. ■

AVERAGE HIGHS AND LOWS IN DEGREES FAHRENHEIT	JAN	MAR	MAY	JUL	SEPT	NOV
GRAND PORTAGE, MN (660 FT.)	5–20	15–35	40–60	50–75	45–65	20–40
DULUTH, MN (790 FT.)	0–20	15–35	40–65	55–75	45–65	20–35

If the wind is coming off Lake Superior (which, again, is about the size of Maine), you can expect to dig out an insulating layer or at least a windproof shell. Veterans of the Superior Hiking Trail have reported drops of nearly 20° in a short amount of time.

Even without Lake Superior nearby, temperatures in northern Minnesota take on characteristics of other more mountainous areas in the United States. Temperatures during a summer day reach the mid sixties or seventies, with the night's lows dipping into the forties. Overall, you should be more concerned about cold than heat. But don't expect to see any flurries during your thru-hike unless you are out there during fall foliage season. Both Grand Portage and Duluth have never seen temperatures reach the 100° mark, but they have both seen record low temperatures colder than –35°.

TERRAIN

The terrain of northern Minnesota is spectacularly challenging and scenic. "Wait, isn't that where that *canoeing* place is?" you may ask. Yes, the Boundary Waters Canoe Wilderness Area is on the North Shore, but so is the highest peak in Minnesota, Eagle Mountain (2,301 feet), which can be reached by completing a twenty-mile road walk off the SHT (see Points of Interest).

The Superior Hiking Trail Association has released an eight-map set that covers the trail end to end. Looking at the maps in order (from north to south) you'll see that the *differences between the highest point and lowest point* within each of the eight sections are 600, 800, 900, 800, 1000, 1,100, 700, and 800 feet, respectively. Overall, the SHT's high point exceeds 1,800 feet on Sundling Creek Ridge and Rosebush Ridge. The low point of the SHT is 600 feet at the current southern terminus near Route 61 on the outskirts of Two Harbors, and the Lake Walk along the shoreline of Lake Superior on the far north section. Short, steep climbing is par for the day's activities. Needless to say, Minnesota is more rugged than most would think. Trails that can be quite muddy take you to expanses of hardwoods such as

TERRAIN HIGHLIGHTS

- Deep maple and aspen forests
- Wind-raked summits
- Gorges
- Rocky outcrops
- Highest waterfall in Minnesota
- Freshwater streams
- Ponds
- Bogs

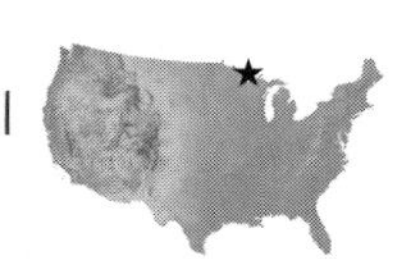

maple and aspen. On your hike you will also ascend to rocky summits that support a softwood forest of spruce, fir, and pine. In addition to plant life, geological features add further beauty to this two-week trip.

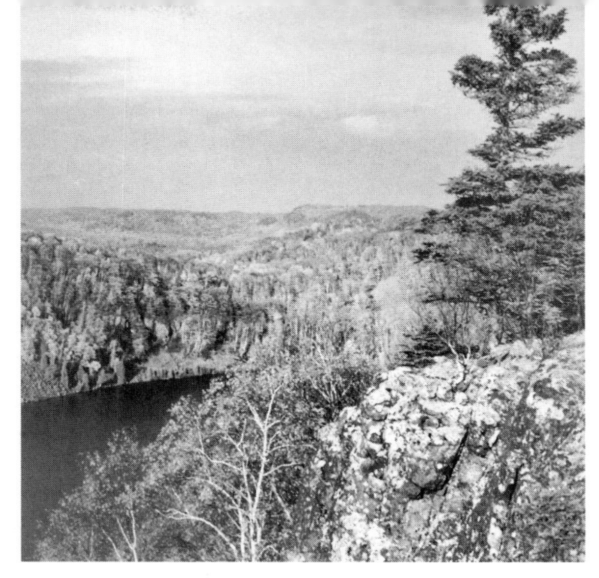

This section of the Superior Hiking Trail, near Silver Bay, Minnesota, is a land of windswept peaks, quiet bogs, and clear lakes. (TIM LARSON/SUPERIOR HIKING TRAIL ASSOCIATION)

WATER

For most of its route, the SHT does not follow the Lake Superior shoreline; however, there is no shortage of water to fill your needs. The trail crosses approximately sixteen sizable rivers from Duluth to Canada, and you'll cross many smaller rivers with each day of hiking. (Volunteers for the Superior Hiking Trail Association plus state and federal employees have done an impressive job of installing bridges on forty major drainages.) As summer drags on, you should expect the water levels to drop. Throughout the entire year, savvy SHT hikers should find and carry extra water before hiking on ridgelines. Each designated campsite usually has a year-round water source, too.

WILDNESS

The secret is out that the north end of Minnesota is a land of peaks, bogs, moose, and mountain views, but that doesn't mean that crowds of hectic hikers spoil the area. Although most sections of the SHT are rarely more than a day's walk from Route 61, the trail travels within five miles of five settlements on its North Shore journey: Two Harbors, Beaver Bay, Schroeder, Grand Marais, and Holland. Two Harbors and Grand Marais are the only sizeable villages, with 3,600 and 1,400 year-round residents, respectively. All in all, you're more likely to tramp through a mud hole than a parking lot. Routing the trail through so much publicly held land, such as the enormous Superior National Forest, helps ensure a truly wild experience. Other than

SCHLIMMER'S SIDE TRAIL

HIGHPOINTER'S TAKE NOTE

Getting to Eagle Mountain—Minnesota's 2,301-foot highpoint—is a twenty-mile side trip from the SHT. Leave the trail near Grand Marais and follow Route 12 north. After a long road walk to the Eagle Mountain hiking trailhead, take the very rocky three-mile route to the top of the North Star State. A plaque marks the summit. A self-issue permit is available for free at the trailhead. ■

CRITTERS

- Beavers
- Black bears
- Loons
- Moose
- Red foxes
- Wolves

the impacts of logging, this area lacks extensive development. There isn't a complete system of trail shelters on the SHT, but there are shelters in nearby state parks. For those looking for even more wildness, there is always the option of exploring Lake Superior's North Shore with map and compass rather than staying on a trail. With many water sources and thousands of acres to wander around in, this area can be a bushwhacker's dreamland.

The SHT is one of the few long-distance trails with a shuttle to help section backpackers and day hikers get around to different parts of the trail. The privately owned Superior Shuttle runs a regular schedule from May to October, visiting trailheads on the SHT. This transportation service will give you a ride for $5 to $20, depending on where you are and where you want to go. Your dog is welcome aboard, too, as long as Fido can scratch up an additional $3.

WILDLIFE

Take a minute and close your eyes. Relax. Imagine a place that is home to large mammals, rock-topped low mountains, swift-running streams, blinding fall foliage, a slew of different birds, and a pristine setting to take it all in. Oh, that's good. Beautiful, isn't it? Now stop imagining it, and go find it on the Superior Hiking Trail.

POINTS OF INTEREST

PICK UP A PADDLE

Boundary Waters Canoe Wilderness Area, near the SHT's northern terminus, is a legendary destination for canoeists and kayakers. After you've completed the Superior Hiking Trail give your boots a break and explore more of Minnesota by paddle.

CASCADE RIVER

You'll pass many waterfalls on your Superior Hiking Trail thru-hike, particularly in the Cascade River State Park. These falls are especially beautiful in spring. Hidden Falls and Secret Falls are highlights.

ROCKY SUMMITS

At 1,500 feet, Carlton Peak provides a 360° view that includes Lake Superior, Britton Peak, and Leveaux Mountain. Other rocky summits along the SHT provide excellent views, too.

IT'S SIMPLY GORGES

You'll visit Devil Track Canyon (the deepest canyon in Minnesota) just northeast of Grand Marais, and you'll see the stunning Kadunce River Gorge on a far north section of trail. Just north of the Kadunce River Gorge, the SHT actually follows the shore of Lake Superior via the Lake Walk.

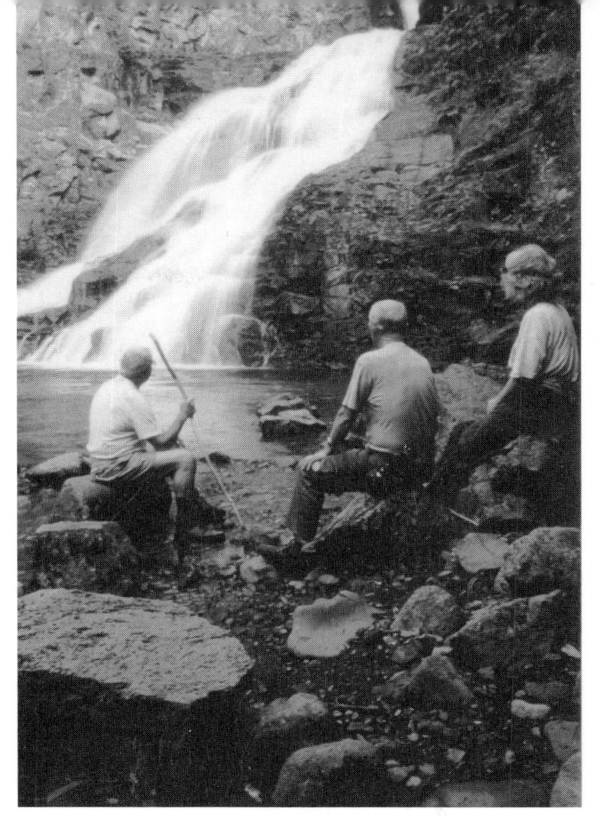

Hikers enjoy cascading Caribou Falls just north of Little Marais, Minnesota. (SUPERIOR HIKING TRAIL ASSOCIATION)

In Their Own Words . . .

The Superior Hiking Trail is a two-hundred-mile footpath that follows the rocky ridgeline high above Lake Superior, along Minnesota's North Shore. The trail connects seven state parks, two state forests, and the Superior National Forest. It features cascading rivers with dramatic waterfalls, sparkling back-country lakes, and diverse forests, including blazing fall maples and white birches.

There are thirty trailheads on the Superior Hiking Trail, giving both day hikers and backpackers convenient access. There are no fees, reservations, or permits required for trail use, or the seventy-five backcountry campsites. Several towns are located within two to three miles of the trail so backpackers can mail themselves parcels for longer trips. A shuttle services the trail from mid-May to mid-October.

Although the trail is not high, as far as elevation goes (this is the Midwest!), it is more challenging than you might think. A good portion of the trail follows the spine of the old Sawtooth Mountains. In addition, the trail has many changes in elevation as it descends steeply into river valleys, crosses the rivers, ascends steeply up the other side, and then travels the ridgeline until the next river.

—Gayle Coyer, Superior Hiking Trail Association executive director

tahoe rim trail

165 MILES | CALIFORNIA NEVADA

TO GO . . .

- loop hike
- Lake Tahoe as a centerpiece
- graded route
- alpine terrain with excellent views

OR NOT TO GO?

- dry sections with blazing summer sun
- multiple-use route is often busy
- time needed to acclimate

Rose Knob Peak (9,696 feet) provides a breathtaking view of Crystal Bay on Lake Tahoe's north shore. Lake Tahoe is the eleventh-deepest lake in the world, measuring 1,650 feet at its deepest point. (STEVE ANDERSEN WWW.TAKEITOUTDOORS.COM)

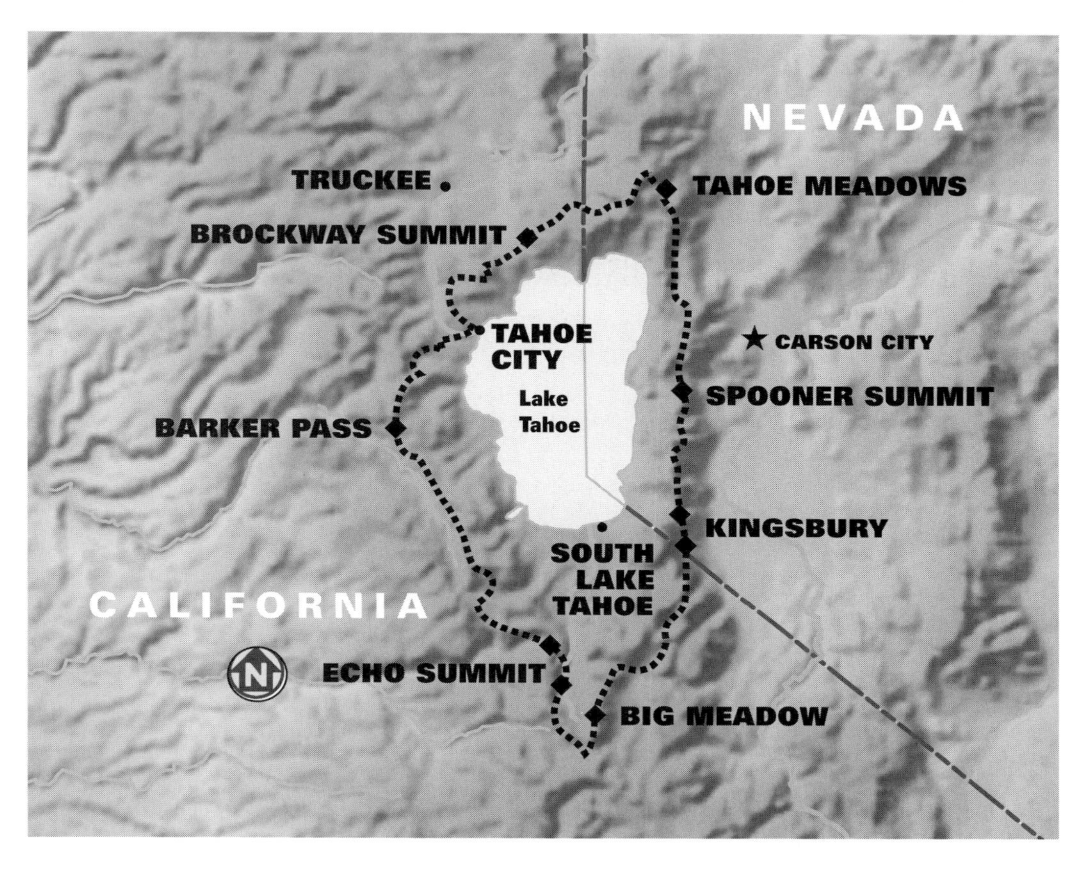

● Towns near or on the trail ★ State capital

▪▪▪▪▪▪▪ Trail route ◆ Trailhead

The Tahoe Rim Trail (TRT), whose center, Lake Tahoe, was described by Mark Twain as the "fairest picture the whole earth affords," is one of the three loop trails in this guide. This trail starts where it ends—that is, if by the end of your trip you successfully end up where you start. The TRT is one of the most beautiful trails, if not *the* most beautiful trail, in this guide. It affords gorgeous views of the Sierra Nevada to the west, and the high peaks of Nevada to the east and south. The Lake Tahoe area is not on such a grand scale as the 14,000-foot peaks of Colorado or California—it's more of a scaled-down version of those places—but the topography's reduced scale loses nothing in overall beauty.

The first person to thru-hike the Tahoe Rim Trail was Steve Andersen in August 1998. Steve has remained purely dedicated to adventuring on the TRT as well as sup-

VITALS

- Expect to cover 16 miles a day
- Expect a thru-hike to take 10 days
- Hiking season: June to October
- Water availability: Seldom
- Resupply opportunities: Sometimes
- First year thru-hiked: 1998
- Approximate yearly thru-hikers: Fewer than 300
- Primary contact: Tahoe Rim Trail Association

LAKE TAHOE

This body of water shared by California and Nevada is the eleventh-deepest lake in the world, measuring approximately 1,650 feet at its deepest point. Lake Tahoe is also one of the largest lakes on our planet in terms of volume. The lake's great depth, combined with a surface dimension exceeding 200 square miles, results in Lake Tahoe being ranked as the twentieth-largest lake in the world and the sixth largest in the United States (the five Great Lakes place first through fifth) in terms of volume of water. The surface elevation exceeds 6,200 feet and varies slightly due to a dam, although this is a naturally formed lake. Lake Tahoe has never frozen over and gets warm enough to swim in during the summer, but don't try to dive down beyond 600 feet, for you'll find the temperature hovering at a chilly 39° year-round. The lake is known for its deep blue hue and crystal clear waters, which are a joy to see on this more-than-two-week trip. The lake is so clear that objects can be seen at depths of more than a hundred feet. This is because more than a third of all rain that falls in the Lake Tahoe Basin actually lands in the lake—so it receives a direct deposit of clear rainwater—and runoff from the surrounding hills passes through granite and marshes, which act as giant filters.

However, Lake Tahoe is threatened. The biggest current threats are nearby traffic congestion, urbanization, destruction of wetlands, cattle grazing, and overall soil erosion. The resulting sediments seep into the lake, clouding the water and influencing cultural eutrophication. Cultural eutrophication is an overnutrientization that can occur in nearly any body of water, and this is why biodegradable soap should not be used anywhere near lakes and streams. Soap nutrients, as well as sediment and fertilizers, leach into the water—in this case, Lake Tahoe—and encourage algae blooms.

Florida and North Carolina share a problem with the Lake Tahoe Basin: fecal coliform invasion caused by farm animal feces getting into water supplies. The waste acts as a fertilizer, and (duh) it *is* fecal matter, so we get tons of cooties in the water, too. So who's going to do something about these problems in the Tahoe Basin? Keep Tahoe Blue. This group, now more than forty years old, states on its website that it is dedicated to "the restoration and preservation of the best natural resources of the Tahoe Basin's waters, forests, and landscape for the enjoyment of present and future generations." So there! Check out the website or drop them a note. They need all the support they can get, because the common belief among scientists studying Lake Tahoe is that the clouding of the lake must stop within ten years or it will be too late to successfully reverse the degradation. ■

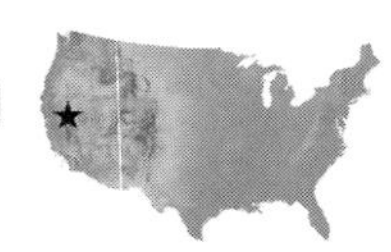

DON'T LEAVE HOME WITHOUT IT

RAD SPEAK

The extreme mountain bikers, skiers, and snowboarders who "hang at Squallywood, shreddin' the pow-pow and launchin' mad kickers in the three percent, dicin' it up and pushin' it to the max extreme" near the Tahoe Rim Trail will think you're a hardcore local if you speak like this.

---

porting the trail's existence. Andersen has now started his third year on the Tahoe Rim Trail Association's board, has covered the entire 165-mile route three and a half times, and has created an elevation profile for the TRT, which can be viewed at www.takeitoutdoors.com. Steve Andersen, like me, has created a lifestyle that enables him to hike in the most beautiful places in the United States while getting paid at the same time. Oh, rough life!

WEATHER

The weather, specifically the temperatures, varies greatly on the Tahoe Rim Trail. In fact, the average low and high temperatures for each month vary the most of any trail in this guide, even surpassing the Colorado Trail's monthly variances. You'll notice, for example, that the TRT has a 35-degree temperature range between the average low and high temperatures in May and a 45-degree temperature range in July. The TRT is one of the few trails in the *Thru Hiker's Guide to America* for which you might bring a down vest and a pair of nylon shorts and end up wearing them both on the same day. Like the higher John Muir Trail to the west, you can expect the sun to be shining on you for most of your trek. Nearby Squaw Valley ski resort, with a base elevation of 6,200 feet and a summit elevation exceeding 9,000 feet, records nearly 300 sunny days a year but also receives 450 inches of annual snowfall. Although it starts getting pretty warm around April, you'll have to wait until mid June to avoid the TRT's many snowfields. If you attempt this hike any earlier, you'll certainly encounter the legendary "Sierra Cement."

TERRAIN

You'll find the terrain on the Tahoe Rim Trail similar to that of the nearby Pacific Crest Trail (which partially coincides with the TRT) and the John Muir Trail, both located high in the Sierra Nevada. Graded for pack stock, the TRT rarely exceeds a 10 percent grade (we Northeasterners can hardly imagine such a thing),

AVERAGE HIGHS AND LOWS IN DEGREES FAHRENHEIT

	JAN	MAR	MAY	JUL	SEPT	NOV
TRUCKEE, CA (5,840 FT.)	15–40	25–50	30–65	40–85	35–75	20–50
SOUTH LAKE TAHOE, CA (6,260 FT.)	15–40	20–45	30–60	40–80	35–70	20–50

TERRAIN HIGHLIGHTS

- > Wildflower fields
- > Endless views
- > Lakes
- > Seasonal streams
- > Conifer forests
- > Alpine terrain
- > Aspen forests

so you can easily cruise this path once you get acclimated. And what better reason to hang out near Lake Tahoe for a couple of days before your thru-hike? At more than 6,000 feet, Lake Tahoe makes a good one- to two-day layover to help you get used to the higher elevations prior to your hike. The low point of the TRT is Tahoe City, a bit higher than 6,300 feet; the high point of the trail exceeds 10,000 feet on Relay Peak. Your route is full of switchbacks on a tread of sand and granite ranging from car-size boulders to pea-size pebbles.

WATER

The Tahoe Rim Trail is mighty dry despite the fact that more than sixty drainages pour into Lake Tahoe from the surrounding mountain ranges. The TRT is not fully dry, of course, but you will be trudging through long waterless areas, especially if you start your thru-hike after July. As the summer progresses, at least two sections exceeding ten miles in length will have no water. Nearly all of the streams on the TRT are seasonal, as are some of the lakes. The only sure place to find lakes full of water is the Desolation Wilderness Area. The output of water sources varies from month to month and year to year. Thru-hikers should take into consideration how much snow has fallen during the past winter to determine what snowfields, and thus what areas of runoff, are left. It would be a good idea to contact the Tahoe Rim Trail Association (TRTA) to get the full scoop on water availability for the current hiking times. During periods of even mild drought, you may have to cache water along the TRT for later use. Again, the TRTA can be of great assistance, as can the U.S. Forest Service, in your attempt to gain up-to-date information about available water.

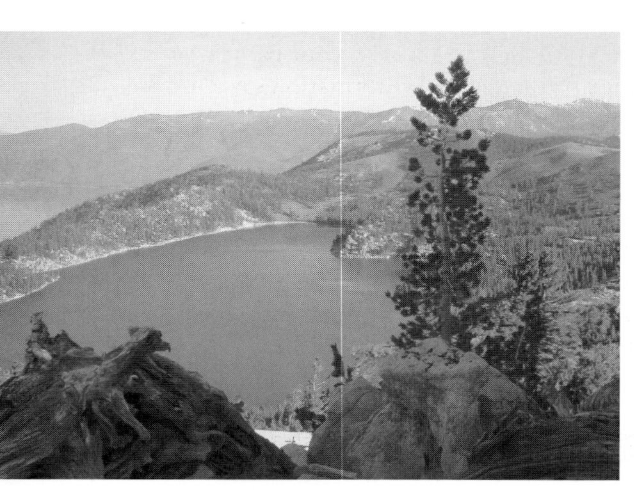

Snow Valley Peak (9,214 feet) offers a fine view of the narrow isthmus separating Marlette Lake and Lake Tahoe (left). (STEVE ANDERSEN WWW.TAKEITOUTDOORS.COM)

WILDNESS

The Tahoe Rim Trail is not classified as a frontcountry trail, but it is also not phenomenally wild in many parts. Why not?

It's a multiple-use trail, so you have to share the tread with our horse packer friends, and about half the route is open to our mountain biking buddies as well. Luckily, motor junkies are not allowed anywhere on it. Mountain bike use is regarded as "heavy" on some sections, and it has come to the point where a northeast section of trail near Tahoe Meadows is closed to bikers on odd days of the month. If you (the hiker) run into horses, simply step off the trail and give the horse and rider a gentle hello. Remember: hikers yield to horses, bikers yield to hikers and horses. The Tahoe Rim Trail Association's fact sheet states that an estimated 3,000 people use the Tahoe Rim Trail each week. That's a lot of people to try to get along with. Be polite. Share the trail.

The TRT passes two easily reachable resupply points at convenient locations when looking at the overall route of the trail. On the northwest side of the loop route, Tahoe City provides ample supplies for backpackers. On the south side of the TRT you can stop at the town of South Lake Tahoe. There are other places to resupply, but these two locations seem to be the most obvious and convenient. Six major paved roads cross the trail, as do many dirt forest roads, but there are no extended road walks on the Tahoe Rim Trail.

You will need a permit to enter the Desolation Wilderness Area in Eldorado National Forest, one of three wilderness areas that the TRT crosses. In most locations, camping is allowed just about anywhere along the trail if you're at least 200 feet from all water and trails, though you should check out all rules and regulations from area to area. If possible, camp on gravel or rock even though it doesn't look that comfortable. It's a durable surface where you'll leave hardly a trace. A fire permit is required—even for a backpacking stove. Even then, camp stoves and fires are sometimes banned during times of high wildfire danger. Also, ask the Tahoe Rim Trail Association and the U.S. Forest Service about where to park your car if you are doing any multiple-day hikes. These groups have valuable information on what trailheads are most often subject to car break-ins by merciless hooligans.

WILDLIFE

The TRT is home to a whole bunch of western critters that you'll have the pleasure of becoming acquainted with on this 150+-mile route. Bears have become a big concern in some areas, so it's highly recommended that you kill them. Just kidding. It's recommended that you hang your food or, better yet, carry a bear canister. Otherwise, your carelessness will kill them when they become so-called problem bears that need to be eliminated.

CRITTERS

- Black bears
- Bobcats
- Coyotes
- Pikas
- Pine martens*
- Porcupines
- Wolverines*
- Yellow-bellied marmots

*Very rare. If you see them, report this to a local U.S. Forest Service office.

There's gold in them thar hills. Looking west from the Nevada side of the trail, hikers see a land unchanged from the prospecting days of old. (STEVE ANDERSEN WWW.TAKEITOUTDOORS.COM)

POINTS OF INTEREST

THE CENTERPIECE

An obvious destination for all Tahoe Rim Trail thru-hikers is Lake Tahoe itself, where ferries take you out for a cruise to give you stunning views of the encircling mountain ranges. Nearly all settlements around the lake are strongly oriented to serve outdoors enthusiasts.

WHAT'S IN A NAME?

Desolation Wilderness is sometimes not as desolate as it sounds, but with three mountain ranges and more than a hundred lakes, you should find some solitude. If not, head off trail through easily navigable terrain. You'll need to get a permit to cross the Desolation Wilderness Area.

WORLD-CLASS SKIING

Squaw Valley, Alpine Meadows, Heavenly, and Northstar-at-Tahoe, among others, offer spectacular downhill skiing replete with chutes and waist-deep powder. You can also rub elbows with people who wear furry boots and light their cigars with $50 bills. Wow!

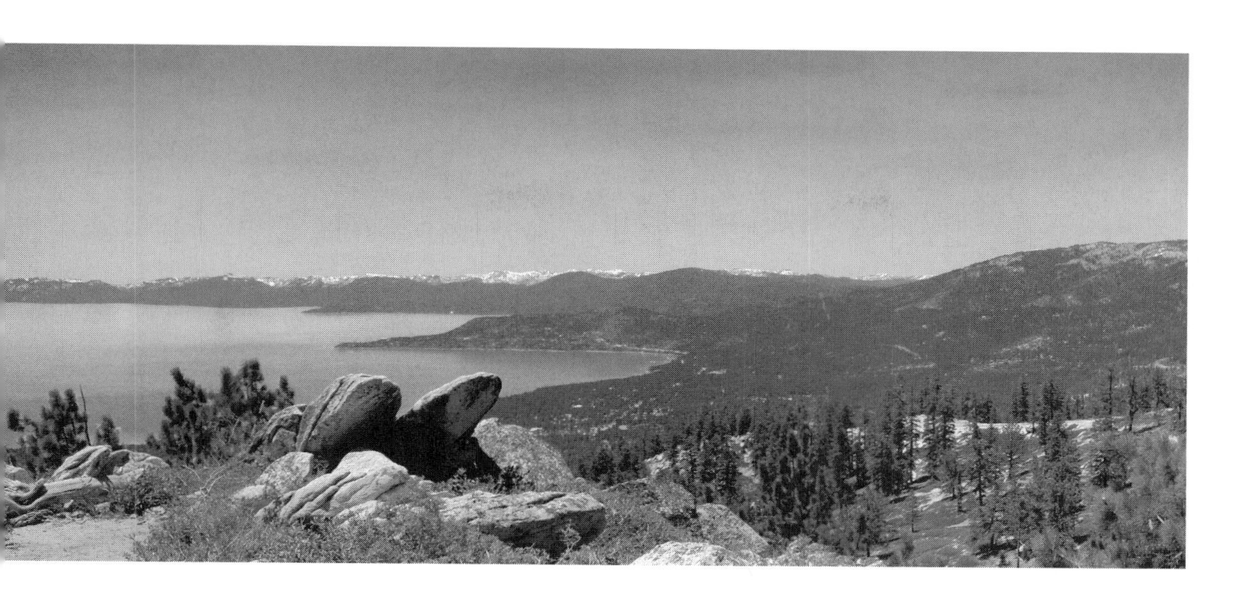

In Their Own Words . . .

The Tahoe Rim Trail is a 165-mile trail circling one of North America's most spectacular sights: Lake Tahoe. It meanders on stark ridges high above the deep blue lake and past glacier-carved lakes in remote wilderness. You will pass through green meadows loaded with wild-flowers and summit a peak of more than 10,000 feet. Along its journey, the trail passes through three Wilderness Areas, two states, and two mountain ranges. The trail provides a tremendous variety of vistas and plant communities, but awesome views of Lake Tahoe for mile after mile are the trail's most sensational features.

What makes the Tahoe Rim Trail especially unique is the fact that it is a big loop going all the way around the lake. If you backpack the entire trail, you can watch where you are going, and where you have been, as you slowly circle the lake. One can hike the entire Tahoe Rim Trail in about two weeks, or access its eight trailheads for a wide variety of day hiking or back-packing adventures. Mountain biking is allowed on over half the trail, and horses and foot traffic are allowed on the entire Tahoe Rim Trail. With its spectacular views, easy accessibility, and incredible summer weather, the Tahoe Rim Trail is a real treat, whether you're hiking for a day or two weeks.

—Tim Hauserman, Lake Tahoe area guide and author of *The Tahoe Rim Trail: A Complete Guide for Hikers, Mountain Bikers, and Equestrians*

tuscarora trail

250 MILES | VIRGINIA
WEST VIRGINIA
MARYLAND
PENNSYLVANIA

TO GO . . .

- fantastic ridgeline hiking
- crowd factor should be low
- near-year-round hiking season
- Appalachian Trail or C and O Canal Towpath hiking options

OR NOT TO GO?

- long, dry sections
- gets pretty hot in summer

From atop its many ridgelines, hikers of the Tuscarora Trail will behold the wide valleys and pastoral landscapes that parallel much of this 250-mile footpath. (DON DESROSIERS)

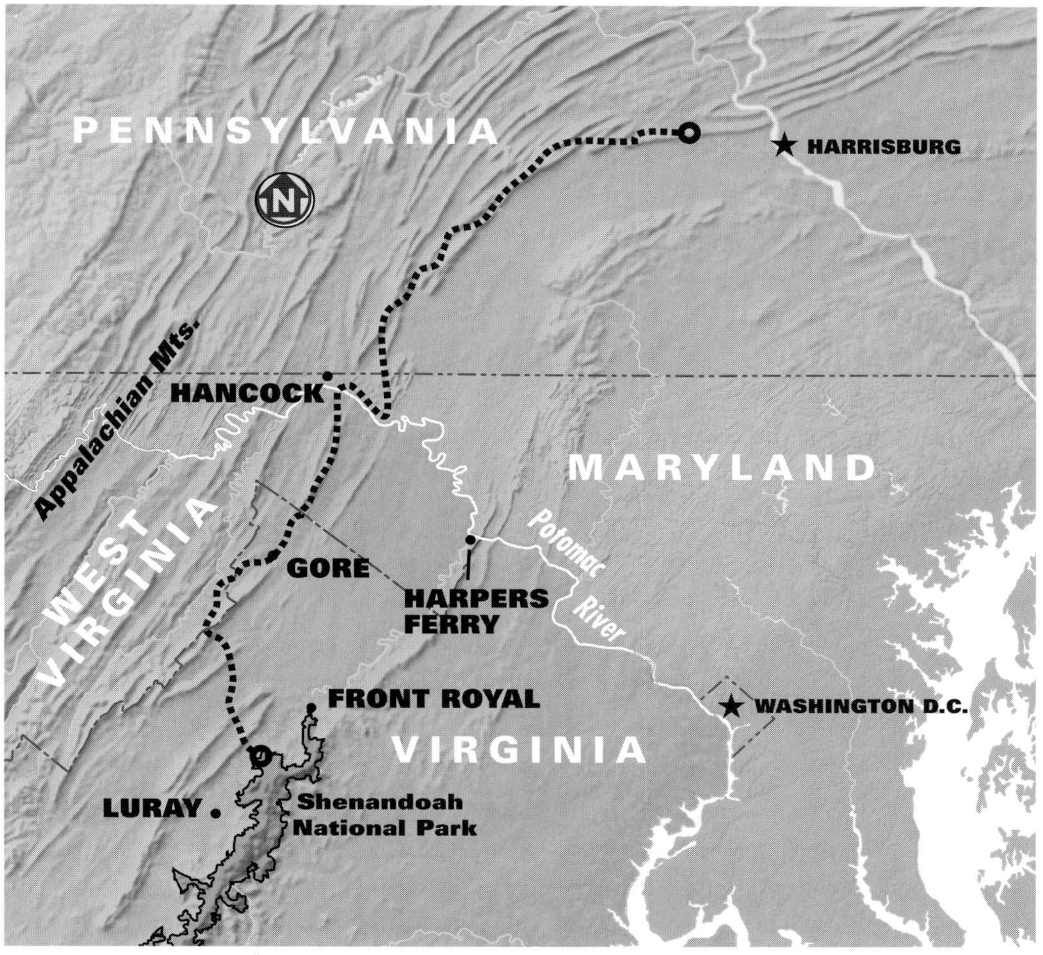

The Tuscarora (pronounced *tusk-ah-roar-ah*) Trail (TT) is a path that was nearly relegated to the history books. In the early 1980s we lost two things: brightly colored polyester suits, and the tread of the Tuscarora Trail. Common sense did away with polyester suits, while briars, bushes, and poison ivy nearly swallowed the TT. But, thanks to the work of the Potomac Appalachian Trail Club, the Keystone Trails Association, and several state and federal land management agencies, the TT is back and better than ever.

The Tuscarora Trail of today actually used to be two trails: the 110-mile Tuscarora Trail in the north and the 140-mile Big Blue Trail in the south. These paths started out as possible Appalachian Trail alternate routes, but then the Appalachian Trail received

VITALS

- Expect to cover 14 miles a day
- Expect a thru-hike to take 18 days
- Hiking season: April to November
- Water availability: Sometimes
- Resupply opportunities: Sometimes
- First year thru-hiked: Unknown
- Approximate yearly thru-hikers: Fewer than 50
- Primary contact: Potomac Appalachian Trail Club

its National Scenic Trail protection in the late 1960s and attention shifted from the Tuscarora Trail route to the AT. The Tuscarora Trail and the Big Blue Trail were regarded as mere blue-blazed Appalachian Trail side trails. During the 1980s, the Tuscarora Trail and the Big Blue Trail didn't get the tender loving care they so deserved and became overgrown. There was a severe drought for part of these decades, and the gypsy moth defoliation of the 1980s didn't help things either.

The Potomac Appalachian Trail Club and the Keystone Trail Association stepped in to save these two fading paths. Between 1994 and 1997, the Tuscarora Trail and the Big Blue Trail were cleared, combined, renamed, and better maintained. We now have the 250-mile Tuscarora Trail that starts on the northern tip of Shenandoah National Park, Virginia, and ends west of Harrisburg, Pennsylvania. A new guidebook was published in 1997, a patch design is currently being worked on, and the Potomac Appalachian Trail Club now maintains the TT. What a success story!

WEATHER

Being somewhat down in the South and traveling along modest elevations, the TT is a three-season trail. You could also try a thru-hike in November, perhaps even early December if you can tolerate cold and occasional sticky snowstorms. Spring is certainly the best time to be on the Tuscarora Trail, with an amazing array of wildflowers to keep your eyes busy. Because a deep snowpack does not last long here, some years you can start hiking on the TT as soon as March. Heat and humidity rule in the valleys and gaps from May to August, but some nice steady breezes on the ridgelines will help keep you cool.

TERRAIN

The terrain of the Tuscarora Trail is challenging. You'll have to contend with steep climbs and descents, limited water on sections, blowdown, and briar growth. However, you will speed right along on smooth sections of rock-slab ridgelines up high or

AVERAGE HIGHS AND LOWS IN DEGREES FAHRENHEIT

	JAN	MAR	MAY	JUL	SEPT	NOV
LURAY, VA (790 FT.)	25–45	30–60	50–80	60–90	50–80	35–60
HARRISBURG, PA (320 FT.)	25–40	35–50	50–75	65–85	60–75	35–55

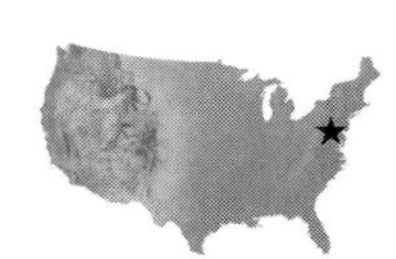

TERRAIN HIGHLIGHTS

- > Hemlock forests
- > Extended ridgelines
- > Historical areas
- > Rock fields
- > Canal towpaths
- > Balsam fir
- > Oak and hickory forests
- > Climbs with switchbacks

canal towpaths down in the valleys. The northern sections tend to be the rockiest. That "Rocksylvania" nickname given by Appalachian Trail thru-hikers, aptly describes the Pennsylvanian portions of the Tuscarora Trail.

The tread consists of singletrack hiking trail, canal towpaths, all-terrain-vehicle trails, and cleared rights-of-way. In Pennsylvania the elevation rarely exceeds 2,000 feet; in Maryland the entire route is below 1,000 feet; and West Virginia's section of the TT never exceeds 2,500 feet. Northern Virginia's elevations range from 1,400 to more than 3,000 feet. The lowpoint of the trail is in Maryland at a stream only 400 feet above sea level; the highpoint is at the southern terminus, on the Appalachian Trail in Virginia, at 3,400 feet. The biggest climbs on the entire TT are between 1,500 and 2,000 vertical feet.

WATER

Water on the TT is not plentiful on certain sections. Because this is mostly a ridgeline trail, only the gaps are guaranteed to hold water for most of the year. A lot of small and/or perennial springs and occasional campgrounds, parks, and homes can give you water, but the ridgelines are the worst. Some sections up to twelve miles in length are dry. Also, the Tuscarora Trail and the Florida Trail share a common problem—areas severely polluted from agricultural runoff. Be sure to treat all water. It's highly recommended that you get the scoop about water quality and availability from the locals in addition to the Potomac Appalachian Trail Club and the U.S. Forest Service.

WILDNESS

The TT is regarded by many mid-Atlantic hikers as much more quiet and desolate than its eastern neighbor, the AT. Only a few shelters are located on this 250-mile trek, which crosses national forests, state game lands, state forests, the Shenandoah National Park (where you need to secure a permit for backcountry camping), wildlife management areas, wildlife sanctuaries, and private holdings. The bad news is that you'll also pass by logged areas, buried gas lines, aboveground power lines, farms, fields, all-terrain-vehicle tracks, and other signs of human meddling. Barbwire fences can be hurdled with the aid of stiles. To spice things up, you'll ford a couple of streams, some of which can be thigh deep at times of high water. As for resupplying, you should be able to grab more food and stock up on potable water at least once a week, depending on how far from the trail you stray.

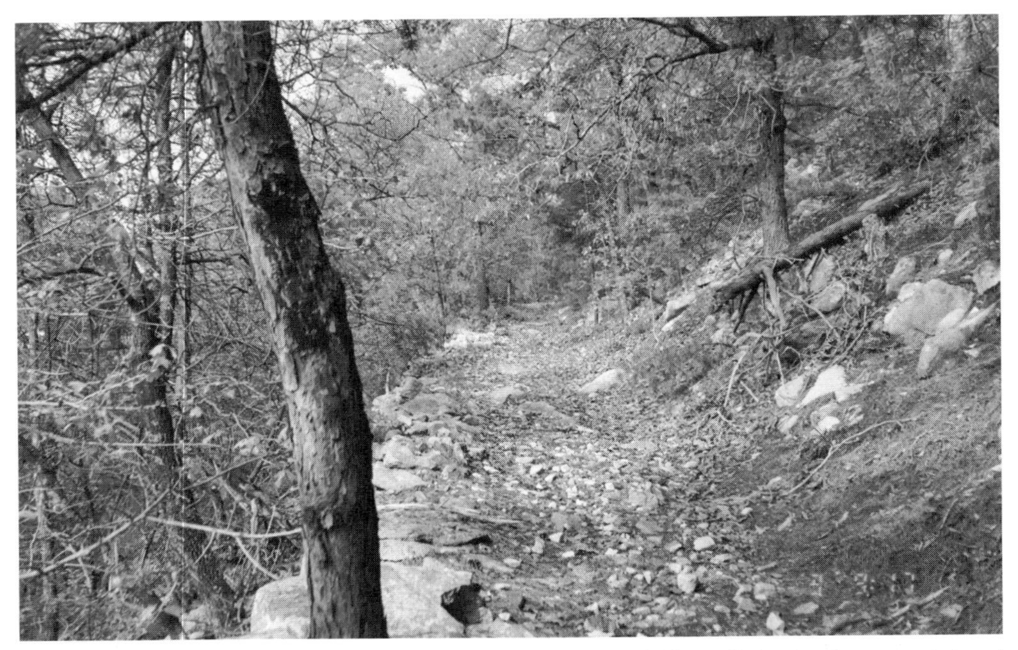

Rocksylvania at its finest. The Keystone State has earned its dubious distinction from rough tread like this. (DON DESROSIERS)

Regarding private lands, the owners have been kind enough to let the TT run through their property. Please leave all gates as you found them, keep pets under control at all times, and just plain behave. The same can be said for being on public land, too, or no matter what trail you're on.

Beyond the TT proper, you have many hiking options. The trail meets with the 2,170-mile Appalachian Trail and the 185-mile C and O Canal Towpath.

The Tuscarora Trail's ability to provide hikers with solitude was duly noted in the December 2003 issue of *Blue Ridge Outdoors*. The Tuscarora Trail was voted "Best Long Distance Hike" in the "Best of the Blue Ridge 2003 Readers' Choice Awards."

DON'T LEAVE HOME WITHOUT IT

CALAMINE LOTION

The Tuscarora Trail provides plenty of opportunities to make contact with poison ivy. Learn to identify this maleficent three-leaf plant, and do your best to avoid it. Failing that, you'll need backup. Pack some calamine lotion into a travel bottle and use it liberally if a rash develops. Just don't mistake this pink liquid for Pepto Bismol. There ain't no ER on the TT.

CRITTERS

- Black bears
- Bobcats
- Grouse
- Rattlesnakes
- Red squirrels
- Turkeys

Still, the Tuscarora offers a disproportionate share of solitude to hikers who want to truly immerse themselves in the wilderness experience. En route from Virginia on the far side of the Shenandoah Valley through Maryland and into Pennsylvania, the Tuscarora offers 252 miles of passage through one of the least populated—and most beautiful—places in the East.

It should also be noted that this issue of *Blue Ridge Outdoors* found the four most unnecessary pieces of gear to be a cell phone, a helmet mirror, a Walkman, and an inflatable pillow. The top event name was "Hilly Hellacious Hundred," the most overused event name was "Turkey Trot," and the best place to make out was "Any Blue Ridge Parkway Overlook." Scandalous!

WILDLIFE

Because the Tuscarora Trail is indeed wilder than its much longer neighbor, the Appalachian Trail, keeping down the noise means you should be able to see some critters on your thru-hike. Mammals, snakes, and birds are just some of the common trail residents.

POINTS OF INTEREST

BACK IN THE DAY

Along the TT you'll see roads constructed as far back as 1772, gaps used for moving troops and supplies during the War of Independence, the Mason-Dixon Line, and old gristmill sites. You'll also walk on a section of trail where George Washington liked to ride his horse.

THE TUSCARORA

The trail's name refers to one group of Native Americans who traversed the area. The Tuscarora resided in the Carolinas with Cherokee and Catawba cultures prior to 1715. Up to that point, the Tuscarora were losing battles with the invading Europeans, so they appealed to Five Nations (the Seneca, Cayuga, Onondaga, Oneida, and Mohawk tribes) in the north for assistance. Five Nations decided they would not supply direct help, but they did invite the Tuscarora to join them. In 1715, Five Nations became Six Nations. Today's Tuscarora Trail does not follow the exact route these traveling Indians walked in the 1700s, because the Indians traveled through the easier valley routes, not the ridgelines. The Tuscarora most likely walked in the wide valleys that now accommodate Interstate 81 and U.S. Route 11. ■

BIG VIRGINS

Hemlocks Natural Area in Pennsylvania is home to virgin stands of hemlock. Set on more than 130 acres of land, this area includes a narrow ravine greater than a mile long.

SUGAR KNOB AREA

Near the West Virginia–Virginia border, the gorgeous ridgelines of the Sugar Knob area have fern fields, springs, and streams up high, and can accommodate campers.

DEEP HOLLOW AREA

Located in northern Virginia, this area has four scree fields, a gorge, the Cat Rock Cliffs, and a shelter with fireplace, spring, and privy.

OVERALL, A NICE RUN

Located just before the TT's southern terminus you'll see Overall Run and its 2,000-foot stretch of cascading waterfalls. One of these falls is the tallest in Shenandoah National Park at ninety-three feet. Overall Run offers views from its many rocky outcrops. This area has one of the highest concentrations of black bears inside the park. Remember that dogs must be kept on a leash while in the national park, please.

In Their Own Words . . .

The Tuscarora Trail started as an emergency solution when it looked as if portions of the Appalachian Trail through northern Virginia would be closed in the late 1960s and early 1970s. A lot of work was done very quickly: Some of it was good, some of it was less so. Those of us who hiked it in the early years recall many sections where you needed several people to find the trail. Send one hiker to the left, one to the right, and one straight ahead. Whoever found a blaze gave out a yell. Fortunately, some of the "less good" portions have been improved over the years. A lot of the road walking is gone, although there may never be a good way around the waterless stretches in Pennsylvania. Such is the nature of the geography.

For the Mid-Atlantic, this is a wonderful trail except during hunting season. Lots of miles without many other people can be found. Not many amenities are on the Tuscarora Trail, but I think that seeing people is surely not the reason I go into the woods. For the distance hiker, some options are a little more limiting: While there are stores and post offices within a reasonable distance of the trail, you'll have to walk a shade farther than if you were hiking the Appalachian Trail. And in many of the Pennsylvania sections, dry conditions along the ridgetops require some planning with regards to water. But with that said, this is a nice place, reasonably close to some large metropolitan areas on the East Coast, that allows you to easily "get away from it all." Using a combination of the Tuscarora Trail and Appalachian Trail, with

the option of including the C and O Canal Towpath, you can combine a month worth of trails into a walk that starts and ends at a subway stop (really, I've done it).

For the day and section hikers, the entire trail can be covered as a series of fairly easy trips. There are many places where it's pleasant to just walk quietly in the woods, to see what there is to see, and to recharge the batteries. And remember, there are no bad days of hiking—some just aren't as nice as others.

—Don Desrosiers, Appalachian Trail and Tuscarora Trail thru-hiker

wonderland trail

95 MILES | WASHINGTON

TO GO . . .

- excellent trail maintenance
- jaw-dropping scenery
- loop hike
- circle the state's high point and climb it if you've got the skills

OR NOT TO GO?

- do not expect to be alone
- climbing 20,000 vertical feet is not easy
- stream fords may be problematic

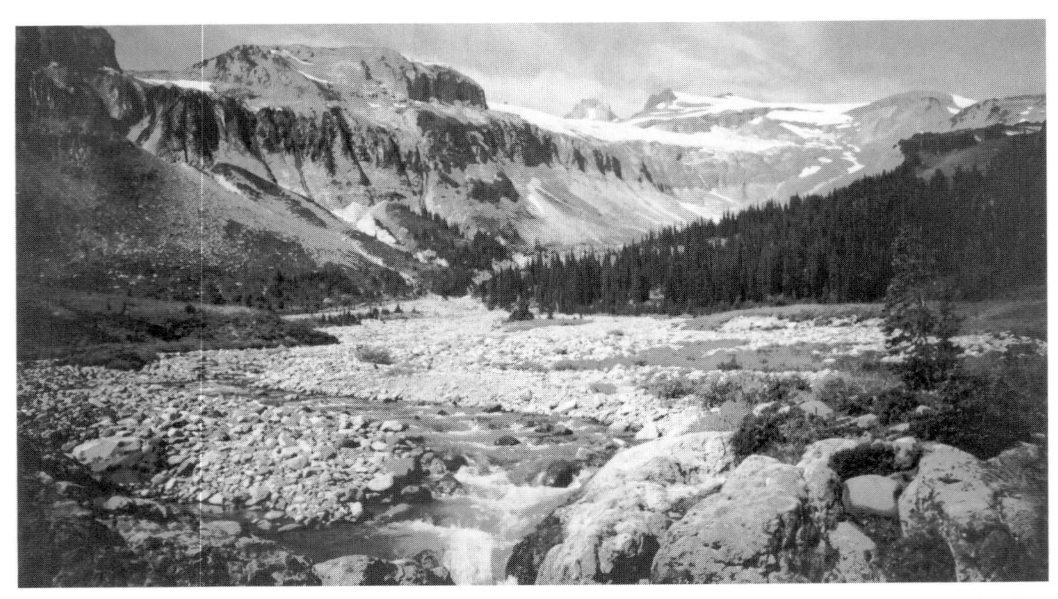

The thru-hiking season on the Wonderland Trail generally starts in July when drainages drop to fordable levels. The bare rock at Indian Bar indicates this stream's potential fury. (M. SHAWN LUTGEN)

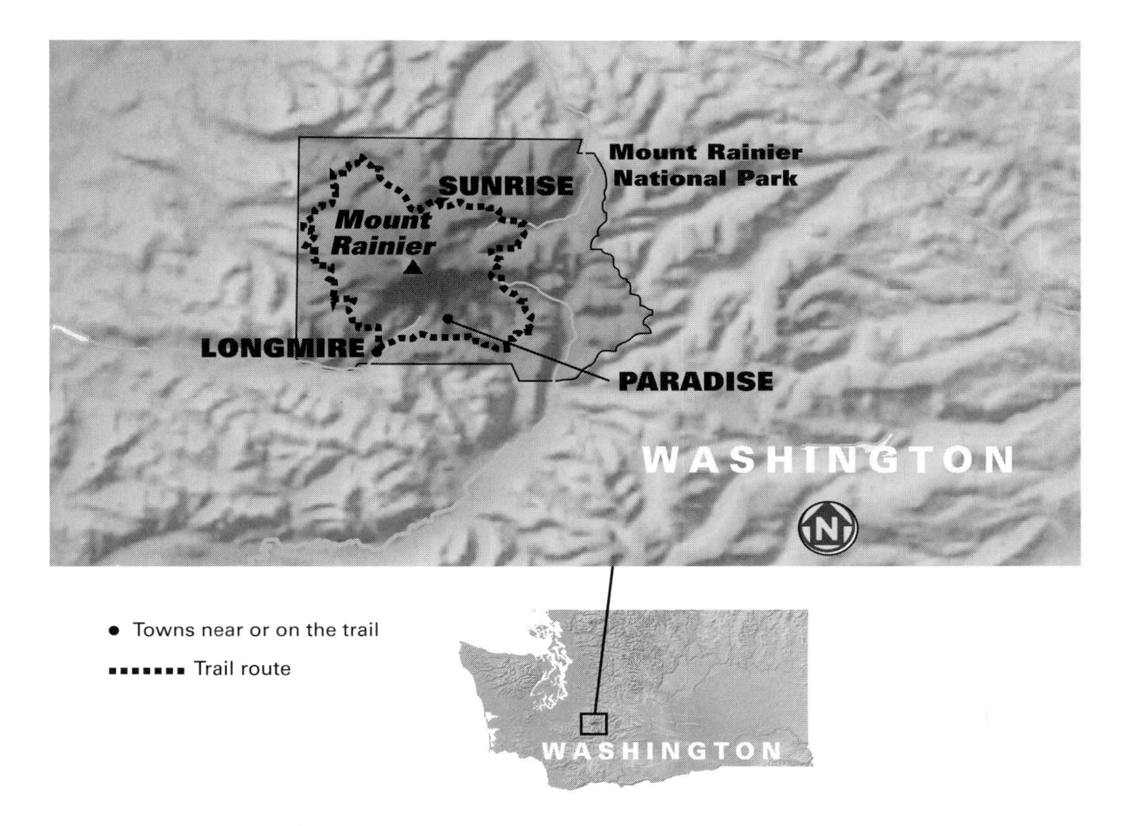

The Wonderland Trail (WT) is the last of three trails in this guide that provide you with a convenient route of travel: the loop. You don't have to worry about getting back to the beginning of the trail from the end of the trail because the end is the beginning (unless you end early, and then the end is, well, the end). The WT circles the massive 14,411-foot volcano Mount Rainier but reaches an elevation of only half that. Still, the overall size and expanse of Mount Rainier should blow most peoples' minds, especially East Coasters. Mount Rainier's base covers more than a hundred square miles, and the peak rises more than 8,000 vertical feet above the surrounding terrain. For days on end, a WT thru-hiker is rewarded with views of the surrounding lands of Washington and Oregon, as well as constant views of glaciers, snowfields, cliffs, and the summit cone of Washington's highpoint.

The WT has been voted the number-one long-distance trail by the readers of *Backpacker* magazine in past issues. The WT was also voted first in best scenery, first in best wildlife, third in best signage/trail marking, and second in best trail/camp/shelter conditions. These figures are quite impressive. No wonder this trail is so popular to hike! The WT also requires the shortest amount of time to complete compared to any other trail in the guide. Averaging fifteen miles a day, you can complete the loop in less than a week.

VITALS

- > Expect to cover 15 miles a day
- > Expect a thru-hike to take 6 days
- > Hiking season: July to October
- > Water availability: Frequent
- > Resupply opportunities: Seldom
- > First year thru-hiked: Unknown
- > Approximate yearly thru-hikers: 200 to 300
- > Primary contact: Mount Rainier National Park

WEATHER

A trail surrounding a peak as massive as Mount Rainier is susceptible to quick changes in weather. It seems that the most dramatic changes in terms of water take place just above you but actually not in the sky. Because Mount Rainier holds tons of snow and ice above the Wonderland Trail, hikers must be aware that things run counter to conditions on most other trails. The hotter it gets here, the wetter it gets, due to melting snow and ice above you. Be aware that drainages increase in depth from the effects of the sun, in addition to the effects of rain. The hiking season starts in July for this reason. Starting your hike in May or June will have you come across dangerous raging brown torrents of runoff in addition to lengthy snowfields.

Temperatures during the hiking season stay around 65° during the day, dropping to near the freezing point when darkness arrives. Using the calculation of a 3.5° drop per thousand feet gained, the tops of the biggest climbs may be 7 to 11° cooler than the bottom of the climbs, and this temperature change may become a 15° difference as you approach ice and snow at the top. As with all mountain weather, it would be best to expect the unexpected, within reason.

TERRAIN

So what is harder: going up the highest peak in Washington or going around it? Well, after the research I did, I would have to say *around it*, although neither option seems particularly easy. A thru-hike of the WT requires you to climb no less than 20,000 vertical feet over snowfields and scree slopes, through streams, and among shaded evergreen forests with a smooth tread often cut into the sides of hills. This 20,000-vertical-foot figure brings the Wonderland Trail into third place in terms of average number of feet climbed per mile (see rankings on page 112).

The vegetation patterns on the WT divide into zones, as on most big hills in

AVERAGE HIGHS AND LOWS IN DEGREES FAHRENHEIT

	JAN	MAR	MAY	JUL	SEPT	NOV
GREENWATER, WA (1,720 FT.)	30–45	35–50	45–60	50–70	45–70	35–50
LONGMIRE RANGER STATION, WA (2,760 FT.)	25–35	30–45	40–60	45–75	40–70	30–40

TERRAIN HIGHLIGHTS

- Snowfields
- Stream crossings
- Glacial runoff
- Old growth conifer forests
- Wildflower meadows
- Signs of debris flows
- Gorgeous views
- Alpine terrain

the Northwest. With a low point of less than 3,000 feet and a crest of nearly 7,000 feet, the Wonderland Trail first leads through old growth forests of hemlock, Pacific yew, and Douglas fir up to 250 feet in height. You'll see Alaska cedars that may be more than a thousand years old. As you climb, here come more softwoods, mostly spruce, fir, and pine. Finally you'll reach tree line around 5,500 feet, primarily hiking among tundra and rock, with some larger growth hiding in cracks and on the leeward side of rock and snow, to escape the wind.

WATER

Mount Rainier and the Wonderland Trail are constantly affected by water, and you will be, too. Runoff shapes the mountain, glaciers creep downward, and heavy rains trigger debris flows. Water helps you maintain health, but it may keep your feet soaked all day and can make stream crossings difficult or (to the optimist) exciting. You'll readily find bodies of water on all sections of the WT, because approximately forty lakes come within a short distance of the trail. If you can't find freshwater, you can always melt snow and ice or use glacial runoff in a pinch. The water coming out of glaciers contains quite a bit of silt and other debris. It's best to strain this water through a bandanna or let it settle in a cooking pot first, so you keep your water filter happy. And, yes, giardia (aka beaver fever) even lives in glacier water. Damn!

WILDNESS

If solitude is one of your top priorities when planning a long-distance hike, the Wonderland Trail is not for you. The WT has three strikes against it concerning wildness, or rather, crowding. If you head out on the WT, realize that you are: (1) in a National Park that more than one million people visit per year; (2) within sixty miles of Bellevue, Centralia, Kent, Olympia, Seattle, and Tacoma with a collective population of approximately one million people; (3) among as many as three hundred people who attempt to hike the Wonderland Trail in a single year. The most obscure trails in this guide may average one end-to-end completer per month, but the Wonderland Trail can average more than one end-to-end completer per day during its peak season.

So although the Wonderland Trail is a grand trail, and Mount Rainier is beyond beauty, the three points above combined with restricted bushwhacking over the fragile terrain of Mount Rainier make for a trip to be shared. If you don't mind that, then go for it. If you can enjoy a wild experience with others around, the WT will keep you happy.

SCHLIMMER'S SIDE TRAIL

HIGHPOINTERS TAKE NOTE

Mount Rainier, the highest summit in Washington, is the peak featured on the state's license plate, and the mountain that claims climbers' lives every year. This enormous peak also has the largest glacial system of any single peak in the conterminous United States. All these claims (except for the death toll) make a lot of people want to climb to the top of it. About 10,000 people try each year, but only half make it. A lot of folks are happy just being near it. Each year more than a million people visit Mount Rainier National Park, which has a yearly budget exceeding eight million dollars.

The most popular route up the mountain starts from the 5,400-foot level at Paradise. From here, you start your ascent toward the top, about seven miles away. Most people camp at Camp Muir, located more than 10,000 feet high; Ingram Flats, about a thousand feet higher than Camp Muir, is a camping option, too. From either of these camps, continue up somewhat steep snow and rock to the crater rim. It's as "easy" as that! Well, besides the thin air, howling wind, numbing cold, and 9,000-vertical-foot climb.

If you want to climb Mount Rainier, there are some logistics involved. First, it costs approximately ten dollars to get into the park and another fifteen dollars to hike to the summit. Everyone needs to secure a climbing permit, and anyone wanting to climb the peak solo has to apply with the National Park Service to do so. Otherwise, the minimum group size is two, the maximum is twelve. You should get your hands on a "blue bag" to poop in, because human waste has become a big problem on the mountain. Besides, if you take the time to poop in a bag and carry it all the way out, you'll be guaranteed good luck on the mountain in return. Really!

Mount Rainier (14,411 feet), the centerpiece of the near-hundred-mile Wonderland Trail, is easily viewed from Nickel Creek. (M. SHAWN LUTGEN)

And you may need good luck with all the weather this area gets. Only a hundred miles from the Pacific Ocean, this peak interrupts the flow of moisture into the interior of Washington, so you may encounter high winds and lots of snow. In the winter of 1971–72, nearby Paradise recorded more than ninety feet of total snowfall. Therefore, it's not shocking that the number-one fatal natural hazard in Washington and Oregon is the avalanche.

Rainier was possibly first summited in 1855, but many regard 1870 as the year of the first successful ascent. Mount Rainier's first winter ascent was completed in 1922 by Jacques Bergues and Jean and Jacques Landry. The first successful ski descent of Mount Rainier was in 1948. Kermit Bengtson, Dave Roberts, Cliff Schmidtke, and Charles Welsh descended the northeast side, Emmons Glacier, and Glacier Basin to complete their downhill run. ■

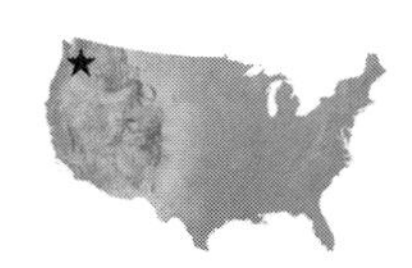

CRITTERS

- > Black bears
- > Douglas squirrels
- > Elk
- > Marmots
- > Mountain beavers
- > Mountain goats
- > Mountain lions
- > Pikas

Located less than eight miles apart are at least fifteen designated campsites complete with water and an outhouse. Off-trail camping is permitted but discouraged. Concerning resupplys, food can be cached in the park at various national park ranger stations, but only if permission is granted first. Contact Mount Rainier National Park for more information.

WILDLIFE

Although Mount Rainier's summit is constantly shrouded in ice and snow, the highest point on the WT is 7,000 feet below the summit, and the world is very much alive down here. Many mammals, large and small, can be seen on a Wonderland Trail hike if you keep an eye out and *keep quiet*. What's amazing about seeing so many different animals, weather, and plant life on your trip is that they are all on just one mountain.

POINTS OF INTEREST

REMAINING GLACIERS

Possibly due to the rise in global temperature, glaciers all over the world are disappearing, including most of the ones located in the Pacific Northwest. But some giants remain on Rainier, including the Nisqually, Ingraham, Emmons, and Winthrop glaciers.

SIGNS OF MUD FLOWS

These destructive flows can be a fifteen-foot wall of mud, water, boulders, and other debris moving downhill faster than you can run. Keep your eyes peeled for these and other signs of Rainier's past life as an active volcano.

FLOWER HUNTING

The large meadows of Indian Henry's Hunting Ground are renowned for their dramatic wildflower displays. From mid-July to late August you'll be dazzled by colorful lupine, paintbrush, mountain asters, and columbine. In September and October, this area comes alive with fall colors.

POINT AND CLICK

From the Reflection Lakes area, you'll be treated to a spectacular whole-mountain view. (That is, if you can see anything. This area is prone to dense fog, even in summer.) The image of Rainier's peak mirrored in these lakes is manna for photographers.

DON'T LEAVE HOME WITHOUT IT

FOUL-WEATHER GEAR

I recommend that you tackle the WT between July and October for good reason. The Paradise area of Mount Rainier National Park receives a whopping 100 inches of annual precipitation; 75 percent of which falls between the months of October and May. If you decide to brave the off season, don't skimp on rain or snow gear.

In Their Own Words . . .

One thing for sure about Mount Rainier's Wonderland Trail is that words and pictures will never be able to tell the whole story. When you walk, eat, and sleep at Mount Rainier's feet, you'll begin to understand that the story of the Wonderland Trail is best relayed through personal experience. But the experience does not come without a price. The trail takes away part of everyone who decides to walk it. It will cost you time, blood, sweat, and even some private tears. In return, you'll get the experience and the trail's permission to share that experience with anyone who will listen.

I thru hiked the trail in early September, in eleven days, clockwise, starting and finishing in Longmire. The trail snaked its way through thick forests, meadows, along ridgelines, across rivers and streams, along the side of glaciers, and across snowfields. The weather changes as much as the trail. Be prepared for it all. Every day is different and a new and exciting view is waiting around every corner and over the next ridge.

Every person that thru hikes the Wonderland Trail will leave with something. Whether it's a new revelation or a new appreciation, the experience will be yours. Personally, I felt an increase in self-confidence, and gained a new appreciation for the relationships I have and the things I have been blessed with. I learned, and was reminded over and over again, that the greater the challenge, the greater the reward will be.

—M. Shawn Lutgen, 2002 Wonderland Trail thru-hiker

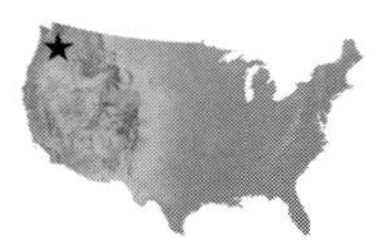

other long-distance adventures

Here is a modest list of other possibilities for the long-distance hiker. No detailed information is given because some of the hikes are extremely long, and even thoroughly covering them as I have the others would not do them justice. Also, most of the trails are currently being developed and face near constant changes. Lengths listed are the approximate projected totals in some cases. These trails range from flat woods walks to trailless routes above 9,000 feet. If the twenty-five trails mentioned previously didn't catch your interest, get ready for an additional fifteen.

Allegheny Trail (AT), PA-WV-VA. 330 miles

West Virginia Scenic Trails Association
PO Box 4042
Charleston, WV 25364
www.wvonline.com/wvsta

American Discovery Trail (ADT), CA-CO-DE-IA-IL-IN-KS-KY-MD-MO-NE-NV-OH-UT-WV. 6,800 miles

American Discovery Trail
PO Box 20155
Washington DC 20041
800-663-2387
www.discoverytrail.org

Appalachian National Scenic Trail (AT), CT-GA-MA-MD-ME-NC-NH-NJ-NY-PA-TN-VA-VT-WV. 2,170 miles

Appalachian Trail Conference
799 Washington Street
PO Box 807
Harpers Ferry, WV 25425
304-535-6331
www.appalachiantrail.org

Benton MacKaye Trail (BMT), GA-NC-TN. 275 miles

Benton MacKaye Trail Association
PO Box 53271
Atlanta, GA 30355
www.bmta.org

Catamount Ski Trail (CST), VT. 300 miles

Catamount Ski Trail Association
1 Main Street, Suite 308A
Burlington, VT 05401
802-864-5794
www.catamounttrail.org

Continental Divide National Scenic Trail (CDT), CO-ID-NM-MT-WY. 3,100 miles

Continental Divide Trail Alliance
PO Box 628
Pine, CO 80470
888-909-CDTA (toll free)
www.cdtrail.org

Eastern Continental Trail (ECT), AL-CT-FL-GA-MA-MD-ME-NB-NC-NH-NJ-NY-PA-PQ-TN-VA-VT-WV. 4,400 miles

Eastern Continental Trail Information
M. J. Eberhart
PO Box 274
Russellville, MO 65074
www.nimblewillnomad.com
Also contact the Florida Trail Association, Appalachian Trail Conference (above), and the International Appalachian Trail.

Great Western Trail (GWT), AZ-ID-MT-UT-WY. 3,000 miles

Great Western Trail Association
PO Box 41
Kaysville, UT 84037
www.gwt.org

North Country National Scenic Trail (NCT), MI-MN-ND-NY-OH-PA-WI. 4,200 miles

North Country Trail Association
229 East Main Street
Lowell, MI 49331
888-454-NCTA (toll free)
www.northcountrytrail.org

Pacific Crest National Scenic Trail (PCT), CA-OR-WA. 2,650 miles

Pacific Crest Trail Association
5325 Elkhorn Boulevard, PMB #256
Sacramento, CA 95842
916-349-2109
www.pcta.org

Pacific Northwest Trail (PNT), ID-MT-WA. 1,200 miles

Pacific Northwest Trail Association
PO Box 1817
Mount Vernon, WA 98273
877-854-9415
www.pnt.org

Potomac Heritage National Scenic Trail (PHT), VA-MD. 700 miles

Potomac Heritage Trail Association
2437 15th Street Northwest
Washington, DC
888-223-4093
www.potomactrail.org

Sierra High Route (SHR), CA. 195 miles

Roper, Steve, and Deborah Kaufman, ed. 1997. *The Sierra High Route: Traversing Timberline Country.* 2d ed. Seattle, WA: Mountaineers.

Tahoe to Yosemite Trail (TYT), CA. 180 miles

Lake Tahoe Basin Management Unit
870 Emerald Bay Road, Suite 1
South Lake Tahoe, CA 96150
530-573-2600
530-573-4036 (hearing impaired)
www.fs.fed.us/r5/ltbmu
Also contact the Tahoe Rim Trail Association and Pacific Crest Trail Association (above).

United States/Canada Border Swath (International Boundary), ND-ID-ME-MI-MN-MT-NH-NY-OH-PA-VT-WA (United States) or AB-BC-MB-NB-OT-PQ-SK (Canada). 3,990 miles

International Boundary Commission
1250 23rd Street Northwest, Suite 100
Washington DC, 20037
202-736-9007
www.internationalboundarycommission.org
The International Boundary Commission has field offices in Montana, Minnesota, and Maine, too. Also contact U.S. Customs and Border Protection at http://cbp.gov/.

recommended resources

INTRODUCTION

BACKPACKING HOW-TO

Getchell, Annie, and Dave Getchell Jr. 2000. *The Essential Outdoor Gear Manual: Equipment Care, Repair, and Selection*, 2 ed. Camden, ME: Ragged Mountain Press.

Jardine, Ray. 2000. *Beyond Backpacking: Ray Jardine's Guide to Lightweight Hiking: Practical Methods for All Who Love the Out-of-doors, from Walkers and Backpackers, to Long-distance Hikers*. LaPine, OR: AdventureLore Press. www.rayjardine.com.

Kestenbaum, Ryel. 2001. *The Ultralight Backpacker*. Camden, ME: Ragged Mountain Press.

O'Bannon, Allen, and Mike Clelland, illus. 2001. *Allen and Mike's Really Cool Backpackin' Book*. Helena, MT: Falcon Pub.

Townsend, Chris. 2005. *The Backpacker's Handbook*, 3 ed. Camden, ME: Ragged Mountain Press.

BACKPACKING ETHICS

Leave No Trace Center for Outdoor Ethics
PO Box 997
Boulder, CO 80306
800-332-4100
www.lnt.org

Waterman, and Guy Waterman. 1993. *Backwoods Ethics: environmental Issues for Hikers and Campers*. 2d ed. rev. Woodstock, VT: Countryman Press.

———. 1993. *Wilderness Ethics: Preserving the Spirit of Wildness*. Woodstock, VT: Countryman Press.

FIRST AID

American Red Cross
2025 E Street, NW
Washington, DC 20006
202-303-4498
www.redcross.org

Wilderness Medical Associates
189 Dudley Road, Suite 2
Bryant Pond, ME 04219
888-WILD-MED
www.wildmed.com

Gill, Paul G., Jr. Wilderness First Aid: A Pocket Guide. Camden, ME: Ragged Mountain Press.

Morrissey, Jim. 2000. *Wilderness Medical Associates Field Guide*. Revised ed. Bryant Pond, ME: Wilderness Medical Associates.

WILDERNESS LEADERSHIP

Wilderness Education Association
900 East 7th Street
Bloomington, IN 47405
812-855-4095
www.weainfo.org

American Alpine Club. Published annually. *Accidents in North American Mountaineering.* New York, NY: American Alpine Club.

TRIP PLANNING

Mueser, Roland. 1998. *Long-Distance Hiking: Lessons from the Appalachian Trail.* Camden, ME: Ragged Mountain Press.

ARIZONA TRAIL

Arizona Trail Association
PO Box 36736
Phoenix, AZ 85067
602-252-4794
www.aztrail.org

Grand Canyon National Park
PO Box 129
Grand Canyon, AZ 86023
928-638-7888
www.nps.gov/grca

Kaibab Plateau Visitor Center
HC 64, Highways AZ 67/US 89A
Jacob Lake, AZ 86022
928-643-7298
In 2003, this forest service center had basic maps of the Arizona Trail available at no cost. Other Arizona Forest Service offices might have these maps as well. The Arizona Public Lands Information Center (APLIC) in Phoenix offers maps, too, but charges for them, and I have found the APLIC to be extremely unreliable overall.

ARIZONA TRAIL THRU-HIKING

Arizona Trail Association. *Essential Information for Long Distance Hikers.* Phoenix, AZ: Arizona Trail Association.

Arizona Trail Association. Fall 2000. "The Arizona trail." *The Distance Hiker's Gazette.* Retrieved August 4, 2002, from www.aldhawest.org/gazette/V5_4_ArizonaTrail.html.

DeLorme. 2004. *Arizona Atlas and Gazetteer.* 6th ed. Yarmouth, ME: DeLorme Mapping Company.

This atlas from DeLorme shows most AZT sections that currently exist.

Lankford, Andrea. 2002. *Biking the Arizona Trail: The Complete Guide to Day-Riding and Thru-Biking.* Englewood, CO: Westcliffe Publishers.

Lorang Jones, Tom. 2003. *The Arizona Trail: The Complete Guide.* Englewood, CO: Westcliffe Publishers.

Townsend, Chris. 2002. *Crossing Arizona: A Solo Hike Through the Sky Islands and Deserts of the Arizona Trail.* Woodstock, VT: Countryman Press.

ARIZONA HISTORY

Barnes, Will C. 1988. *Arizona Place Names.* Tucson, AZ: University of Arizona Press.

GRAND CANYON NATIONAL PARK

Butchart, Harvey. 1998. *Grand Canyon Treks: 12,000 Miles Through the Grand Canyon.* Bishop, CA: Spotted Dog Press.

Ghiglieri, Michael P., and Thomas M. Myers. 2001. *Over the Edge: Death in the Grand Canyon: Gripping Accounts of All Known Fatal Mishaps in the Most Famous of the World's Seven Natural Wonders* . Flagstaff, AZ: Puma Press.

Powell, John Wesley. 2002. *The Exploration of the Colorado River and Its Canyons*. Washington, DC: Adventure Classics/National Geographic.

SOUTHWEST NATURE GUIDE

Alden, Peter, et al. 1999. *National Audubon Society Field Guide to the Southwestern States*. New York, NY: Knopf.

UNITED STATES–MEXICO BORDER

Langewiesche, William. 1993. *Cutting for Sign*. New York, NY: Pantheon.

BAKER TRAIL

Hostelling International Pittsburgh
830 East Warrington Avenue
Pittsburgh, PA 15210
412-431-1267
www.hipittsburgh.org

Rachel Carson Trail Conservancy
PO Box 35
Warrendale, PA 15086
www.rachelcarsontrail.com

Allegheny National Forest
PO Box 847
Warren, PA 16365
814-723-5150
www.fs.fed.us/r9/forests/allegheny/

Pennsylvania Bureau of State Parks
PO Box 8551
Harrisburg, PA 17105-8551
www.dcnr.state.pa.us/stateparks/

BAKER TRAIL THRU-HIKING

Pittsburgh Council of American Youth Hostels, and Jim Ritchie (Ed.). 1999. *Baker Trail Guide Book*. Pittsburgh, PA: Hostelling International Pittsburgh.

Rachel Carson Trails Conservancy. 1999. *Guide to the Baker Trail*. Pittsburgh, PA: Hostelling International Pittsburgh.

PENNSYLVANIA GEOLOGY

Van Diver, Bradford B. 1990. *Roadside Geology of Pennsylvania*. Missoula, MT: Mountain Press.

PENNSYLVANIA HIKING

Ostertag, Rhonda and George Ostertag. 2002. *Hiking Pennsylvania*. 2nd ed. Guilford, CT: Falcon Publishing.

BUCKEYE TRAIL

Buckeye Trail Association
PO Box 254
Worthington, OH 43085
800-881-3062 (in Ohio)
www.buckeyetrail.org

BUCKEYE TRAIL THRU-HIKING

Berger, Karen. 2002. "Boomerang Backpacking: The Buckeye Trail." GORP. Retrieved April 24, 2002, from www.gorp.com/gorp/activity/hiking/features/loops8.htm.

Buckeye Trail Association.

Complete set of twenty-four section maps. These maps show the Buckeye Trail route plus mileage, directions, campsites, and facilities.

Hutchins, B. & M. *Burr Oak to Milford.* This guide covers 242 total miles of the BT.

———. *Following the Miami &Erie Canal from Lake Loramie State Park to*

Napoleon. This guide covers nearly 99 miles of the BT.

———. *Milford to Lake Loramie State Park*. This guide covers more than 125 miles of the BT.

Pond, Robert J. 2003. *Follow the Blue Blazes: A Guide to Hiking Ohio's Buckeye Trail*. Athens, OH: Ohio University Press.

Wildernet. 2002. "Ohio: Buckeye Trail." Retrieved April 24, 2002, from www.wildernet.com/pages/area.cfm?areaID=OHBT&CU_ID=1.

OHIO HIKING

Ramey, Ralph. 1997. *Fifty Hikes in Ohio: Day Hikes and Backpacking Trips Throughout the Buckeye State* . 2d ed. Woodstock, VT: Backcountry Publications.

OHIO HISTORY

Kytle, Elizabeth. 1996. *Home on the Canal*. Baltimore, MD: Johns Hopkins University Press.

COHOS TRAIL

Cohos Trail Association
252 Westmoreland Road
Spofford, NH 03462
www.cohostrail.org

White Mountain National Forest
719 Main Street
Laconia, NH 03246
603-528-8721
www.fs.fed.us/r9/white

COHOS TRAIL THRU-HIKING

Cohos Trail Association. 2004. Cohos Trail Maps. Spofford, NH: Cohos Trail Association.

Nilsen, Kim Robert. 2000. *The Cohos Trail: The Guidebook to New Hampshire's Great Unknown*. North Hampton, NH: Nicolin Fields Pub.

NEW ENGLAND LOGGING HISTORY

Pike, Robert E. 1967. *Tall Trees, Tough Men*. New York, NY: W. W. Norton.

NEW HAMPSHIRE HIKING

Daniell, Gene, and Steven D. Smith, eds. 1992. *AMC White Mountain Guide: Hiking Trails in the White Mountain National Forest*. 27th ed. Boston, MA: Appalachian Mountain Club Books.

NORTHEAST ALPINE GUIDE

Slack, Nancy G. and Allison W. Bell. 1993. *85 Acres: A Field Guide to the Adirondack Alpine Summits*. Lake George, NY: Adirondack Mountain Club.

NORTHEAST NATURE GUIDE

Kalinowski, Tom. 1999. *Adirondack Almanac: A Guide to the Natural Year*. Utica, NY: North Country Books.

WHITE MOUNTAIN HISTORY

Howe, Nicholas. 2000. *Not Without Peril: One Hundred and Fifty Years of Misadventure on the Presidential Range of New Hampshire*. Boston, MA: Appalachian Mountain Club.

Julyan, Robert, and Mary Julyan. 1993. *Place Names of the White Mountains*. Rev. ed. Hanover, NH: University Press of New England.

Waterman, Laura, and Guy Waterman. 1989. *Forest and Crag: A History of*

Hiking, Trail Blazing, and Adventure in the Northeast Mountains. Boston, MA: Appalachian Mountain Club.

COLORADO TRAIL

Colorado Trail Foundation
710 10th Street, #210
Golden, CO 80401
303-384-3729
www.coloradotrail.org

COLORADO TRAIL THRU-HIKING

Colorado Trail Foundation. 2002. *The Colorado Trail: The Official Guidebook*. 6th ed. Golden, CO: Colorado Mountain Club Press.

Colorado Trail Foundation, ed. 2003. *Colorado Trail: The Trailside Databook*. 2nd ed. Golden, CO: Colorado Mountain Club Press.

Denise, Robert P. 1993. *Hiking the Colorado Trail: A Guide for Long and Short Hiking Trips Along the Colorado Trail*. Fort Collins, CO: Lothlórien Press.

Hammick, Bruce. Fall 2002. "Should I hike the Colorado trail?" The Distance Hikers Gazette. Retrieved April 28, 2002, from www.aldhawest.org/gazette/V4_3_Hammick.html.

Shaw, Christine. 2002. "Hiking the Colorado Trail: Expedition Planner." GORP. Retrieved April 18, 2002, from www.gorp.com/gorp/location/co/hik_colorado7.htm.

COLORADO HIKING AND MOUNTAINEERING

Borneman, Walter R., and Lyndon J. Lampert. 1998. *A Climbing Guide to Colorado's Fourteeners*. 20th anniversary ed. Boulder, CO: Pruett Publishing.

Garratt, Mike, and Bob Martin. 1992. *Colorado's High Thirteeners: A Climbing and Hiking Guide*. 3rd ed. Boulder, CO: Johnson Books.

Roach, Gerry. 1999. *Colorado's Fourteeners: From Hikes to Climbs*. 2nd ed. Golden, CO: Fulcrum Publishing.

COLORADO MOUNTAIN HISTORY

Bueler, William M. 2000. *Roof of the Rockies: A History of Colorado Mountaineering*. 3rd ed. Golden, CO: Colorado Mountain Club Press.

Hart, John L. Jerome. 1972. *Fourteen Thousand Feet: A History of the Naming and Early Ascents of the High Colorado Peaks*. Denver, CO: Colorado Mountain Club.

COLORADO WILDFLOWER GUIDE

Robertson, Leigh. 1999. *Southern Rocky Mountain Wildflowers:* A Field Guide to Common Wildflowers, Shrubs, and Trees. Estes Park, CO: Rocky Mountain Nature Association.

FLORIDA TRAIL

Florida Trail Association
5415 SW 13th Street
Gainesville, FL 32608
877-HIKE-FLA
www.florida-trail.org

Big Cypress National Preserve
HCR 61, Box 110
Ochopee, FL 34141
(239) 695-1201
www.nps.gov/bicy

Ocala National Forest
Salt Springs Visitor Center
14100 N. State Highway 19
Salt Springs, FL 32134
352-685-3070
www.fs.fed.us/r8/florida

FLORIDA TRAIL THRU-HIKING

Cordes, Kathleen Ann. 2001. *America's National Scenic Trails.* Norman, OK: University of Oklahoma Press.

Florida Trail Association. Complete set of Florida National Scenic Trail maps. Gainesville, FL: Florida Trail Association.

———. *Thru-Hiker Maps.* Gainesville, FL: Florida Trail Association. This packet includes maps and arrangements for crossing private land.

Florida Trail Association, Kent L. Wimmer, and Joan Hobson, eds. 2001. *Trail Manual for the Florida Trail System.* 4th ed. Gainesville, FL: Florida Trail Association.

Friend, Sandra, ed. 2004. *Florida Trail Companion Guide for Long Distance Hikers.* Gainesville, FL: Florida Trail Association.

Friend, Sandra. 2004. *The Florida Trail: The Official Hiking Guide.* Englewood, CO: Westcliffe.

———. 2003. *Along the Florida Trail.* Englewood, CO: Westcliffe.

Guhse, Rick. *Florida Trail Handbook.* Gainesville, FL: Florida Trail Association.

FLORIDA NATURE GUIDE

Alden, Peter, et. al. 1998. *National Audubon Society Field Guide to Florida.* New York, NY: Knopf.

ICE AGE TRAIL

Ice Age Park and Trail Foundation
207 East Buffalo Street, Suite 515
Milwaukee, WI 53202
800-227-0046
www.iceagetrail.org

Chequamegon-Nicolet National Forest
Medford-Park Falls Ranger District
850 North 8th, Hwy 13
Medford, WI 54451
(715) 748-4875
www.fs.fed.us/r9/cnnf

Ice Age National Scenic Trail
National Park Service
700 Rayovac Drive, Suite 100
Madison, WI 53711
608-441-5610
www.nps.gov/iatr

Wisconsin Department of Natural Resources
101 South Webster Street
Madison, WI 53707
608-266-2621
www.dnr.state.wi.us/

ICE AGE TRAIL THRU-HIKING

Cordes, Kathleen Ann. 2001. *America's National Scenic Trails.* Norman, OK: University of Oklahoma Press.

DeLorme. 2001. *Wisconsin Atlas and Gazetteer.* 9th ed. Yarmouth, ME: DeLorme Mapping Company. This atlas from DeLorme shows most Ice Age Trail sections that currently exist.

GORP. 2002. "National Scenic Trails: Ice Age Trail." GORP. Retrieved May 2, 2002, from www.gorp.com/gorp/resource/us_trail/ice_age.htm.

Ice Age Park and Trail Foundation. 2002.

"Ice Age Trail: History of Wisconsin's Glacial Landscape." Retrieved April 18, 2002, from www.iceagetrail.org/infocenter/landscape.html.

———. Summer 2002. *Mammoth Tales.* Milwaukee, WI: Ice Age Park and Trail Foundation.

———. 2003. *Ice Age Trail Companion Guide: 2004.* Milwaukee, WI: Ice Age Park and Trail Foundation.

Lotto, Sandy. Summer 2002. "A Dream Come True—The Ice Age Trail." *Northbound.* Retrieved September 14, 2003, from www.treesfortomorrow.com/pubs/trail.pdf.

WISCONSIN GEOLOGY

Campbell, James. November 2000. "The Ice Age Trail: Land of Cool Carvings." *Backpacker.*

Dott, Robert H., Jr., and John W. Attig. 2004. *Roadside Geology of Wisconsin.* Missoula, MT: Mountain Press Pub.

WISCONSIN HIKING

Hintz, Martin. 1997. *Hiking Wisconsin.* Champaign, IL: Human Kinetics.

Morgan, John, and Ellen Morgan. 2004. *50 Hikes in Wisconsin: Walks, Hikes, and Backpacks in the Badger State.* Woodstock, VT: Countryman Press.

INTERNATIONAL APPALACHIAN TRAIL

IAT/SIA Maine Chapter
27 Flying Point Road
Freeport, ME 04032
www.internationalat.org/SIAIAT

Baxter State Park
64 Balsam Drive
Millinocket, ME 04462
207-723-5140
www.baxterstateparkauthority.com

Mount Carleton Provincial Park
11 Gagnon Street
Saint-Quentin, NB E8A 1N4
Canada
506-235-6040
www.out-there.com/carleton.htm

Parc national de la Gaspésie
900, route du Parc
Sainte-Anne-des-Monts, Québec, G0E 2G0
Canada
866 PARC GAS

U.S. Customs and Border Protection
Houlton Sector Headquarters
96 Calais Road
Hodgdon, ME 04737
207-532-6521
www.cbp.gov/xp/cgov/enforcement/border_patrol/border_patrol_sectors/houlton_sector_me/
(This sector covers all of Maine.)

INTERNATIONAL APPALACHIAN TRAIL THRU-HIKING

Baxter State Park Authority. "Thru-Hiking in Baxter State Park." www.baxterstateparkauthority.com/hiking/thru-hiking.html.

Dykstra, Monique. 2002. *Alone in the Appalachians: A City Girl's Trek from Maine to the Gaspesie.* San Diego, CA: Raincoast Books.

IAT/SIA. 2000. *Bilingual Hiking Glossary.* Freeport, ME: Maine Chapter of IAT/SIA.

IAT/SIA and Suzanne Goulet (Ed.). 2002. *A Thru-Hiker's Companion Guide to the*

International Appalachian Trail. 2d ed. Freeport, ME: Maine Chapter of IAT/SIA. An extensive, free thru-hiker's guide is currently available on the IAT/SIA website.

Mann, Paul. October 1998. "The Province of Dreamers." *Backpacker.* 49–56.

Waterman, Guy, and Laura Waterman. October 1977. "Time for a change." *Off Belay.*

NORTHEAST ALPINE GUIDE

Slack, Nancy G. and Allison W. Bell. 1993. *85 Acres: A Field Guide to the Adirondack Alpine Summits.* Lake George, NY: Adirondack Mountain Club.

NORTHEAST MOUNTAIN HISTORY

Waterman, Laura, and Guy Waterman. 1989. *Forest and Crag: A History of Hiking, Trail Blazing, and Adventure in the Mountains of the Northeast.* Boston, MA: Appalachian Mountain Club.

NORTHEAST NATURE GUIDE

Kalinowski, Tom. 1999. *Adirondack Almanac: A Guide to the Natural Year.* Utica, NY: North Country Books.

JOHN MUIR TRAIL

Pacific Crest Trail Association
5325 Elkhorn Boulevard, PMB 256
Sacramento, CA 95842
916-349-2109
www.pcta.org

Inyo National Forest
351 Pacu Lane, Suite 200
Bishop, CA 93514
760-873-2485
www.fs.fed.us/r5/inyo

Sequoia and Kings Canyon National Park
47050 Generals Highway
Three Rivers, CA 93271
559-565-3341
www.nps.gov/seki/index.htm

Yosemite Association
PO Box 230
El Portal, CA 95318
209-379-2646
www.yosemite.org

Yosemite National Park
PO Box 577
Yosemite NP, CA 95389
209-372-0200
209-372-4726 (hearing impaired)
www.nps.gov/yose/index.htm

JOHN MUIR TRAIL THRU-HIKING

Schaffer, Jeffrey P., et al. 1995. *The Pacific Crest Trail.* Volume One: California. 5th ed. Berkeley, CA: Wilderness Press.

Winnett, Thomas and Kathy Morey. 1998. *Guide to the John Muir Trail.* 3rd ed. Berkeley, CA: Wilderness Press.

JOHN MUIR

Muir, John. 2001. *The Mountains of California.* New York, NY: Modern Library.

SIERRA NEVADA HIKING AND MOUNTAINEERING

Porcella, Stephen and Cameron Burns. 1995. *Hiking and Climbing California's Fourteeners.* Evergreen, CO: Chockstone Press.

Secor, R. J. 1999. *The High Sierra: Peaks, Passes, and Trails.* 2nd ed. Seattle, WA: Mountaineers.

SIERRA NEVADA HISTORY

Browning, Peter. 1991. *Place Names of the Sierra Nevada: From Abbot to Zumwalt.* 2nd ed. Berkeley, CA: Wilderness Press.

Clyde, Norman. 1998. *Close Ups of the High Sierra*. Bishop, CA: Spotted Dog Press.

LONE STAR HIKING TRAIL

Lone Star Hiking Trail Club
1100 Augusta #66
Houston, TX 77057
www.lshtclub.com

Sam Houston National Forest
394 FM 1375 West
New Waverly, TX 77358
888-361-6908
www.fs.fed.us/r8/texas/recreation/sam_houston/samhouston_gen_info.shtml

The free national forest map features the LSHT.

LONE STAR HIKING TRAIL THRU-HIKING

Brewington, Don. 1999. "A Hiker's Guide for the Lone Star Trail." Houston, TX: Lone Star Hiking Trail Club.

This thru-hiking guide is available for free on the Lone Star Hiking Trail Club's website, www.lshtclub.com/Hiker's%20Guide.htm.

TEXAS NATURE GUIDE

Werler,. John E. and James R. Dixon. 2000. *Texas Snakes: Identification, Distribution, and Natural History*. Austin, TX: University of Texas Press.

Price, Steve. 1996. *Seasonal Guide to the Natural Year: A Month by Month Guide to Natural Events. Texas*. Golden, CO: Fulcrum Publishing.

LONG PATH

New York-New Jersey Trail Conference
156 Ramapo Valley Road
Mahwah, NJ 07430
201-512-9348
www.nynjtc.org/trails/longpath/

For Catskills Forest Preserve information contact:

NYS Department of Environmental Conservation (DEC), Division of Lands and Forests
21 South Putt Corners Road
New Paltz, NY 12561-1696
(845) 256-3000
www.dec.state.ny.us/website/dlf/publands/cats/

For information on Greene and Delaware counties:

NYS Department of Environmental Conservation (DEC), Division of Lands and Forests
Rte 10, HCR 1
Stamford, NY 12167
(607) 652-7365

LONG PATH THRU-HIKING

New York-New Jersey Trail Conference. 2002. *The Long Path Guide*. 5th ed. Mahwah, NJ: New York-New Jersey Trail Conference.

CATSKILL HIKING

McAllister, Lee, and Myron Steven Ochman. 1989. *Hiking the Catskills: A Guide for Exploring the Natural Beauty of America's Romantic and Magical Mountains on the Trail and "Off the*

Beaten Path." New York, NY: The Whole Concept Design Studios.
This book is currently out of print, but I highly recommend attempting to find a copy. It's one of the best guidebooks I have ever read.
Wadsworth, Bruce, and the Schenectady Chapter of the Adirondack Mountain Club. 1994. *Guide to Catskill Trails.* 2d ed. Lake George, NY: Adirondack Mountain Club.

LONG PATH HISTORY

Scherer, Glenn, ed.. 1995. *Vistas and Vision: A 75 Year History of the NY-NJ Trail Conference.* New York, NY: New York-New Jersey Trail Conference.

NORTHEAST MOUNTAIN HISTORY

Waterman, Laura, and Guy Waterman. 1989. *Forest and Crag: A History of Hiking, Trail Blazing, and Adventure in the Northeast Mountains.* Boston, MA: Appalachian Mountain Club.

NORTHEAST NATURE GUIDE

Kalinowski, Tom. 1999. *Adirondack Almanac: A Guide to the Natural Year.* Utica, NY: North Country Books.

LONG TRAIL

Green Mountain Club
4711 Waterbury-Stowe Road
Waterbury Center, VT 05677
802-244-7037
www.greenmountainclub.org

Green Mountain National Forest
231 North Main Street
Rutland, VT 05701
802-747-6700
802-747-6765 (hearing impaired)
www.fs.fed.us/r9/gmfl/green_mountain/index.htm

Vermont Department of Forests, Parks, and Recreation
103 South Main Street
Waterbury, VT 05671-0601
www.state.vt.us/anr/fpr/

LONG TRAIL THRU-HIKING

Green Mountain Club. 2003. *Long Trail Guide.* 25th ed. Waterbury Center, VT: Green Mountain Club.
Norton, Russell. 2001. *Long Trail End-to-Ender's Guide.* 10th ed. Waterbury Center, VT: Green Mountain Club.
Wilderness Map Company. 2004. *Vermont's Long Trail: Illustrated Hiking Map & Guide.* Twin Mt, NH: Wilderness Map Company.

LONG TRAIL HISTORY

Curtis, Jane, et al. 1985. *Green Mountain Adventure, Vermont's Long Trail.* Lebanon, NH: Whitman Press.
Lanza, Michael. May 2004. "Speed freak." *Backpacker.* 78–82, 116–19.

NORTHEAST ALPINE GUIDE

Slack, Nancy G. and Allison W. Bell. 1993. *85 Acres: A Field Guide to the Adirondack Alpine Summits.* Lake George, NY: Adirondack Mountain Club.

NORTHEAST MOUNTAIN HISTORY

Waterman, Laura, and Guy Waterman. 1989. *Forest and Crag: A History of*

Hiking, Trail Blazing, and Adventure in the Northeast Mountains. Boston, MA: Appalachian Mountain Club.

NORTHEAST NATURE GUIDE

Kalinowski, Tom. 1999. *Adirondack Almanac: A Guide to the Natural Year*. Utica, NY: North Country Books.

MASON-DIXON TRAIL

Mason-Dixon Trail System, Inc.
719 Oakbourne Rd
West Chester, PA 19382
www.angelfire.com/pa2/yorkhikingclub/mdts.html

Maryland Department of Natural Resources
580 Taylor Avenue
Tawes State Office Building
Annapolis, MD 21401
410-260-8367
877-620-8DNR (in Maryland)
www.dnr.state.md.us

Pennsylvania Department of Conservation and Natural Resources
Rachel Carson State Office Building
PO Box 8767
400 Market Street
Harrisburg, PA 17105
www.dcnr.state.pa.us

MASON-DIXON TRAIL THRU-HIKING

Mason-Dixon Trail System, Inc. 1996. *Maps to the Mason-Dixon Trail System*. West Chester, PA: Mason-Dixon Trail System Inc.

These maps come complete with trail descriptions on the back.

PENNSYLVANIA GEOLOGY

Van Diver, Bradford B. 1990. *Roadside Geology of Pennsylvania*. Missoula, MT: Mountain Press.

PENNSYLVANIA HIKING

Ostertag, Rhonda, and George Ostertag. 2002. *Hiking Pennsylvania*. 2nd ed. Guilford, CT: Falcon Publishing.

METACOMET-MONADNOCK TRAIL

Appalachian Mountain Club—Berkshire Chapter
PO Box 9369
North Amherst, MA 01059
413-549-4124
www.amcberkshire.org

Metacomet-Monadnock Trail Conference
14 Country Lane
South Hadley, MA 01075
http://amcberkshire.org/mmtrail

Massachusetts Department of Conservation and Recreation
251 Causeway Street, Suite 600
Boston, MA 02114
617-626-1250
www.mass.gov/dcr/

METACOMET-MONADNOCK TRAIL THRU-HIKING

Ryan, Christopher J. 2003. *Metacomet-Monadnock Trail Guide: A Trail Guide with Maps of the 117 Mile Long-Distance Footpath Through the Three County/Pioneer Valley Region of Western Massachusetts and the Monadnock Region of Southwest New Hampshire* . 10th ed.

Amherst, MA: Berkshire Chapter, Appalachian Mountain Club.

AREA ACTIVITIES

Monkman, Jerry, and Marcy Monkman. 2002. *Discover Southern New Hampshire: AMC Guide to the Best Hiking, Biking, and Paddling.* Boston, MA: Appalachian Mountain Club Books.

NATURE GUIDE

Kalinowski, Tom. 1999. *Adirondack Almanac: A Guide to the Natural Year.* Utica, NY: North Country Books.

NORTHEAST HISTORY

Waterman, Laura, and Guy Waterman. 1989. *Forest and Crag: A History of Hiking, Trail Blazing, and Adventure in the Mountains of the Northeast.* Boston, MA: Appalachian Mountain Club.

MID STATE TRAIL

Mid State Trail Association, Inc.
PO Box 167
Boalsburg, PA 16827
The MSTA's "rarely regular news publication," The Brushwacker, can be found onthe Internet at http://phoenix.goucher.edu/MSTA.

Pennsylvania Department of Conservation and Natural Resources
Rachel Carson State Office Building
PO Box 8767
400 Market Street
Harrisburg, PA 17105
www.dcnr.state.pa.us

MID STATE TRAIL THRU-HIKING

Thwaites, Tom. 2001. *Map and Guide Set to Mid State Trail in the Seven Mountains of Pennsylvania.* 10th ed. Boalsburg, PA: Mid State Trail Association, Inc.

Mid State Trail Association, Inc. 2002. *Maps to the Mid State Trail System.* Boalsburg, PA: Mid State Trail Association, Inc.

PENNSYLVANIA GEOLOGY

Van Diver, Bradford B. 1990. *Roadside Geology of Pennsylvania.* Missoula, MT: Mountain Press.

PENNSYLVANIA HIKING

Ostertag Rhonda, and George Ostertag. 2002. *Hiking Pennsylvania.* 2nd ed. Guilford, CT: Falcon Publishing.

MOUNTAINS-TO-SEA TRAIL

Friends of the Mountains to Sea Trail
3585 US 401 South
Louisburg, NC 27549
www.ncmst.org

North Carolina Division of Parks and Recreation
State Trails Program
12700 Bayleaf Church Road
Raleigh, NC 27614
919-846-9995
http://ils.unc.edu/parkproject/trails/home.html

MOUNTAINS-TO-SEA TRAIL THRU-HIKING

De Hart, Allen. 2000. *Hiking North Carolina's Mountains-to-Sea Trail.* Chapel Hill, NC: University of North Carolina Press.

DeLorme. 2003. *North Carolina Atlas and Gazetteer*. 6th ed. Yarmouth, ME: DeLorme Mapping Company.
This atlas from DeLorme shows many MST sections that currently exist, though not the entire end-to-end route.
Dossey, Donald E., and John I. Hillyer. 1998. *The Mountains-to-Sea Trail: Western North Carolina's Majestic Rival to the Appalachian Trail*. Asheville, NC: Outcomes Unlimited Press.

APPALACHIAN MOUNTAIN HISTORY

Kephart, Horace. 2001. *Our Southern Highlanders: A Narrative of Adventure in the Southern Appalachians and a Study of Life Among the Mountaineers*. New and enl. ed. Alexander, NC: Land of the Sky Books.
Schwarzkopf, S. Kent. 1985. *A History of Mt. Mitchell and the Black Mountains: Exploration, Development, and Preservation*. Raleigh, NC: North Carolina Division of Archives and History.

APPALACHIAN NATURE GUIDE

Bradley, Jack, and Carrie Cook. 1994. *Alpine Forest*. Raleigh, NC: North Carolina Division of Parks and Recreation.
Smith, Richard M. 1998. *Wildflowers of the Southern Mountains*. Knoxville, TN: University of Tennessee Press.

NORTHVILLE-PLACID TRAIL

Adirondack Mountain Club
814 Goggins Road
Lake George, NY 12845
518-668-4447
www.adk.org
www.geocities.com/schdyadk/ (click on Schenectady chapter, trail details)

New York State Department of Environmental Conservation
Adirondack Office
1115 NYS Route 86
PO Box 296
Ray Brook, NY 12977
518-897-1200
www.dec.state.ny.us

NORTHVILLE-PLACID TRAIL THRU-HIKING

Case, Jeffrey, and Donna Case. eds. 2002. *Guide to Adirondack Trails: Northville-Placid Trail*. 3d ed. rev. Lake George, NY: Adirondack Mountain Club.

ADIRONDACK HIKING

Cagle, Laurence T. 2004. *Adirondack Trails: Central Region Guide*. 3rd ed. Lake George, NY: Adirondack Mountain Club.
Aprill, Dennis. 2000. *Paths Less Traveled: The Adirondack Experience for Walkers, Hikers and Climbers of All Ages*. New enlarged ed. Mt. Kisco, NY: Pinto Press.
Goodwin, Tony. ed. 2004. *Adirondack Trails: High Peaks Region*. 13th ed. Lake George, NY: Adirondack Mountain Club.

ADIRONDACK HISTORY

Carson, Russell M. L. 1973. *Peaks and People of the Adirondacks*. Glens Falls, NY: Adirondack Mountain Club.

ADIRONDACK NATURE GUIDE

Kalinowski, Tom. 1999. *Adirondack Almanac: A Guide to the Natural Year*. Utica, NY: North Country Books.

NORTHEAST MOUNTAIN HISTORY

Waterman, Laura, and Guy Waterman. 1989. *Forest and Crag: A History of Hiking, Trail Blazing, and Adventure in the Mountains of the Northeast*. Boston, MA: Appalachian Mountain Club.

OUACHITA TRAIL

Ouachita Mountain Hikers
PO Box 371
Hot Springs, AR 71902
www.msdriscoll.com/hsv/hike/

Ouachita National Forest
PO Box 1270
Hot Springs, AR 71902
501-321-5202
www.fs.fed.us/oonf/ouachita

Ozark Society
PO Box 2914
Little Rock, AR 72203
501-666-2989
www.ozarksociety.net

Tim Ernst
Cloudland.net Publishing
HC 33, Box 50-A
Pettigrew, AR 72752
870-861-5536
www.cloudland.net

OUACHITA TRAIL THRU-HIKING

Ernst, Tim. 2000. *Ouachita Trail Guide*. 3d ed. Pettigrew, AR: Cloudland.net.

Lantz, Gary. December 1998. "A Trail of True Grit." *Backpacker*. 88–94.

ARKANSAS AND OKLAHOMA HIKING

Ernst, Pam. 2003. *Arkansas Dayhikes for Kids and Families: 89 Easy Trails in "the Natural State."* Pettigrew, AR: Cloudland.net.

Ernst, Tim. 2003. *Arkansas Hiking Trails: A Guide to 78 Selected Trails in "the Natural State."* 3rd ed. Pettigrew, AR: Cloudland.net.

———. 2003. *Ozark Highlands Trail Guide*. 4th ed. Pettigrew, AR: Cloudland.net.

OZARK HIGHLANDS TRAIL

Ozark Highlands Trail Association
Tim Ernst and Cloudland.net Publishing
HC 33, Box 50-A
Pettigrew, AR 72752
870-861-5536
www.hikearkansas.com/ohta.html

Ozark-St. Francis National Forests
605 West Main Street
Russellville, AR 72801
479-968-2354
www.fs.fed.us/oonf/ozark

Ozark Society
5210 Sherwood Road
Little Rock, AR 72207
501-666-2989
www.ozarksociety.net

OZARK HIGHLANDS TRAIL THRU-HIKING

Ernst, Tim. 2003. *Ozark Highlands Trail Guide.* 4th ed. Pettigrew, AR: Cloudland.net.

ARKANSAS AND OKLAHOMA HIKING

Ernst, Pam. 2003. *Arkansas Dayhikes for Kids and Families: 89 Easy Trails in "the Natural State."* Pettigrew, AR: Cloudland.net.
Ernst, Tim. 2003. *Arkansas Hiking Trails: A Guide to 78 Selected Trails in "the Natural State."* 3rd ed. Pettigrew, AR: Cloudland.net.
———. 2000. *Ouachita Trail Guide.* 3d ed. Pettigrew, AR: Cloundland.net.

RIVER-TO-RIVER TRAIL

River-to-River Trail Society
1142 Winkleman Road
Harrisburg, IL 62946
www.rivertorivertrail.org

Shawnee National Forest
50 Highway 145 South
Harrisburg, IL 62946
800-MY-WOODS
www.fs.fed.us/r9/forests/shawnee

RIVER-TO-RIVER TRAIL THRU-HIKING

O'Dell, John. 1995. *River to River Trail Guide: Southern Illinois : Battery Rock on the Ohio River to Grand Tower on the Mississippi River.* Harrisburg, IL: River to River Trail Society.
Rice, Larry. February 1998. "A Trail of Two Rivers." *Backpacker.* 66–70.

ILLINOIS HIKING

Kurz, Don. Tim Ernst, ed.. 2004. *Illinois Wildflowers.* Cave Mountain, AR: Cloudland.net Pub.
McPherson, Alan. 1993. *Fifty Nature Walks in Southern Illinois.* Vienna, IL: Cache River Press.

SHORE-TO-SHORE TRAIL

Huron-Manistee National Forests
1755 South Mitchell Street
Cadillac, MI 49601
www.fs.fed.us/r9/hmnf/

Michigan Department of Natural Resources
Parks and Recreation
PO Box 30257
Mason Building, Third Floor
Lansing, MI 48909
517-373-9900
www.michigan.gov/dnr

Michigan Trail Riders Association
3010 North M-52
Stockbridge, MI 49285
517-851-7554
www.mtra.org

SHORE-TO-SHORE TRAIL THRU-HIKING

Michigan Trail Riders Association. Michigan Trail Riders Association maps. Stockbridge, MI: Michigan Trail Riders Association.

THRU-HIKING AND MICHIGAN HIKING

Modrzynski, Mike. 1996. *Hiking Michigan.* Helena, MT: Falcon Press.

SUPERIOR HIKING TRAIL

Superior Hiking Trail Association
PO Box 4
731 7th Avenue
Two Harbors, MN 55616
218-834-2700
www.shta.org

Superior National Forest
8901 Grand Avenue Place
Duluth, MN 55808
218-626-4300
218-626-4399 (hearing impaired)
www.superiornationalforest.org

Superior Shuttle Service
2618 Highway 61 East
Two Harbors, MN 55616
218-834-5511
http://superiorshuttle.com/

Minnesota Pollution Control Agency
520 Lafayette Road
St. Paul, MN 55155
651-296-6300
www.pca.state.mn.us

Sierra Club North Star Chapter
2327 East Franklin Avenue, Suite 1
Minneapolis, MN 55406
612-659-9124
www.northstar.sierraclub.org

SUPERIOR TRAIL THRU-HIKING

Superior Hiking Trail Association. 2004. *Guide to the Superior Hiking Trail: Linking People with Nature by Footpath Along Lake Superior's North Shore.* Two Harbors, MN: Ridgeline Press.

Superior Hiking Trail Association. Superior Hiking Trail maps. Two Harbors, MN: Superior Hiking Trail Association.

LAKE SUPERIOR

McGuffin, Gary, and Joanie McGuffin. 1995. *Superior: Journeys on an Inland Sea*. Minocqua, WI: NorthWord Press.

MINNESOTA HIKING

Link, Mike and Kate Crowley. 1999. *Hiking Minnesota*. Champaign, IL: Human Kinetics.

TAHOE RIM TRAIL

Tahoe Rim Trail Association
DWR Community Non-Profit Center
948 Incline Way
Incline Village, NV 89451
775-298-0012
www.tahoerimtrail.org

Eldorado National Forest
100 Forni Road
Placerville, CA 95667
530-622-5061
530-621-5297 (hearing impaired)
www.fs.fed.us/r5/eldorado

Humboldt-Toiyabe National Forest
1200 Franklin Way
Sparks, NV 89431
775-331-6444
775-355-5305 (hearing impaired)
www.fs.fed.us/r4/htnf

Keep Tahoe Blue
955 Emerald Bay Road
South Lake Tahoe, CA 96150
530-541-5388
www.keeptahoeblue.com

Lake Tahoe Basin Management Unit
35 College Drive
South Lake Tahoe, CA 96150
530-543-2600
www.fs.fed.us/r5/ltbmu

Tahoe National Forest
631 Coyote Street
Nevada City, CA 95959
530-265-4531
530-478-6118 (hearing impaired)
www.fs.fed.us/r5/tahoe

TAHOE RIM TRAIL THRU-HIKING

Hauserman, Tim. 2002. *The Tahoe Rim Trail: A Complete Guide for Hikers, Mountain Bikers, and Equestrians.* Berkeley, CA: Wilderness Press.

Schaffer, Jeffrey P., et al. 1995. *The Pacific Crest Trail.* Volume One: California. 5th ed. Berkeley, CA: Wilderness Press.

Purdue, Matt. June 1998. "Share and share alike." *Backpacker.* 18.

Wade, Judy. 2002. "Tahoe Rim Trail." *GORP.* Retrieved June 6, 2002, from www.gorp.com/gorp/location/ca/tahoerim.htm.

LAKE TAHOE HISTORY

Lekisch, Barbara. 1988. *Tahoe Place Names: The Origin and History of Names in the Lake Tahoe Basin.* Lafayette, CA: Great West Books.

TUSCARORA TRAIL

Potomac Appalachian Trail Club
118 Park Street SE
Vienna, VA 22180
703-242-0693
www.patc.net

Shenandoah National Park
3655 U.S. Highway 211 East
Luray, VA 22835
540-999-3500
www.nps.gov/shen

TUSCARORA TRAIL THRU-HIKING

Burnham, Bill. May 2000. "Nibble While You Walk." *Backpacker.*

Johnston, Elizabeth, and Tom Lupp. 1998. *The Tuscarora Trail: A Guide to the South Half in West Virginia and Virginia.* 3rd ed. Vienna, VA: Potomac Appalachian Trail Club.

Lupp, Tom. 1998. *The Tuscarora Trail: A Guide to the North Half in Maryland and Pennsylvania.* 3rd ed. Vienna, VA: Potomac Appalachian Trail Club.

APPALACHIAN HISTORY

Adams, Noah. 2001. *Far Appalachia: Following the New River North.* New York, NY: Delacorte Press.

Brooks, Maurice. 1995. *Appalachians.* Morgantown, WV: Seneca Books.

Strain, Paula M. 1993. *The Blue Hills of Maryland: History Along the Appalachian Trail on South Mountain and the Catoctins.* Vienna, VA: Potomac Appalachian Trail Club.

THE TUSCARORA

Graymont, Barbara (Ed.). 1994. *Fighting Tuscarora: The Autobiography of Chief Clinton Richard.* Syracuse, NY: Syracuse University Press.

Wissler, Clark. 1996. *Indians of the United States.* Revised ed. New York, NY: Random House.

WONDERLAND TRAIL

Mount Rainier National Park
Tahoma Woods, Star Route
Ashford, WA 98304
360-569-2211
360-569-2177 (hearing impaired)
www.nps.gov/mora

Northwest Interpretive Association
Mount Rainier National Park
Longmire, WA 98397
360-569-2211, ext. 3320
www.nps.gov/mora/NWIA/nwia.htm

WONDERLAND TRAIL THRU-HIKING

Filley, Bette. 1998. *Discovering the Wonders of the Wonderland Trail*. Issaquah, WA: Dunamis House.

MOUNT RAINIER

Filley, Bette. 1995. *Big Fact Book About Mount Rainier*. Issaquah, WA: Dunamis House.

Gauthier, Mike. 1999. *Mount Rainier: A Climbing Guide*. Seattle, WA: The Mountaineers Books.

Smoot, Jeff. 1993. *Adventure Guide to Mount Rainier*. Guilford, CT: Falcon Press.

PACIFIC NORTHWEST HISTORY

Beckey, Fred, et al. 1999. *The Range of Glaciers*. Portland, OR: Oregon Historical Society.

schlimmer's favorite trail reads

While recovering from a trail injury, being tent bound on those rainy or snowy days on the trail, or attempting to function in the real world, a good book can help keep your sanity and boredom in check. Below are what may be my favorite books, all nonfiction and in alphabetical order by author. Subjects range from polar exploration to seafaring adventure. All of these books are guaranteed to keep your mind satisfied. Approximately half the titles gained a spot on *National Geographic*'s One Hundred Greatest Adventure Books of All Time. All of these books are available in paperback editions of backpacker-friendly weight and dimension.

Ambrose, Stephen. 1996. *Undaunted Courage: Meriwether Lewis, Thomas Jefferson, and the Opening of the American West*. New York, NY: Touchstone.

Brown, Dee. 1970. *Bury My Heart at Wounded Knee: An Indian History of the American West*. New York, NY: Henry Holt.

Buhl, Hermann, and Hugh Merrick, trans. 1954. *Nanga Parbat Pilgrimage: The Lonely Challenge*. Seattle, WA: The Mountaineers.

Callahan, Steven. 1999. *Adrift: Seventy-six Days Lost at Sea*. New York, NY: Mariner Books.

De Poncins, Gontran. 1941. *Kabloona*. Alexandria, VA: Time Life.

Glick, Daniel. 2001. *Powder Burn: Arson, Money, and Mystery in Vail Valley*. New York, NY: Public Affairs.

Herzog, Maurice. 1997. *Annapurna: The Epic Account of a Himalayan Conquest and its Harrowing Aftermath*. New York, NY: Lyons Press.

Junger, Sebastian. 1998. *The Perfect Storm: A True Story of Men Against the Sea*. New York, NY: Harper Collins.

Krakauer, Jon. 1997. *Into the Wild*. New York, NY: Knopf.

Kropp, Goran. 2000. *Ultimate High*. New York, NY: Discovery Channel.

Lansing, Alfred. 1999. *Endurance*. 2d ed. New York, NY: Carroll and Graf.

Peacock, Doug. 1990. *Grizzly Years: In Search of the American Wilderness*. New York, NY: Henry Holt and Company.

Powell, John Wesley. 1895. *The Exploration of the Colorado River and Its Canyons*. Washington, DC: National Geographic.

Rawicz, Slavomir. 1997. *The Long Walk*. New York, NY: Lyon Press.

Read, Piers Paul. 1975. *Alive*. New York, NY: Harper Collins.

index

Numbers in **bold** refer to pages with illustrations

about the author

E. Schlimmer examined more than 130 pieces of literature and traversed more than 3,000 miles of trails to complete research for this comprehensive, one-of-a-kind guide. To date, his most ambitious adventure has been a solo 2,250-mile off-road mountain bike expedition along the entire United States–Mexico border, a story that headlined national mountain biking and adventure magazines. As a hiker, E. Schlimmer has become one of only four people to climb all 770 peaks above 3,000 feet in the Northeast. His employment has included work as an Appalachian Trail caretaker, backcountry forest ranger, trail crew leader and, more recently, freelance writer and public speaker. He often resides in the Adirondack Mountains of New York State.